COMPARATIVE PERSPECTIVES ON
SOCIAL
PROBLEMS

COMPARATIVE PERSPECTIVES ON

SOCIAL
PROBLEMS

Edited and with Introduction by

VYTAUTAS KAVOLIS
Dickinson College

LITTLE, BROWN AND COMPANY Boston

FIRST PRINTING

Printed simultaneously in Canada by
Little, Brown & Company (Canada) Limited

PRINTED IN THE UNITED STATES OF AMERICA

PREFACE

This book is a modest introduction to the study of social problems from a cross-cultural and, to a lesser extent, historical point of view. It contains a structural framework for organizing data on the human inadequacies of social environments; illustrates the variety of approaches developed by representatives, of the several social sciences, active in the field; and presents a sample of the substantive findings that seem most relevant to the concerns of students of social problems in the contemporary world.

A distinctive feature of this reader is the integration of the empirical findings of anthropologists, psychologists, political scientists, and even historians with those of the sociologists. The field of social problems lends itself better than most other branches of sociology to such integration; and, since most of the cross-cultural studies of pathological behavior have been conducted by non-sociologists, it is indeed necessary to draw upon other disciplines in a comparative survey of social problems.

I have not aimed at a formalization of theory. It has seemed more essential, at this time, to move toward the identification of the structural, processual, and psychosocial variables out of which a *general* theory of the pathologies of social life could be constructed when more becomes known about the effects of these variables on people and the interrelationships among the variables themselves. I view this general theory as a necessary foundation for the more specialized explanations of particular "problems." I would therefore prefer to abandon the traditional organization of the field in terms of a sequence of problems, and deal with it by analyzing components of social organization and types of social processes in terms of the effects each of them has on the whole range of destructive and self-destructive behavior. Gestures toward this approach are made in the introductory essay.

A number of excellent studies had, expectably, to be omitted because of limitations of space. I particularly regret my inability to include some provocative gems about the means by which various societies have attempted to cope with their social problems.

I am grateful to Alex Inkeles for critical comments, to H. Wade Seaford, Jr., for advice on anthropological selections, to the Dickinson College Faculty Research Fund for financial assistance, and to Mrs. Isabel Goodhart for her secretarial contributions.

Vytautas Kavolis
Dickinson College

TABLE OF CONTENTS

COMPARATIVE PERSPECTIVES ON
SOCIAL
PROBLEMS

I

Introduction

1   VYTAUTAS KAVOLIS

The Comparative Approach to Social Problems

Social problems have been conceived of as (1) behavior deviating from
whatever norms happen to be institutionalized in a social setting; (2)
conditions judged by a group to be radically undesirable and susceptible
to amelioration by social action; and (3) destructive and self-destructive
behavior of persons, groups, or whole societies.

These may be called respectively the deviance, the public-awareness,
and the pathology conceptions of social problems. Each conception has
its own virtues and deficiencies. The deviance approach focuses attention
on the variability of standards of "normality" accepted in different social
settings and on the psychosocial mechanisms which produce nonconformity to them. Deviant behavior is frequently caused by some "felt
difficulty in fulfilling role obligations."[1] It may dramatically reinforce
existing normative standards or, when it occurs on a larger scale, generate

[1] William J. Goode, "A Theory of Role Strain," *American Sociological Review*, 25 (1960), pp. 483-496.

pressures toward change in the social system.[2] Prevalent reactions to deviance affect what happens to the individual defined as "deviant."[3]

The concept of deviance is most helpful in understanding the individual case — how has a particular person acquired a deviant role and how is he affected by it. But the concept of deviance includes a variety of behaviors that are neither destructive in their consequences nor judged by societies or significant groups therein to be radically undesirable (e.g., the nonconformity of the dance musician to ordinary middle-class career expectations).[4] On the other hand, extremely destructive forms of behavior, such as genocide and warfare, will not be defined as social problems if they are institutionalized in a society and accepted by the majority (or by the leaders whom the majority acknowledges to be legitimate) as either normal or at least legally sanctioned behavior.

The public-awareness view of social problems has the merit of drawing attention to what members of a society subjectively perceive to be a condition they should attempt to correct. Those who conceive of a condition as a social problem in this sense are likely to support ameliorative action, while others, in all likelihood, will not. Hence this perspective on social problems may be most relevant to the activist concerned with programs of amelioration. It aids in understanding and influencing social reactions. But, by itself, it provides neither an analytical perspective for understanding the causes of the conditions regarded as social problems nor a general criterion for judging them to be social problems.

The third conception of social problems — as the varieties of destructive and self-destructive behavior — provides a universal criterion for evaluating social arrangements by their human costs. If it were possible to arrive at a cross-culturally valid definition of "destructive or self-destructive behavior," then conditions causally associated with such behavior could be identified as pathogenic (or having pathogenic aspects), regardless of whether they were institutionalized in a society and supported by its cultural traditions or not, and whether anyone in the society in which they occurred was aware of their pathogenic effects. With this perspective on social problems, no longer would the sociologist stand theoretically helpless — as the "deviationists" must — in relation to prejudice in South Africa, slavery in the pre-Civil War American South, Nazi con-

[2] Talcott Parsons, *The Social System* (Glencoe, Ill.: The Free Press, 1951), pp. 249-325; Albert K. Cohen, *Deviance and Control* (Englewood Cliffs, N.J.: Prentice-Hall, 1966).

[3] Edwin M. Lemert, *Social Pathology* (New York: McGraw-Hill Book Co., 1951), Chaps. 2-4; Edwin M. Schur, *Crimes Without Victims: Deviant Behavior and Public Policy* (Englewood Cliffs, N.J.: Prentice-Hall, 1965).

[4] Howard S. Becker, *Outsiders: Studies in the Sociology of Deviance* (New York: The Free Press, 1963), pp. 79-119.

centration camps, genocide under Stalin, or the pathologies arising from conformity to "normal" middle-class values.[5]

I do not accept the view that to define pathology in terms of destructiveness is a culture-bound judgment. To regard *destruction of life, health, or sense of personal identity* (a definition with a hard core and stretchable boundaries) as the universal criterion of pathological behavior constitutes the most general extension of the implications of the major ethical systems of mankind. With respect to this criterion, exceptions have to be justified, not the criterion itself; but the criterion has been frequently held to apply only to members of one's own group. What we are doing is universalizing the criterion of pathology — applying it to all societies, including those that have not generalized their moral norms sufficiently to make them applicable to outsiders as much as to themselves.

Nor can it be legitimately assumed that the social-pathology approach necessarily incorporates a conservative bias in favor of preserving existing institutions.[6] What is pathological is not behavior which deviates from established custom or disrupts social stability but that which is destructive or self-destructive in its consequences. Whenever established institutions (or innovations) promote such behavior, they must be regarded as pathogenic. Conflict, in this theoretical perspective, is not in itself pathological (unless it generates violence). Lack of conflict may be pathogenic if it perpetuates a high incidence of self-destructive behavior.

The "field" of social pathology may be defined as the study of the destructive or self-destructive behavior of individuals (pathological behavior) and of the social and cultural conditions, or processes, which cause or contribute to such behavior (pathogenic conditions). If the goal is to understand how particular conditions have pathogenic effects on individuals, studying one type of pathological behavior in isolation from others is insufficient. It is only by investigating the overall effects of a social condition, on all types of pathological behavior, that the social pathologist can determine to what extent and in what manner the condition is pathogenic. A theoretical framework is needed within which any given social condition can be related to all types of pathological behaviors (if a relationship can be demonstrated to exist).

In organizing the data for such a framework, it is helpful to distinguish self-directed destructiveness from other-directed destructiveness, and spon-

[5] Erich Fromm, *The Sane Society* (Greenwich, Conn.: Fawcett Publications, 1955).

[6] An accusation that has been justly directed against an earlier generation of American social pathologists. C. Wright Mills, "The Professional Ideology of Social Pathologists," in his *Power, Politics and People*, ed. Irving Louis Horowitz (New York: Ballantine Books, 1963), pp. 525-552.

taneous pathological behavior from organized pathologies. Self-destruc-
tiveness refers to all forms of behavior by which an individual destroys
or damages his own life, health, or sense of personal identity. Such forms
of behavior range from suicide at the highest level of intensity, through
alcoholism and neurosis at intermediate levels, to various kinds of "inauthentic" actions, alien to the "true nature" of the personality, that the
individual performs either because he is forced by external circumstances
or because he does not "know" himself. Only the higher and intermediate levels of intensity will be considered systematically in this article, as
little reliable cross-cultural research has been done on "inauthentic"
behavior, except on alienation.

Other-directed destructiveness is another umbrella term referring to all
activities by which an individual destroys or damages the life, health, or
sense of personal identity of another person or persons. Such activities
include, at one extreme, the various forms of murder (including socially
sanctioned killing, as in warfare) and, at the other extreme, the withdrawal of social esteem from a specific person or group of persons. (This
may be a rational action when it has been "earned" by the specific behavior of such a person or persons, but even then it is other-destructive.)
I would classify racial discrimination and most forms of crime as other-
directed destructive behavior of intermediate intensity. However, racial
discrimination is easily intensified to the level of genocide; and the intensity of aggression inherent in crime varies from high to low. Some
activities officially designated as crimes, such as school truancy, are purely
self-destructive. Some crimes do not affect either the self or others de-
structively (e.g., the crime of offering a glass of wine to a seventeen-year-
old in Pennsylvania). On the other hand, numerous other-destructive
activities have historically not been regarded as crimes (war, economic
exploitation of the easily victimized).

Spontaneous pathological behavior is exhibited when an individual
"chooses," in part voluntarily, to engage in a destructive or self-destructive course of action, or when he unconsciously develops, without having
the ability to choose, the symptoms of a self-destructive disease. Organized pathology exists when the individual is either "morally" obligated or
"politically" coerced by the group or organization to whose authority or
power he is subject to commit destructive or self-destructive acts (or to
encourage others to commit such acts). The purest cases of organized
pathology are found in concentration camps and the institution of slavery. While the victims of these institutions are coerced into self-destructive behavior, their masters, by accepting their position within these
institutions, assume the obligation to engage in other-destructive behavior, essentially (though not wholly) regardless of their personal malev-
olence or lack thereof. Both the victims and the masters of pathological

institutions are required, by the conditions of operation of such institutions, to engage in pathological behavior.

On a level of intensity, but with broadly comparable psychological effects, is the organized pathology of imperialism and colonialism, the most prominent representative of which, after the virtual demise of West European colonial empires, is the Soviet Union, with its at least fifteen nations held by force in the same relationship to the Great Russians as the natives of Mozambique are to the Portuguese — "crushed with their inessentiality."[7]

Organized pathology is not necessarily, at any given time, socially disreputable. Respected organizations may require their members to participate, or unintentionally promote, pathological behavior. The Catholic church does so when it requires its clerical members, against their growing opposition, to persuade its lay members not to use effective methods of fertility control. The rationale of this requirement is moral upgrading of the faithful. The socially relevant result is a sizable contribution to over-population, malnutrition of children, illegal abortions that damage the health or destroy the lives of pregnant women, and revolutionary political extremism, especially in Latin America. Some readers might find that the rats of Rajasthan constitute an emotionally more acceptable illustration of the point that is being made here.[8]

These examples suggest to what extent the deviance perspective may be irrelevant to understanding the causes of major social pathologies. Yet one of the measures of the rationality of a social order is the degree to which its definitions of socially unacceptable deviance correspond with what can be empirically shown to be pathological behavior. In a rational society, presumably, only the pathological would be regarded as seriously deviant, and the only socially consequential deviance would be that of demonstrably destructive or self-destructive behavior. However, since societies are not rationally organized, both the deviance and the pathology perspectives are necessary to understand their problems.

In studying social pathology, we aim at establishing the characteristics of social structure and process as well as those of cultural orientation which promote pathological behavior wherever they occur. To eliminate accidental patterns of findings that hold in a particular time and place but lack general validity, systematic cross-cultural study of the various forms of pathological behavior is necessary. Such studies should eventu-

[7] Frantz Fanon, *The Wretched of the Earth* (New York: Grove Press, 1966), p. 30.

[8] "Food is scarce in this desert town, as it is in much of India. . . . But the rats in this desert state of Rajasthan face no food problem. They are considered to be holy creatures, and they are fed by faithful worshippers. The rodent population of Rajasthan is said to outnumber the human population: 25 million rats to 20.1 million people." *The New York Times*, August 21, 1968, p. 16.

ally lead to a theoretical integration of the knowledge of pathological behavior in preliterate, historical, and modern societies accumulated by
half a dozen scholarly disciplines. It should be possible, on the basis of
such a theoretical system, to predict how much of what types of pathology would be likely to occur if we constructed a society with certain specified characteristics. This article contains a series of notes toward such a
theory of the general pathogenic aspects of society and culture.

1. SOCIAL ORGANIZATION AND PATHOLOGICAL BEHAVIOR

In this section, several types of spontaneous pathological behavior will be
related to pathogenic factors within the organization and functioning of
five principal subsystems of society.

The Family and Kinship System

It may be partly a reflection of the professional ideology of American
behavioral scientists that more cross-cultural research has been done on
the family and kinship systems as generators of pathological behavior
than on the political and economic systems. Much of this work has centered on the childhood backgrounds of adult pathologies.

Among the socialization variables, child indulgence has been shown to
be associated with low adult theft rates (in preliterate societies), and
"love-oriented techniques" of discipline with less suicide,[9] suggesting that
the more supportive, less restrictive child-rearing methods tend to reduce
both other- and self-directed aggressiveness.[10] Conversely, severe punishment in childhood is associated with high adult theft rates,[11] and the
suppression of child aggressiveness has been cited as a possible reason for
the high suicide rate of Sweden.[12] The more restrictive, less supportive

---

[9] Margaret K. Bacon, Irvin L. Child, and Herbert Barry III, "A Cross-Cultural
Study of Correlates of Crime," *The Journal of Abnormal and Social Psychology*,
66 (1963), p. 295; David Lester, "Suicide, Homicide and the Effects of
Socialization," *The Journal of Personality and Social Psychology*, 5 (April, 1967),
p. 467.

[10] Field's finding that childhood indulgence is associated with adult drunkenness
has been convincingly rejected by Barry *et al.* Peter B. Field, "A New Cross-
Cultural Study of Drunkenness," in David J. Pittman and Charles R. Snyder,
eds., *Society, Culture, and Drinking Patterns* (New York: John Wiley & Sons,
1962), p. 66; Herbert Barry III, Charles Buchwald, Irvin L. Child, and Margaret
K. Bacon, "A Cross-Cultural Study of Drinking: IV. Comparisons with Horton's
Ratings," *Quarterly Journal of Studies on Alcohol*, Supplement No. 3 (1965), p.
71.

[11] Bacon *et al., op. cit.*, pp. 295-297.

[12] Herbert Hendin, *Suicide and Scandinavia* (Garden City, N.Y.: Anchor
Books, 1965).

type of child socialization seems to increase both other- and self-directed aggressiveness. (Extreme indulgence, however, may have a similar effect.)[13] This dimension of socialization appears then to influence the amount of pathological behavior in society rather than the direction of pathological behavior.

Four characteristics of the family structure are linked with *other-directed* aggressiveness: (1) societies with polygynous family systems produce much feuding and fear of witchcraft;[14] (2) low salience of the father in a mother-based family is associated with criminality and violence in males;[15] (3) a sharp segregation of sex roles in marriage correlates with both physical violence and political extremism;[16] and (4) low maternal sexual gratification (in preliterate societies, a post-partum sex taboo extending for ten months or longer, and in urban societies, less sexual satisfaction in marriage reported by lower-class women) is associated with projective other-directed aggressiveness (fear of sorcerers in the first case, political extremism in the second).[17]

These four apparently pathogenic variables in family organization are interrelated but not identical. In particular, the latter three can occur in monogamous family systems as well as under polygyny. In general, other-directed aggressiveness of males is frequent where their mothers had been placed, relative to their fathers, in a socially inferior or highly segregated position, reducing their effectiveness as socializers of male children. Self-destructive behavior, such as drunkenness and suicide, occurs where adult males are provided with relatively weak restraints and little supportiveness

[13] S. H. Posinsky, "Navaho Infancy and Childhood," *Psychiatric Quarterly*, 37 (1963), pp. 306-321.

[14] Keith F. Otterbein and Charlotte Swanson Otterbein, "An Eye for an Eye, A Tooth for a Tooth: A Cross-Cultural Study of Feuding," *American Anthropologist*, 67 (December, 1965), p. 1474; Robert A. LeVine, "Witchcraft and Co-Wife Proximity in Southwestern Kenya," *Ethnology*, 1 (January, 1962), pp. 39-45.

[15] Bacon *et al.*, *op. cit.*, pp. 292-294; Beatrice B. Whiting, "Sex Identity Conflict and Physical Violence: A Comparative Study," *American Anthropologist*, 67 (December, 1965), pp. 123-140.

[16] B. Whiting, *op. cit.*; Lee Rainwater, "Marital Sexuality in Four Cultures of Poverty," *Journal of Marriage and the Family*, 26 (November, 1964), pp. 457-466; Seymour Martin Lipset, *Political Man: The Social Bases of Politics* (Garden City, N.Y.: Anchor Books, 1963), pp. 87-126.

[17] John W. M. Whiting, "Sorcery, Sin, and the Superego: A Cross-Cultural Study of Some Mechanisms of Social Control," *Nebraska Symposium on Motivation 1959*, ed. Marshall R. Jones (Lincoln: University of Nebraska Press, 1959), pp. 174-195; Rainwater, *op. cit.*; Lipset, *op. cit.* Aggressiveness is projective when it results in empirically unjustified perception of others as threatening aggression; this perception then legitimates an attack against those perceived as threatening. It is in this sense that the fear of witchcraft is an other-destructive pathology.

by the kinship system.[18] These variables seem to constitute determinants
of the direction of pathological behavior, without necessarily affecting the
amount of pathological behavior. When both types of pathogenic conditions are present — inferior or segregated mothers and lack of kinship
controls over the adult males themselves — the amount of pathological
behavior should increase.

A number of Western studies imply that whatever the organization of
the family system might be, a low degree of attachment to it by an
adult individual increases his chances of self-destructive behavior, such as
suicide. (The preservative effect of marriage, in Western societies, tends
to increase with age, and appears to be greater for men than for women.)[19]
However, the unmarried Chinese in Singapore were found to have lower
rates of schizophrenia than the married,[20] and in Nigeria marriage also
does not seem to decrease suicide.[21] These non-Western studies suggest
that differences in family systems, or in the articulation of the family
with other social institutions, determine the extent to which an individual
benefits from his attachment to it. Given a highly patriarchal or tradi-
tionalist family system in a rapidly changing society, some degree of detachment from it may be beneficial for an adult.

Western findings on the relationship between suicide and old age are
also inconsistent with the patterns discovered in the African societies in
which old age is prestigious. In the latter, suicide rates decline in middle
and old age,[22] contrary to the Western pattern of consistent increases
(for males) with advancing age. With respect to suicide, an increase in
social rewards (a gratifying experience) can apparently compensate for
the decline in physiological vitality due to aging (a frustrating experience). The distribution of social rewards determines the differential prevalence of social pathology. However, if high status is directly associated
with suicide (as in Western societies), African data might be interpreted
as suggesting that what keeps the suicide rate low in old age is not the
societal prestigiousness of old age but the possession by oldsters of signifi-

[18] Field, op. cit.; David C. McClelland, William Davis, Eric Wanner, "A
Cross-Cultural Study of Folk-Tale Content and Drinking," Sociometry, 29 (De-
cember, 1966), pp. 308-333; Emile Durkheim, Suicide: A Study in Sociology
(New York: The Free Press of Glencoe, 1963), pp. 171-202.

[19] Louis I. Dublin and Bessie Bunzel, To Be or Not To Be: A Study of Suicide
(New York: Harrison Smith and Robert Haas, 1933), pp. 127-130; Vera Norris,
Mental Illness in London (London: Oxford University Press, 1959), p. 256.

[20] H. B. M. Murphy, "Culture and Mental Disorder in Singapore," in Marvin
K. Opler, ed., Culture and Mental Health (New York: The Macmillan Co.,
1959), pp. 311-314.

[21] T. Asuni, "Suicide in Western Nigeria," International Journal of Psychiatry,
1 (1965), pp. 57-58.

[22] Paul Bohannan, ed., African Homicide and Suicide (Princeton, N.J.: Princeton University Press, 1960), p. 121.

cant roles in the "intimacy structures" of the family system. This type of social reward is independent of the overall status of the family in society.

The Stratification System

If we turn to comparative research on stratification systems as the locus of pathogenesis, we immediately discover that a larger proportion of such studies have been conducted in modern nations than in preliterate societies (as might be expected because of the much more strategic importance of stratification systems in urban societies). One of the main findings that emerges from these studies is that, while systems of stratification (that is, an unequal distribution of wealth, power, and prestige) have been universal above the level of the simplest nomadic bands, the *degree* of inequalitarianism determines the extent to which a stratification system is pathogenic. In preliterate societies, a high degree of status inequality goes with greater frequency of theft.[23] An extremely unequal distribution of agricultural land ownership is correlated, in modern states, with high rates of violent political deaths.[24] These findings could be interpreted by assuming either that inequalitarian societies produce more unfavorable gratification-frustration ratios for their members, or that the experience of inequality imposed by others and by the society on low-status groups is subjectively perceived by their members as legitimating aggression against others and the society. A form of self-destructive behavior, drunkenness, is less prevalent in the more hierarchical preliterate societies,[25] but it is not yet possible to tell whether inequalitarian systems generally minimize self-destructive behavior.

In modern stratification systems, the position occupied by an individual is an important determinant of his susceptibility to pathological behavior. The lower (unskilled-labor) class appears to generate more pathological behavior than does the middle class, especially with respect to recidivist juvenile delinquency, interpersonal violence, racial prejudice, and mental illness. However, in India the rate of first admissions to psychiatric hospitals is higher for the upper castes.[26] If this finding reflects the actual disorder prevalence rather than differential access to treatment, one might hypothesize that the upper strata are under greater strain in the early phases of the modernization of traditional societies, but that in advanced industrial societies, such as the United States, the lower classes become exposed to greater strain registering in psychiatric symptoms.

[23] Bacon *et al.*, *op. cit.*, p. 291.

[24] Bruce M. Russett, "Inequality and Instability: The Relation of Land Tenure to Politics," *World Politics*, 16 (April, 1964), pp. 442-454.

[25] McClelland *et al.*, *op. cit.*, p. 331.

[26] Sharadamba Rao, "Caste and Mental Disorders in Bihar," *American Journal of Psychiatry*, 122 (1966), pp. 1045-1055.

Divorce rates seem to be related to the modernization process in a similar manner.[27]

In Western urban societies, suicide is apt to increase toward both extremes of the status distribution; so do first admissions to mental hospitals for alcoholism in Britain.[28] The primary locus of narcotics addiction within class systems has been variable: slanted toward the middle and higher classes in Britain,[29] toward the lower in Hong Kong[30] as well as, at least since World War II, in the United States (where patterns of drug consumption may now be changing in the British direction). While racial prejudice is more intense in the lower class in both the United States and South Africa,[31] a religio-ethnic prejudice, anti-Semitism, in Germany and Austria has drawn more of its organized support from the middle and the lower-middle classes.[32] This comparison might suggest that the middle class tends to become involved with the more organized, and the lower class with the more spontaneous, expressions of prejudice. White collar crime, such as price-fixing, embezzlement, and bribery, is a middle- or upper-class offense. Thus lower-class status is not consistently related to higher rates of *all* types of pathological behavior, but it is associated more frequently than middle-class status with other-directed, spontaneous violence.

It seems reasonable to hypothesize that low status in urban societies is more likely to be subjectively perceived as legitimating other-directed aggression (since the lower-status person is chiefly frustrated by limitations, which he resents, imposed on him by others or the social system). "When behavior is subjected to strong external restraints by virtue either of subordinate status or intense involvement in social relationships with other persons, the restraining objects can be blamed for frustration, thereby legitimating outward expression of the resultant aggression."[33] But the higher rates of psychiatric disorders in the lower classes cannot

[27] William J. Goode, "Marital Satisfaction and Instability: A Cross-Cultural Class Analysis of Divorce Rates," *International Social Science Journal*, 14 (1962), pp. 507-526.

[28] M. W. Susser and W. Watson, *Sociology in Medicine* (London: Oxford University Press, 1962), p. 95.

[29] Edwin M. Schur, *Narcotic Addiction in Britain and America: The Impact of Public Policy* (Bloomington: Indiana University Press, 1966), pp. 122-126.

[30] Albert G. Hess, *Chasing the Dragon: A Report on Drug Addiction in Hong Kong* (New York: The Free Press, 1965), pp. 62, 65-66, 80.

[31] Thomas F. Pettigrew, "Personality and Sociocultural Factors in Intergroup Tensions," *The Journal of Conflict Resolution*, 2 (March, 1958), pp. 29-42.

[32] Peter G. J. Pulzer, *The Rise of Political Anti-Semitism in Germany and Austria* (New York: John Wiley & Sons, 1964), p. 281.

[33] Andrew F. Henry and James F. Short, Jr., *Suicide and Homicide: Some Economic, Sociological, and Psychological Aspects of Aggression* (New York: The Free Press of Glencoe, 1964), p. 103.

be explained in this manner since they are forms of self-destructive be-havior. Furthermore, low status is associated with psychophysiological symptoms even when it is assigned on the basis of sex rather than income or occupation.[34] Low status thus appears not only to legitimate other-directed aggression, but, to some extent, also to generate self-destructive behavior; it is an "objectively damaging" condition.

While the pathologies of low-status groups typically entail direct action or a spontaneous response to immediately experienced social conditions, the upper strata (or revolutionary leaders aspiring to dominant status in a society) may indirectly, but with far greater impact, cause pathological behavior *in others* by failing to lead their societies toward necessary changes[35] or by establishing pathogenic institutions and making policy decisions necessitating organized violence. "The true anti-Semites of the Roman Empire were . . . the intelligentsia"; "the medieval witchhunts were mostly arranged by scholars"; and in Germany, "*one-fourth* of the SS elite had previously received the doctorate."[36] Gurr has pointed out that civil violence which arises out of subjective deprivation felt by "elite-aspirants" tends to be more highly organized and intense than civil violence occurring in response to deprivations experienced by the "masses."[37] Insofar as many studies of social problems neglect these aspects of the pathology of stratification systems, they tend to carry an inbuilt anti-lower-class bias.

In American studies, social mobility within a stratification system and mobility-striving have been found to be associated with racial prejudice. In Sweden, however, neither of these two variables was related to group prejudice.[38] The differences in the findings may have to do with the less ethnically diversified nature of the Swedish society or with the relative

---

[34] Thomas S. Langner, "Psychophysiological Symptoms and the Status of Women in Two Mexican Communities," Jane M. Murphy and Alexander H. Leighton, eds., *Approaches to Cross-Cultural Psychiatry* (Ithaca, N.Y.: Cornell University Press, 1965), pp. 360-392.

[35] Cf. Alvin Boskoff, "Social Indecision in Two Classical Societies," in Werner J. Cahnman and Alvin Boskoff, eds., *Sociology and History: Theory and Research* (New York: The Free Press of Glencoe, 1964), pp. 246-257; Crane Brinton, *The Anatomy of Revolution* (New York: Vintage Books, 1952), pp. 264-275.

[36] Edward H. Flannery, *The Anguish of the Jews: Twenty-three Centuries of Anti-Semitism* (New York: The Macmillan Co., 1965), p. 19; Hermann Mann-heim, *Comparative Criminology* (Boston: Houghton Mifflin Co., 1965), p. 634; William Kornhauser, *The Politics of Mass Society* (New York: The Free Press of Glencoe, 1959), p. 188.

[37] Ted Gurr, "Psychological Factors in Civil Violence," *World Politics*, 20 (January, 1968), pp. 276-277.

[38] Melvin Seeman, Dennis Rohan, and Milton Argeriou, "Social Mobility and Prejudice: A Swedish Replication," *Social Problems*, 14 (Fall, 1966), pp. 188-197.

security (both economic and psychological) offered to the individual by the welfare state. The Swedish-American comparison suggests that whatever pathogenic effects social mobility may have can be offset by specific combinations of other social factors. A mobile social order does not necessarily generate a high level of group prejudice. Social mobility is, however, associated with higher suicide rates in New Zealand as well as in the United States.[39] Industrialization, which produces more mobile societies, tends to increase suicide, but not homicide, rates.[40] Thus social mobility appears more consistently to promote self-destructive than other-destructive behavior.

Barriers to social mobility, on the other hand, are associated with higher rates of juvenile delinquency in Israel[41] as well as in the United States. An increased closure of mobility channels has been cited as one of the chief reasons for the revolutionary participation of the eighteenth-century French bourgeoisie.[42] Barriers to upward mobility may be generally conducive to other-directed aggression for both lower and middle classes, though the aggressiveness may be expressed in different specific ways by each class. Downward mobility has been found to be associated with homicide, suicide, and crimes against property in Ceylon,[43] thus with both self- and other-destructive behavior. Status loss or insecurity is also linked with male suicides in Africa, while female suicides are more affected by "family strife."[44] It seems entirely plausible that the causation of male self-destructive behavior should be anchored more in the stratification system, while female pathologies are more closely linked with the family and kinship system with which women tend to be more closely involved.

The Economic System

Economic variables — if they are to be detached from those pertaining primarily to stratification systems — have not been extensively investi-

[39] Austin L. Porterfield and Jack P. Gibbs, "Occupational Prestige and Social Mobility of Suicides in New Zealand," *The American Journal of Sociology*, 66 (September, 1960), pp. 147-152.

[40] Richard Quinney, "Suicide, Homicide, and Economic Development," *Social Forces*, 43 (March, 1965), pp. 401-406; Yrjö Littunen and Eugene L. Gaier, "Social Control and Social Integration," *The International Journal of Social Psychiatry*, 9 (1963), p. 169.

[41] Shlomo Shoham, Nahum Shoham, and Adnan-El-Razek, "Immigration Ethnicity and Ecology as Related to Juvenile Delinquency in Israel: An Explorative Study," *British Journal of Criminology*, (October, 1966), pp. 391-409.

[42] Elinor G. Barber, *The Bourgeoisie in 18th-Century France* (Princeton, N.J.: Princeton University Press, 1955), pp. 112-126.

[43] Arthur Lewis Wood, *Crime and Aggression in Changing Ceylon* (Philadelphia: American Philosophical Society, 1961), pp. 101-103.

[44] Bohannan, *op. cit.*, p. 262.

gated in the cross-cultural studies of social pathology. Economic insecurity seems to be associated with drunkenness in preliterate societies.[45] Unemployment is linked with suicide in Hong Kong[46] and with delinquency in the Soviet Union.[47] "Studies of the behavior of the unemployed in countries in which extremist movements are weak, such as the United States and Britain, indicate that apathy was their characteristic political response. . . . On the other hand, German data suggest a high correlation between working-class unemployment and support of Communists, and middle-class unemployment and support of Nazis."[48] Occupations that demand individual responsibility tend to have high suicide rates.[49] Alienation from work in Sweden, however, does not produce intergroup hostility or political apathy, as it tends to do in the American society.[50] This may be due to such variables as differences in the cultural meaning of work or the presence of a working-class party, capable of compensating for feelings of alienation from work, in Sweden.

The relative paucity of cross-cultural data on specifically economic sources of individual pathologies may to some degree reflect an "anti-materialist" bias in the choice of problems for research. But the negative findings that have been made suggest, at least, that economic factors are not ubiquitous in the genesis of individual pathologies.

The Political System

Swanson's study of sorcery in preliterate societies indicates that there is no correlation between economic insecurity and witchcraft; rather, the latter is associated with a deficiency in political organization — the lack of institutionalized means for adjudication of conflicts of interest between groups.[51] The apparently greater disposition of the urban lower classes

[45] Donald Horton, "The Functions of Alcohol in Primitive Societies: A Cross-Cultural Study," *The Quarterly Journal of Studies of Alcohol,* 4 (1943), pp. 199-320.

[46] P. M. Yap, *Suicide in Hong Kong* (Hong Kong: Cathay Press, 1958), pp. 33-36.

[47] Peter Juviler, "Delinquency and the Family in the U.S.S.R.," paper presented at the 1967 meeting of the American Sociological Association, p. 13.

[48] Lipset, *op. cit.,* p. 116.

[49] Robert E. L. Faris, *Social Disorganization* (New York: The Ronald Press Co., 1948), pp. 210-212.

[50] Melvin Seeman, "On the Personal Consequences of Alienation in Work," *American Sociological Review,* 32 (April, 1967), pp. 273-285.

[51] Guy E. Swanson, *The Birth of the Gods: The Origins of Primitive Beliefs* (Ann Arbor: University of Michigan Press, 1960), pp. 137-152. For the displaced peasants and unskilled workers who participated in the violent chiliastic movements of medieval Europe, there also "existed no regular, institutionalised methods of voicing their grievances or pressing their claims." Norman Cohn, *The Pursuit of the Millennium,* 2nd ed. (New York: Harper & Bros., 1961), p. 315.

toward political extremism and racial prejudice can also be explained, in part, as outward aggressiveness in response to a frustrating lack of access to legitimate power structures (through which conflicts of interest are adjudicated in modern societies).

Grygier has attempted to show that the extreme oppression experienced in concentration camps greatly increased the likelihood of criminality after liberation.[52] A less extreme oppressiveness may be one reason why "the physical crime rate in the sprawling African townships around Johannesburg," in South Africa, "is the highest in the world."[53] Powerlessness promotes other-directed aggression: as the Hindu population of Mauritius attained political ascendancy over the Muslim and mixed colored population, the rates of delinquency of the former declined and those of the latter increased.[54]

The nature of the political system seems to affect the direction of pathological behavior. A comparison of the suicide and homicide rates in the European, Anglo-Saxon, and Latin American societies during the 1950's suggests that stable democracies have the highest average suicide rate and stable dictatorships the highest average homicide rate, while politically unstable nations are intermediate in both respects. (The latter, however, appear to have the highest overall rate of extreme aggressiveness, suicide added to homicide.)[55] This pattern may be due in part to the greater industrialization and prosperity of the stable democracies; and it does not explain why the American murder rate is closer to the average for *unstable* democracies. Altogether, not much research has been done on political structure as the background of individual pathologies.

The Community System

To some extent, the local community can be regarded as the resultant of intersecting kinship, stratification, economic, and political systems. Community integration is usually correlated with strong family solidarity,

[52] Tadeusz Grygier, *Oppression: A Study in Social and Criminal Psychology* (London: Routledge & Kegan Paul, 1954), p. 108.

[53] "Violence Mounts in South Africa," *The New York Times*, November 24, 1967, p. 19. "Apathy, fear and mendacity, punctuated by outbreaks of murderous rage, characterize the personality formed by age-long oppression." Stanislav Andreski, "Genealogy of Public Vices in Latin America," The Sociological Review Monograph No. 11, *Latin American Sociological Studies*, ed. Paul Halmos (Keele, Staffordshire: University of Keele, 1967), p. 77.

[54] T. C. N. Gibbens and R. H. Ahrenfeldt, eds., *Cultural Factors in Delinquency* (Philadelphia: J. B. Lippincott Co., 1966), pp. 46, 124.

[55] Quinney, *op. cit.*, p. 402; Lipset, *op. cit.*, p. 32. The unweighted mean homicide rate per 100,000 in 12 stable democracies is 1.1, the suicide rate 11.6; in 16 unstable political systems (which have had both democratic and dictatorial periods, or in which democracy is internally threatened by powerful anti-democratic movements), the two rates are 6.3 and 10.2; in 7 stable dictatorships, they are 10.3 and 4.1.

prosperity, and "vigorous and well-attended associations."[56] One reason for the high psychiatric disorder rate in the lower class is the frequently, though not always, deteriorated community organization among the impoverished.

The cohesiveness of the local community is also determined by ethnic homogeneity and by the degree of commitment to a collectively shared purpose, and these can vary independently of the other subsystems of the society. As measured by these variables, communal cohesiveness has been found to be associated with low delinquency rates in Israel, where it is a more important influence on delinquency than the rural-urban difference is.[57] Mental health of immigrant groups is better where they constitute a larger percentage of the total population and can provide more communal support for the individual against the pressures of the surrounding society.[58] In both Nigeria and rural northeast America, the poorest mental health is found in the most "disintegrated" communities.[59] Cohesiveness-reducing experiences, such as geographic mobility, tend to be associated with higher suicide rates.[60] Low communal cohesiveness appears to promote both self- and other-destructive behavior.

In part for this reason, various pathologies, particularly of the other-directed type, have tended in the past to be more prevalent in modern urban than in *traditional* rural communities. This comparison in prevalence of pathology is most striking with respect to juvenile delinquency and crimes against property;[61] however, "in Trinidad and Tobago alcoholism is commoner in rural than in urban areas";[62] there has been more rural violence in Colombia;[63] and the Netherlands and Ireland have had higher rural than urban rates of suicide.[64] Rural communities may lose their advantage when their traditional integrated way of life is radically disturbed by the forces of modernization.

Within urban communities, slum areas are particularly pathogenic,

---

[56] Alexander H. Leighton, T. Adeoye Lambo, Charles C. Hughes, Dorothea C. Leighton, Jane M. Murphy, and David B. Macklin, *Psychiatric Disorder among the Yoruba: A Report from the Cornell-Aro Mental Health Research Project in the Western Region, Nigeria* (Ithaca, N.Y.: Cornell University Press, 1963), p. 231.

[57] Shoham *et al.*, *op. cit.*

[58] H. B. M. Murphy, *op. cit.*, pp. 309-310.

[59] Leighton *et al.*, *op. cit.*, pp. 233-234.

[60] Peter Sainsbury, *Suicide in London: An Ecological Study* (New York: Basic Books, 1956), p. 41.

[61] Mannheim, *op. cit.*, pp. 548-551.

[62] M. H. Beaubrun, "Discussion: Socioeconomic Change, Population Explosion and the Changing Phases of Mental Health Programs in Developing Countries," *American Journal of Orthopsychiatry*, 36 (1966), p. 87.

[63] Richard S. Weinert, "Violence in Pre-Modern Societies: Rural Colombia," *The American Political Science Review*, 60 (June, 1966), pp. 340-347.

[64] Dublin and Bunzel, *op. cit.*, p. 82.

though it has been suggested that where the family system remains relatively strong, as traditionally in India, pathological phenomena other than famine appear "to be not as serious as in the slums of the West."[65] Conversely, the "tribally-oriented" African urban migrants, who "do not form communities very readily" on a non-tribal basis in cities, appear to undergo "greater social disorganization" than is evident in European slums.[66] Political organization, traditions of learning, and a strong kinship system may partly offset some of the pathogenic processes in impoverished urban areas.[67]

Determinants of Amount and Direction of Pathological Behavior

The cross-cultural studies reviewed suggest that five variables are associated with both self- and other-destructive behavior: (1) child socialization high on punishment and low on emotional supportiveness; (2) low (and perhaps very high) status within urban class systems; (3) downward mobility; (4) low community cohesiveness; and (5) economic insecurity. These variables might therefore be regarded as the most generally pathogenic, as maximizers of the *amount* of pathology.

The variables that appear to contribute more to self-directed destructiveness are (1) low (or extremely high) degree of control by the family system over adults; (2) relatively equalitarian stratification systems; (3) high status within urban class systems; (4) upward mobility; (5) occupations high on individual responsibility; and (6) stable democracy. The variables that seem more likely to result in other-directed aggression include (1) a "structurally inefficient" type of family characterized by an unbalanced or segregated relationship between the spouses; (2) low maternal sexual gratification; (3) highly inequalitarian stratification systems; (4) barriers to upward mobility; (5) lack of an organized legitimate power structure or of participation therein; and (6) political oppression. While these variables appear to be the determinants of the *direction* of pathological behavior, they may also affect its overall amount. To what extent they do so still remains to be determined.

The spontaneous tendency to engage in other-destructive behavior can always, in principle, be transformed by a strategic elite or group of elite-aspirants into *organized* other-destructive behavior — into an ideologically

[65] Marshall B. Clinard, *Slums and Community Development: Experiments in Self-Help* (New York: The Free Press, 1966), p. 88.

[66] W. Clifford, "Crime and Criminology in Central Africa," in Tadeusz Grygier, Howard Jones, John C. Spencer, eds., *Criminology in Transition: Essays in Honour of Hermann Mannheim* (London: Tavistock Publications, 1965), p. 217.

[67] Oscar Lewis, *La Vida: A Puerto Rican Family in the Culture of Poverty — San Juan and New York* (New York: Vintage Books, 1968), p. xlix.

legitimated social movement. But it should not be assumed that all organized pathology derives, in any ultimate sense, from the sources of aggression in frustrating individual experiences. War, for example, can be initiated on the basis of "rational" strategic considerations.

2. SOCIAL CHANGE AND PATHOLOGICAL BEHAVIOR

The direction of social change seems to affect the prevalence of particular types of pathologies: homicide rates are higher in preindustrial societies, and suicide rates in advanced industrial nations. One explanation of this pattern is that the social system of the advanced industrial society either presupposes or produces a stronger tendency in the personality structure to inhibit extreme other-directed aggression; thus the tendency to exhibit self-directed aggression becomes more prevalent. (However, the personalities of some residents of any advanced industrial society — the rural-bred and the slum dweller among them — have been formed by the fragments of an earlier type of social system which still defines some of the basic parameters of their life).

Particular types of pathologies increase or decline as society evolves toward greater technological mastery and internal complexity. Some types of pathology (witchcraft) become esoteric rarities while others (extremist political movements) emerge into prominence. But there is no convincing evidence that the total amount or the degree of intensity of social pathology produced in a society is affected by its level of evolutionary development, although pathologies seem to increase, temporarily, in particularly stressful, transitional times (as suicide did in Japan between 1938 and 1958, whereupon it subsided dramatically). Some of the apparent increase in pathologies in modern societies is an illusion caused by the ever-growing public awareness of social problems.

The effects of the direction of social change will not be further pursued in this article. The following section will focus on the pathogenic aspects of several types of rapid change itself and on some variables that seem to be capable, or incapable, of restraining the pathogenic effects of change.

Some Types of Rapid Change

The kind of breakdown of relatively static, heavily traditionalized social structures that occurs during the Westernization of tribal societies and of preindustrial civilizations seems frequently to increase the prevalence of mental illness, drunkenness,[68] homicide, suicide, crimes against property,[69]

[68] H. B. M. Murphy, "Social Change and Mental Health," *Causes of Mental Disorders: A Review of Epidemiological Knowledge, 1959* (New York: Milbank Memorial Fund, 1961), pp. 280-329; Horton, *op. cit.*
[69] Wood, *op. cit.*, pp. 103-106.

and projective aggressiveness (distrust of people, fear of supernatural forces);[70] that is, both self-destructive and other-destructive behavior, of both the direct and the projective type. However, "the incidence of major psychoses . . . is surprisingly resistant to social change";[71] and in some cases rapid modernization and acculturation of tribal and traditional societies have been associated with reductions in homicide, suicide, and drunkenness.[72] In accounting for such cases, Graves has suggested that "where traditional social and personal control systems are weak, as among many primitive groups, acculturation may also serve to promote the development of new controls, and thereby make the group better able to prevent disruptive individual behavior,"[73] such as drunkenness.

Alexander Leighton has pointed out that if "cultural change" is not accompanied by "social disintegration," an increase in pathologies need not occur. By social disintegration he refers to a disorganization of the community and family systems, and to cultural disorientation. Leighton also suggests that "the capacity of a social system to undergo cultural change without disintegration is dependent upon the mental health of the component individuals . . . the higher the prevalence of psychiatric disorders, the greater the risk of social disintegration." However, "in a number of communities we have studied," he writes, "the evidence suggests that [social] disintegration has preceded an increase of [psychiatric] disorder prevalence. . . ."[74] Reduction in social control and in the provision of consistent socioemotional supports by the community and family systems emerges as a specifically pathogenic dimension of social change. If this is so, one way to reduce the pathogenic effects of rapid change in the "public" (political and economic) sectors of society would be to maintain relative stability in the particular components of the "intimacy structures" (the family and community systems) with which the individual identifies himself. Observations made in various European societies during and after World War II lead to the conclusion that the psychiatrically disturbing effects of even the most rapid and radical change in the conditions of life — emigration and war — can be withstood by

[70] Seymour Parker and Tom T. Sasaki, "Society and Sentiments in Two Contrasting Socially Disturbed Areas," in Jane M. Murphy and Alexander H. Leighton, eds., *Approaches to Cross-Cultural Psychiatry* (Ithaca, N.Y.: Cornell University Press, 1965), pp. 329-357.

[71] Beaubrun, *op. cit.*, p. 87.

[72] Bohannan, *op. cit.*, pp. 264-265; Theodore D. Graves, "Acculturation, Access, and Alcohol in a Tri-Ethnic Community," *American Anthropologist*, 69 (June-August, 1967), pp. 306-321.

[73] Graves, *op. cit.*, p. 319.

[74] Alexander Leighton, "Cultural Change and Psychiatric Disorders," in A. V. S. de Reuck and Ruth Porter, eds., *Transcultural Psychiatry* (Boston: Little, Brown & Co., 1965), pp. 217-219, 224.

adults and children living in stable families.[75] Israeli findings that "new immigrants preserving their inner cohesion, special cultural homogeneity and agencies of social control" have low delinquency rates[76] also point up the beneficent effects of the stability of the intimacy structures in periods of rapid change in the economic and political conditions. These effects may be particularly salient for children and adolescents.

While social control by the kinship and community systems appears to be of strategic importance in affecting variations in the rates of pathological behavior, an intensification of *political* controls does not necessarily prevent an increase of individual pathological behavior in periods of rapid social change. Juvenile delinquency increased in the Soviet Union during the collectivization of agriculture in the years 1931-1935 in spite of "a simultaneous increase in state coercion."[77] In contrast, delinquency remained roughly constant and the adult crime rate (of the males only) declined significantly during the years of the Nazi transformation in Germany, 1933-1940,[78] a political discontinuity which, in contrast to Stalin's collectivization campaign, was sustained by considerable popular support. This comparison suggests the more general hypothesis that voluntary involvement of large sections of the population in a "successful" political transition may reduce its pathogenic potential *for them* (though possibly at an entirely disproportionate cost for the "outsider," as the European Jews discovered). "Crises in societal patterns or in individual experience that involve important losses, separations or disruptions and are not compensated by new social resources and a new sense of belonging and commitment are particularly significant for mental health and illness."[79]

Periods of unsuccessful revolutionary action, on the other hand, like the post-1905 years in Russia and 1923 in Germany, show increases in crime and delinquency.[80] Unsuccessful wars and defeats in war tend to have a similar effect.[81] Perhaps, then, social movements need to be successful in some measure in moving toward their goals if they are to help preserve their members and the society at large from individual pathologies. While successful social movements of the extremist variety have in the past produced pathological social institutions and organizations specializing in the destruction of lives in the normal course of their func-

[75] Murphy, *op. cit.*
[76] Shoham *et al.*, *op. cit.*, p. 399.
[77] Juviler, *op. cit.*, p. 8.
[78] Chalmers Johnson, *Revolutionary Change* (Boston: Little, Brown & Co., 1966), pp. 133.
[79] Marc Fried, "Effects of Social Change on Mental Health," *American Journal of Orthopsychiatry*, 34 (1964), p. 23.
[80] Juviler, *op. cit.*; Johnson, *op. cit.*
[81] Mannheim, *op. cit.*, p. 595.

tioning (the Inquisition, concentration camps, or totalitarian states), *unsuccessful* social movements tend to generate individual pathologies.

Research concerned with individual pathologies, such as suicide and alcoholism, frequently suggests that the family and community systems have a greater influence than economic and political systems in promoting or restraining pathological behavior. This does not seem to be the case with white-collar crime[82] and with the collective political pathologies, such as extremist movements. If one compares Talcott Parsons' classic analyses of social strains in pre-Nazi Germany and in America during the 1950's, one is led to hypothesize that two conditions extraneous to the family and community systems — economic prosperity and the legitimation of current political institutions by the prevailing cultural tradition — help to reduce the amount and violence of political pathology in periods of rapid change.[83]

But while national prosperity may inhibit society-directed political violence,[84] it seems to promote certain kinds of spontaneous attacks on property and the person. The delinquency rates have been increasing everywhere in Europe (except in Italy and Denmark) as well as in Israel, Japan, and Puerto Rico since the 1950's — a period of incipient mass affluence.[85] Sex crimes "known to the police" appear to be more frequent in the more prosperous industrial than in preindustrial societies; and the only type of crime with consistently increasing rates in Boston from 1849 to 1951 has been forcible rape.[86] In contrast to the utilitarian, gainful nature of most adult crimes, the majority of youthful delinquencies and

[82] John C. Spencer, "White-Collar Crime," in Tadeusz Grygier, Howard Jones, John C. Spencer, eds., *Criminology in Transition: Essays in Honour of Hermann Mannheim* (London: Tavistock Publications, 1965), p. 259; J. S. Nye, "Corruption and Political Development: A Cost-Benefit Analysis," *The American Political Science Review*, 61 (June, 1967), p. 418.

[83] Talcott Parsons, "Democracy and Social Structure in Pre-Nazi Germany," *Essays in Sociological Theory*, rev. ed. (Glencoe, Ill.: The Free Press, 1954), pp. 104-123; "Social Strains in America," in Daniel Bell, ed., *The Radical Right* (Garden City, N.Y.: Anchor Books, 1964), pp. 209-238. Also see Lipset, *op. cit.*, pp. 64-86.

[84] While rapid change in a number of "ecological variables" such as educational level or calory consumption is directly correlated with internal political violence, the rate of growth in national income is inversely associated with it. Ivo K. Feierabend and Rosalind L. Feierabend, "Aggressive Behavior within Polities, 1948-1962: A Cross-National Study," *The Journal of Conflict Resolution*, 10 (September, 1966), p. 266.

[85] Gibbens and Ahrenfeldt, *op. cit.*, pp. 32, 41, 43, 112, 117, 121, 127-130, 134-135; "The Youth Problem: Juvenile Delinquency in Eastern Europe," *East Europe*, 9 (June, 1960), pp. 3-13.

[86] Gibbens and Ahrenfeldt, *op. cit.*, p. 90; Theodore N. Ferdinand, "The Criminal Patterns of Boston Since 1849," *The American Journal of Sociology*, 73 (July, 1967), pp. 84-99.

sexual misconduct may be characterized as expressive "crimes of leisure." They might be expected to increase as the culture of leisure (with its focus on sensuous gratification detached from a communal purpose) develops in a consumption-oriented society and as both the burden and the symbolic significance of productive labor decline (in late imperial Rome as well as in advanced industrial societies). In contrast, utilitarian crime would probably decline with a more equalitarian distribution of affluence and esteem, if the finding that in preliterate societies theft is directly associated with the degree of status inequality, holds for industrial societies.[87]

Both Kornhauser and Lipset have stressed the importance of political, economic, and communal discontinuities in producing political extremism.[88] Mental illness among immigrants tends also to be more frequent in countries in which pressures for rapid acculturation exist.[89] But under certain conditions discontinuities may be beneficent, and the *persistence* or excessively slow change of a normative standard or an institutional structure may be pathogenic. The obvious example is a family system attuned to the need for maximizing reproduction in a high-mortality environment. When mortality is sharply reduced by medical advances, this type of family reproduces itself toward famine — unless it *rapidly* reorganizes itself around a new set of norms supportive of planned fertility reduction. Further evidence is supplied by LeVine who has observed that "anti-European violence" is reduced in the decolonializing societies in Africa when the "switch from paternalism to self-rule" is "carried off quickly and consistently," without generating conflicting expectations.[90]

Such observations suggest that when a relationship of relative equilibrium exists between two sociological variables — static conditions or processes — and when one variable changes sharply in such a way that, if the social system is to survive, the other will have to change at some time, the potential for pathology is reduced if the second variable also changes rapidly. It is the lack of change in the second variable that is typically responsible for the pathogenic process of polarization (discussed below). Studies cited before also indicate that if the results of social change can be incorporated into an ongoing organization of activities, such as a family, community, or state system, and legitimated by a convincing dem-

[87] Bacon *et al.*, *op. cit.*, p. 291.

[88] Kornhauser, *op. cit.*, pp. 129-174; Lipset, *op. cit.*, pp. 53-57. No relationship between "rapidity of modernization" and "Communist Party strength" has been found in Robert M. Marsh and William L. Parish, "Modernization and Communism: A Re-Test of Lipset's Hypothesis," *American Sociological Review*, 30 (December, 1965), p. 942.

[89] Fried, *op. cit.*, p. 10.

[90] Robert A. LeVine, "Anti-European Violence in Africa: A Comparative Analysis," *The Journal of Conflict Resolution*, 3 (December, 1959), p. 427.

onstration that they are congruent with a system of values adhered to by most members of the society in which they occur, then both the experience of discomfort due to change and the resulting potential for pathology are further reduced.[91]

Some Mechanisms of Causation

A psychosocial mechanism generated by social change that has frequently been assumed to affect pathological behavior is the *aspirations gap* — a sharp increase in the normally expectable discrepancy between aspiration and attainment. These disjunctions between expectation and reality are likely to arise particularly in the early part of periods of rapid economic improvement and political modernization, when not only economic and political, but also social and cultural, aspirations grow more rapidly than attainments, and political aggressiveness increases.[92] The aspirations gap develops also in periods when attainments decline sharply — after military defeats and during severe economic depressions, when crime rates tend to be high.[93] In both kinds of situations, an increase in subjective frustration seems to increase the disposition toward pathological behavior. In the classical case, the individual is thwarted by what he perceives as externally imposed barriers to the realization of his aspirations; hence, his aggressiveness, to the extent that it is motivated by the aspirations gap, is likely to take the other-directed form.

Another psychosocial mechanism activated in times of rapid change might be called *psychological invalidation of institutionalized standards of behavior*. Institutionalized norms lose the semblance of authority when they change (because they then prove not to possess any permanent validity), but they lose the essence of authority (that is, are perceived as irrelevant by contemporaries) when they remain stable in a period of rapid change, and therefore cease to articulate between new situations of action and old emotions or new emotions and old situations.

A "withdrawal of allegiance from one or another part of prevailing social standards " — Merton's definition of anomie[94] — does not necessarily produce frustration, although it may do so when an aspirations gap results

[91] Eaton and Weil suggest this in their discussion of the Hutterite method of "controlled acculturation." Joseph W. Eaton, in cooperation with Robert J. Weil, *Culture and Mental Disorders: A Comparative Study of the Hutterites and Other Populations* (Glencoe, Ill.: The Free Press, 1955), pp. 188-207.

[92] James C. Davies, "Toward a Theory of Revolution," *American Sociological Review*, 27 (February, 1962), pp. 5-19; and Feierabend, *op. cit.*, pp. 249-271.

[93] Mannheim, *op. cit.*, pp. 586-595.

[94] Robert K. Merton, "Anomie, Anomia, and Social Interaction: Contexts of Deviant Behavior," in Marshall B. Clinard, ed., *Anomie and Deviant Behavior* (New York: The Free Press of Glencoe, 1964), p. 83.

from it. The psychological dissolution of a set of norms may also remove a source of frustration that was previously regarded as unavoidable. But certainly, with psychological invalidation of norms, the effectiveness of traditional social controls over both the destructive and self-destructive behavior of individuals and groups is reduced. In a social setting in which variables promoting other-directed aggression are present (see previous section), anomie should bring about an increase in other-destructive behavior; this behavior can be studied in slum dwellers or revolutionary peasants. In a situation in which variables promoting self-directed aggression are found, the result should be an increase in self-destruction; well-educated and relatively privileged groups may move in this direction in a period of rapid change. The romanticization of suicide in the Paris Bohème of the nineteenth century[95] or the cult of narcotics in the hippie subculture of affluent American adolescents are cases in point. If, however, "invalidated" norms are coercively imposed on such groups, an attack against their upholders is felt to be legitimate, indeed morally obligatory.

To a certain extent it can be validly argued that in periods of rapid change pathological behavior is produced not by the changes themselves but by the rigidities of social structure and attitudes that are upheld in spite of their demonstrated ineffectiveness in coping with change. While conservatism is identified with traditional virtues, it may in fact contribute to modern pathologies. Thus in Latin America the traditional opposition (now changing) of the Catholic church and nationalistic politicians to effective contraception is one of the chief reasons why abortion, according to some studies, "is the leading cause of death among Latin American women between the ages of 15 and 45."[96] In Japan "delinquents who have been interviewed" by De Vos "were seemingly more likely to be from rather traditionally oriented families than from families whose behavior has been modified by modern trends."[97] In Israel the *non*delinquents were more likely than the delinquents to reject "the outwardly formalized norms of society."[98] In Ceylon, Straus found the more

[95] César Graña, *Bohemian versus Bourgeois: French Society and the French Man of Letters in the Nineteenth Century* (New York: Basic Books, 1964).

[96] Paul L. Montgomery, "For the Latins the Birth Rate Spells Disaster," *The New York Times*, September 17, 1967, Sec. E, p. 7.

[97] George A. De Vos, "Deviancy and Social Change: A Psychocultural Evaluation of Trends in Japanese Delinquency and Suicide," in Robert J. Smith and Richard K. Beardsley, eds., *Japanese Culture — Its Development and Characteristics* (Chicago: Aldine Publishing Co., 1962), p. 166.

[98] Shlomo Shoham and Leon Shasholsky, "A Cross Cultural Analysis of Delinquents and Nondelinquents in Israel," p. 6, paper presented at the 1967 Annual Meeting of the American Sociological Association at San Francisco.

"Westernized" university students to have "the fewest indicators of psychological disability."[99] In the "disintegrated" village communities of Nigeria that were also "changing" in their cultural and economic orientations, there was an average level of mental health, while in the socially "disintegrated" villages that had retained a "traditional" cultural orientation an extremely high level of psychiatric symptoms was prevalent.[100] (If one has to live in a disintegrated community, it may be literally healthier to forget the traditional standards around which the community may have been integrated in the past.) The sociopsychological mechanism operating in these diverse situations may be conceptualized as the *resistance gap* — a sharply increased disjunction between internalized normative standards and the objective requirements of the changed situation of action. The mechanism is similar to the aspirations gap, except that a backward-looking orientation, not a utopian one, is the pathogenic agent in this case. William F. Ogburn has conceived of this mechanism as "cultural lag," though he tied it more closely to technological changes and regarded it as more unavoidable than I do.

When various groups within a society change at different rates, an *attitudinal polarization* between slowly changing "traditionalists" and rapidly changing "modernizers" may occur. This is especially likely when one or the other side adopts an inflexible position and pursues it "extremistically" — in utter disregard of the interests and values of the other side and everyone else. Such a polarization, which Sorokin regarded as characteristic of periods of social and natural "calamities,"[101] intensifies reciprocal other-directed aggressiveness among representatives of the polarized groups. This mechanism operated during the rise of Nazism in Germany and also promoted rural violence in Colombia where 135,000 persons were killed between 1949 and 1958 in a mutual genocide which, contrary to the Marxist assumption that all struggle is ultimately class struggle, had no basis in economic (or for that matter, racial) differences.[102]

When attitudinal polarization is transformed into political polarization, with powerful movements representing the opposite extremes, the communal involvement of the individual adherents of the conflicting camps is likely to be intensified. Their susceptibility to individual pathologies as-

[99] Murray A. Straus, "Westernization, Insecurity, and Sinhalese Social Structure," *The International Journal of Social Psychiatry*, 12 (1966), p. 137.

[100] Leighton *et al.*, *Psychiatric Disorder among the Yoruba*, pp. 239-240.

[101] Pitirim A. Sorokin, *Man and Society in Calamity: The Effects of War, Revolution, Famine, Pestilence Upon Human Minds, Behavior, Social Organization and Cultural Life* (New York: E. P. Dutton & Co., 1942).

[102] Talcott Parsons, "Some Sociological Aspects of the Fascist Movement," *Essays in Sociological Theory*, rev. ed. (Glencoe, Ill.: The Free Press, 1954), pp. 124-141; Weinert, *op. cit.*

sociated with the lack of communal involvement, such as suicide, is reduced. In nineteenth-century France, suicide tended to decline in times of internal disorder and political crisis; and there is a slight negative correlation between the relative size of the Communist vote and the rates of such self-destructive behaviors as suicide and alcoholism.[103] This indeed is one of the psychological attractions of political extremism and other forms of group warfare.

Organized Pathologies and Social Change

Rapid social change, by breaking the restraining hold of custom and the bonds of mutual concern that frequently characterize social relationships in stable traditional societies, provides an opportunity for the establishment of exceedingly pathological institutions (the Inquisition, concentration camps) and may also increase the virulence of existing pathological institutions (e.g., chattel slavery, which has appeared in a "harsh form . . . in expansive, fluid societies, such as the Roman Republic and the United States").[104] Institutions may be called pathological by their very nature when they produce pathological behavior not by their failures but when they function as they have been designed to. Such institutions demand pathological behavior as an obligation of membership.

But social change can also provide the means for eliminating or modifying highly pathogenic institutions which in a relatively unchanging society, such as ancient Egypt, might remain unchallengeable. This is why classical capitalism and totalitarianism have been susceptible to evolution, in some cases, toward more beneficent social systems. The opposite type of evolution is also possible: initially beneficent organizations and institutions can evolve pathologically. The Mafia of Sicily originated as an organization "of resistance to political and social oppression" and developed in a pathological direction, becoming an exploitative criminal organization.[105] Organizations of militant "liberators" have rather frequently exhibited this tendency (Ghana under Nkrumah). When in the latter part of the Middle Ages the church, disturbed by the growth of cities and of heretical movements, began sponsoring the Crusades and the persecution of witches (usually women, old and odd),[106] the humanizing institution which it was in the Dark Ages evolved in a pathological direction — and it took several centuries to reverse the trend.

[103] Robert E. L. Faris, *Social Disorganization* (New York: The Ronald Press Co., 1948), pp. 214-216; Kornhauser, *op. cit.*, p. 91.
[104] David Brion Davis, *The Problem of Slavery in Western Culture* (Ithaca, N.Y.: Cornell University Press, 1966), p. 30.
[105] Gibbens and Ahrenfeldt, *op. cit.*, p. 64.
[106] George Rosen, *Madness in Society: Chapters in the Historical Sociology of Mental Illness* (Chicago: University of Chicago Press, 1968), Chap. 1.

The conditions which facilitate the development of institutions and organizations in a beneficent or in a pathogenic direction have not yet been systematically identified. The decline in the utility of their pathogenic aspects to their leaders and the existence of legitimated internal criticism seem to promote the former course; lack of success in goal attainment and absolute power of the ruling elites, the latter. In open societies pathological institutions can presumably be reformed by relatively pacific social pressures; in closed societies their abolition has frequently required violence from within or without. The difference between open and closed societies is, however, not always empirically clear; it took violence to abolish slavery in the American democracy, and some totalitarian societies (the Soviet Union after Stalin, Yugoslavia) have shown themselves to be capable of peaceful reforms of a limited scope. The relationship between social change and organized pathology is inherently an ambiguous one, not easy to subsume under a specific formula.

3. CULTURAL FACTORS AND PATHOLOGICAL BEHAVIOR

If the subjective perception of a situation affects the likelihood of pathological behavior occurring in it, cultural factors that shape subjective perceptions should influence pathological behavior *independently* of social structure or changes in it. In this section, a few of the ways in which cultural factors affect pathological behavior will be considered.

Explicit Ideologies

The relationship between ideologies of social superiority, racism,[107] militarism,[108] revolutionary romanticism, or fashionable despair[109] and the forms of pathological behavior corresponding to them would seem to be evident. Such collectively shared and historically transmitted ideologies (and also the more transient fashions diffused by the mass media of communication) may legitimate pathological tendencies originating in immediate social experiences. They may also cause pathological behavior in persons who are simply conforming to the ideology of a group with which they identify but are not otherwise pathologically disposed.[110] Traditional

[107] Even the Spanish Inquisition was "in origin, the offspring" of the "desire for racial purity. . . ." R. Trevor Davies, *The Golden Century of Spain, 1501-1621* (New York: Harper Torchbooks, 1961), p. 11.

[108] Preliterate "societies that expect more kinds of satisfactions from successful warfare tend to be societies which fight more frequently and which make more preparation for war." Raoul Naroll, "Does Military Deterrence Deter?" *Trans-Action*, 3 (January/February, 1966), p. 19.

[109] Graña, *op. cit.*, pp. 71-82; Fritz Stern, *The Politics of Cultural Despair: A Study in the Rise of the Germanic Ideology* (Berkeley: University of California Press, 1963).

[110] Cf. Pettigrew, *op. cit.*

ideological polarization may produce extreme group violence within the same social class among persons with identical economic interests.[111] In periods of extreme social stress, ideologies are apt to intensify spontaneously emergent tendencies toward extreme forms of behavior (not all of which, however, are pathological).[112]

Moderate and humane ideologies may help in alleviating pathogenic conditions. But such ideologies have less appeal in times of extreme crisis (and for persons and groups in a condition of high subjective frustration, including the "alienated intellectuals"). Furthermore, humane ideologies do not necessarily humanize their adherents: Christianity has traditionally promoted anti-Semitism,[113] and the perpetrators of mass murder against millions of peasants in Eastern Europe have regarded themselves as Marxists.[114] Van den Berghe has argued that "the egalitarian and libertarian ideas of the Enlightenment," while conflicting with racism, have also "contributed to its development," so that "the lot of the slave has typically been better in aristocratic societies . . . than in *Herrenvolk* democracies like the United States" until World War II.[115] Indeed, in both ancient Greece and the American South before the Civil War, "freedom and slavery seemed to advance together."[116] Ideology, both sacred and secular, has probably tended throughout history to have a more compelling effect when it was used to justify pathological action than as an appeal to desist from such action. However, commitment to a collectively held ideology and its reinforcement by ritual means seem to reduce the likelihood of individual pathologies such as delinquency and psychiatric disorders, which can be precipitated by a lacking sense of participation and purpose.[117]

The modern "ideologies of secular promise," which legitimate the expectation of much higher levels of gratification (economic or social-

[111] Weinert, *op. cit.*, pp. 340-341.

[112] Sorokin insists that in periods of extreme crisis average behavior has tended to polarize at the extremes of destructiveness versus self-sacrificing altruism or creativity. *Man and Society in Calamity.*

[113] James Parkes, *The Conflict of the Church and the Synagogue: A Study of the Origins of Antisemitism* (Cleveland: The World Publishing Co., 1961), p. 375. A careful study suggests that "at least one-fourth of America's anti-Semites have a religious basis for their prejudice. . . ." Charles Y. Glock and Rodney Stark, *Christian Beliefs and Anti-Semitism* (New York: Harper & Row, 1966), p. 205.

[114] Cf. Czeslaw Milosz, "The Lesson of the Baltics," *The Captive Mind* (New York: Vintage Books, 1955), pp. 213-240.

[115] Pierre L. Van den Berghe, *Race and Racism: A Comparative Perspective* (New York: John Wiley & Sons, 1967), pp. 17-18.

[116] David Brion Davis, *op. cit.*, p. 36.

[117] Shoham *et al.*, *op. cit.* In Nigeria, the presence of religious ritual is associated with community integration, and the latter with good mental health. Leighton *et al.*, *Psychiatric Disorder among the Yoruba*, p. 231.

emotional) than are attainable, may promote pathological behavior by increasing, at least temporarily, the aspirations gap. In this manner, the Marxist promise of an ideal future society may contribute as much to juvenile delinquency in the U.S.S.R. as the "American Dream" does in the United States. On the other hand, the absence of such ideologies may increase the unnecessary willingness to bear *avoidable* deprivations, to accept some kind of "self-destruction." To what extent ideologies of secular promise will have pathological effects probably depends on the opportunity structure for attaining their promise, and also on the inner capacities of the personality to cope with the ideological promise, the social opportunity structure, and the generally expectable discrepancy between the two. All of these dimensions are variables; but there are certainly limits to the extent to which opportunity structures for attaining social esteem, freedom, romantic love, or creative self-expression can be adapted to the ideological promise. On the whole, a gradualist "ideology of imperfect promise" would seem to offer the least pathogenic guide for navigating between the resigned acceptance of unnecessary deprivation and an aggressive reaction to disappointed expectations of instant gratification.

Pervasive Cultural Influences

Broad cultural traditions affect socially organized pathologies by unintentionally — even unconsciously — creating in various strategic elites dispositions of action favorable to one or another kind of pathology. A careful statistical study has revealed that from 1820 to 1949 "Christians fought Christians more than would be expected from their population" (as well as fighting Moslems more than would be expected), whereas "Moslems fought Moslems less" than the expected amount. The Confucian-Taoist-Buddhist religion of China, on the other hand, "stands out conspicuously as being either itself a pacifier, or else associated with one. . . ."[118] Although the industrial revolution which was occurring during this period in the Christian West may have contributed to the warlikeness of the Western societies, it seems psychologically plausible — and consistent with the still earlier historical record — to assume that the activistic, this-worldly orientation that Western societies have derived in part from their Judeo-Christian backgrounds may favor the acceptance of organized violence as a means of policy (in spite of the conscious stress on the "Prince of Peace" theme in the Christian tradition). Christianity may also have contributed to bellicosity by promoting repressive sex norms.[119]

[118] Lewis F. Richardson, *Statistics of Deadly Quarrels* (Pittsburgh: The Boxwood Press, 1960), pp. 239, 245.

[119] A relationship between restrictive sex norms and bellicosity (as well as the capacity to create more complex technological and social systems) has been found in preliterate societies by Philip E. Slater, in "Culture, Sexuality and Narcissism:

In a similar manner, cultural values, through their effects on subconscious motivation, produce dispositions toward particular kinds of individual pathologies.[120] Much of the research on the relations between cultural values and pathological behavior has been concerned with values prominent in Western societies. Studies of suicide in Scandinavia and Japan suggest that a strong "preoccupation with success and achievement" contributes to high suicide rates.[121] This cultural value seems to be as strongly held in the United States, where the suicide rate has only amounted to 50-65 per cent of the Japanese and Swedish rates during the 1950's; thus an achievement orientation is not sufficient to account for high rates. Achievement motivation correlates, in contemporary states, with internal political violence, ulcers, and hypertension, but not with deaths due to murder, suicide, and alcoholism. These findings suggest that achievement values inhibit direct aggression, so that direct aggression is exhibited only when ideologically justified — as violence required for fighting oppression; alternatively, inhibited aggressiveness is turned toward oneself in the "hidden" form of psychophysiological symptoms. In preliterate societies, an achievement orientation is associated with drunkenness but not with the frequency of theft and personal crime. Rather, theft is linked with a strong "sense of property," with materialistic values. A pronounced cultural need for dominating other people is correlated, in sixteen modern nations, with high rates of death due to murder, suicide, and alcoholism, as well as with high divorce rates — all, perhaps, expressions of disappointed desires to dominate a refractory social environment. Achievement, property, and power values do not necessarily go together, but they are all highly developed in the American society, which has extremely or moderately high rates of all the pathologies just mentioned. A culturally shaped tendency to perceive the environment as threatening goes with a high frequency of both drunkenness and crime in preliterate societies[122] and also in the urban slums. It is as if the anxiety produced

---

A Cross-Cultural Study," unpublished manuscript. G. Rattray Taylor, *Sex in History* (New York: The Vanguard Press, 1954), p. 301, has suggested that permissive sex norms produce a tendency to direct aggression inward, restrictive norms to direct it outward.

[120] On a typology of the ways in which culture may affect mental health, see Alexander H. Leighton and Jane H. Hughes "Cultures as Causative of Mental Disorders," *Causes of Mental Disorders: A Review of Epidemiological Knowledge, 1959* (New York: Milbank Memorial Fund, 1961), pp. 341-365.

[121] Hendin, *op. cit.*; De Vos, *op. cit.*, p. 164.

[122] Betty A. Nesvold, "Scalogram Analysis of Political Violence: A Cross-National Study," p. 19, paper prepared for delivery at the 1967 Annual Meeting of the American Political Science Association, Chicago, September 5-9; Bacon *et al.*, "Crime," pp. 297-300; Bacon *et al.*, "Drinking," pp. 34-38; S. A. Rudin, "National Motives Predict Psychogenic Death Rates 25 Years Later," *Science*, 160, No. 3830 (24 May, 1968), pp. 901-903.

or reinforced by the cultural tradition causes tendencies to escape through self-destructive behavior or to strike back aggressively. Alcoholic addiction tends to be rare, but narcotics use prevalent, in societies with little sense of sin, as in China.[123]

Conflict between different value systems, apparently regardless of the specific content of these systems, seems to promote juvenile delinquency in Israel[124] as well as in the United States. The conflict between obedience and achievement values is associated with drunkenness in preliterate societies,[125] and the simultaneous presence of both "self-orientation" and "dependency" among Japanese youth has been cited among the reasons for their high suicide rate.[126] The question whether *specific* types of culture conflict promote particular types of pathologies has not been systematically investigated.

Cultural factors affect not only the prevalence, but also the *form*, of pathological behavior. The symptoms, though probably not the amount, of psychiatric disease are influenced by cultural tradition.[127] Psychiatric disturbances are more likely to take the manic depressive form in Christian, particularly Protestant sectarian, societies that inculcate a tendency to seek the causes of failure within one's own mind, interpreting them at the same time as moral deficiencies.[128] While schizophrenia occurs everywhere, depressive psychoses have been thought to be relatively rare in societies which lack the cultural tradition of self-blame.[129] In Ghana, however, such a tradition is associated with high rates of depression and suicide, contrasting with low reported rates in most of sub-Saharan Africa.[130] A study of crimes committed in the Netherlands during the years 1910-1915 and 1919 reveals that "Catholics have a high rate of crimes of violence, Protestants of sexual offenses and Jews of fraud" (i.e.,

---

[123] Raymond G. McCarthy, ed., *Drinking and Intoxication: Selected Readings in Social Attitudes and Controls* (New Haven, Conn.: College and University Press, 1959), pp. 121-122; Bernard Barber, *Drugs and Society* (New York: Russell Sage Foundation, 1967), p. 139.

[124] Shoham *et al.*, *op. cit.*, p. 405.

[125] McClelland *et al.*, *op. cit.*

[126] Mamoru Iga and Kenshiro Ohara, "Suicide Attempts of Japanese Youth and Durkheim's Concept of Anomie: An Interpretation," *Human Organization*, 26 (Spring/Summer, 1967), p. 62.

[127] On Irish-Italian differences in the symptomatology of schizophrenia, see Marvin K. Opler, *Culture & Social Psychiatry* (New York: Atherton Press, 1967), pp. 289-303.

[128] Eaton and Weil, *op. cit.*

[129] E. D. Wittkower and J. Field, "Some Problems of Transcultural Psychiatry," in Marvin K. Opler, ed., *Culture and Mental Health: Cross-Cultural Studies* (New York: The Macmillan Co., 1959), p. 493.

[130] S. Kirson Weinberg, "Cultural Aspects of Manic Depression in West Africa," *Journal of Health and Human Behavior*, 6 (Winter, 1965), pp. 247-257.

commercial white-collar crimes).[131] These differences, however, may be attributed at least in part to social position rather than religious background.

The type of cultural values formally adhered to may, in certain areas of pathological behavior, make no difference. Thus religious values do not detain American adolescents from delinquency, and delinquent and non-delinquent youths in Israel do not differ significantly in their "societal values."[132] The *intensity* of adherence to some set of culturally elaborated values may, in such cases, restrain more than the type of values adhered to (so long as the values are not themselves pathological; that is, so long as they do not positively require some kind of pathological behavior).

The cultural attitude toward a condition or form of behavior influences the extent to which it becomes pathogenic. Where the bribing of officials (a type of white-collar crime) is sanctioned by a favorable community attitude, it may or may not interfere with economic development, but it does not generate a subjective sense of resentment that might lead to pathological behavior.[133] Where nonconformity to traditional norms is defined as less seriously deviant, it occurs more frequently but has a less disturbing effect on the personalities of those who engage in it (e.g., produces less guilt) and on their subsequent social behavior.[134] On the other hand, when a "culture of violence" becomes established as a traditional expectation, it is likely to increase the spontaneous generation of violent acts — and also to define the proper objects of aggression, whether neighbors or political leaders.[135] The "culture of poverty" — a particular set of attitudes characterized by mistrust, resignation, avoidance of organization, and sexual promiscuity — intensifies the pathogenic effects of poverty itself.[136] Subcultural norms positively sanctioning a type of pathological behavior, such as juvenile vandalism or the use of narcotics, will

[131] Michael Argyle, *Religious Behavior* (Glencoe, Ill.: The Free Press, 1959), p. 99. In Israel, where the Jews are less exclusively urban than they were in Europe, the difference between the rates of crimes against the person and against property has disappeared. Mannheim, *op. cit.*, p. 570.

[132] Thomas M. Gannon, S.J., "Religious Control and Delinquent Behavior," *Sociology and Social Research,* 51 (July, 1967), p. 426; Shoham and Shasholsky, *op. cit.*, p. 5.

[133] Nye, *op. cit.*

[134] Harold T. Christensen and George R. Carpenter, "Value-Behavior Discrepancies Regarding Premarital Coitus in Three Western Cultures," *American Sociological Review,* 27 (1962), pp. 67-70; Nye, *op. cit.*, p. 423.

[135] Merle King, "Violence and Politics in Latin America," The Sociological Review Monograph 11, *Latin American Sociological Studies,* ed. Paul Halmos (Keele, Staffordshire: University of Keele, 1967), pp. 119-132; Marvin E. Wolfgang and Franco Ferracuti, *The Subculture of Violence: Towards An Integrated Theory in Criminology* (London: Social Science Paperbacks, 1967).

[136] Lewis, *op. cit.*

tend to make these pathologies more prevalent and resistant to attempts at rehabilitation.

A cultural attitude defining a form of behavior that is not pathological in its effects on the society or the personality — whether political dissent or moderate consumption of alcoholic beverages — as pathological in its moral effects (that is, as "immoral") will cause it to be treated as if it were pathological, and will probably to some extent force it to become pathological. (If members of groups which prohibit alcohol do drink, they are more likely to become alcoholics than members of the groups which permit drinking). The prohibition of a form of behavior may also produce foci of pathology in areas of social life not covered by the prohibition, as in the Islamic countries where opium use and addiction have been stimulated by the prohibition of alcohol.[137] Pathological forms of behavior, such as mental illness, tend to appear in a less severe form when the cultural attitude toward them is not categorically rejective.[138]

4. SOCIAL CONTROL OF PATHOLOGICAL BEHAVIOR

The culturally prescribed mode of treatment of the pathologies that have occurred in a society affects their virulence, direction, and, less demonstrably, their prevalence. Some punishment or deprivation of rights is a typical component of the treatment of individual (but not of organized) pathologies and of nonpathological acts disapproved of in a society. Thus while 99 per cent of preliterate societies punish for such destructive behavior as rape of a married woman, 92 per cent also punish for a nonpathological but disapproved act such as sexual relations during menstruation.[139] Since punishment is a means of dealing with what is socially disapproved and not with what is pathological in its effects, nonpathological acts may be punished and pathological behavior (such as exploitation and prejudice) remain unpunished.

Punishment is, of course, more effective in dealing with the partly voluntaristic pathologies than with wholly involuntary "sickness" (e.g., an addiction after it has developed). Both certainty and severity of punishment, but especially the former, appear to be associated with lower homicide rates.[140] (This relationship could reflect the tendency for more tightly organized communities to have less crime and more certain punishment, without punishment itself being the deterrent of crime.) To be

[137] Bernard Barber, op. cit., pp. 139-143.

[138] Julian Silverman, "Shamans and Acute Schizophrenia," American Anthropologist, 69 (February, 1967), pp. 21-31.

[139] Julia S. Brown, "A Comparative Study of Deviations from Sexual Mores," American Sociological Review, 17 (April, 1952), p. 138.

[140] Jack P. Gibbs, "Crime, Punishment, and Deterrence," Southwestern Social Science Quarterly, 48 (March, 1968), pp. 515-530.

effective, punishment must also be "commensurate with the crime," "symbolize the ethical condemnation of legitimate society," and "be in accord with the values of the groups with which the individual identifies himself."[141]

A *predominantly* punitive method of treatment of pathologies tends to increase their virulence (and the difficulty of rehabilitation of persons subject to them) without necessarily reducing their prevalence. This is especially true with regard to "sickness." In Britain, where narcotics addiction is treated medically rather than punitively as in the United States, it is less pathological in its consequences and far less prevalent[142] (though in both countries recent increases have occurred). The more punitive treatment of drunkenness in Finland than in Denmark has not prevented it from being a greater "public nuisance" in the former country.[143]

Ineffectiveness of punishment by itself is also implied in a study of forty preliterate societies by Palmer, who found "a positive relationship both between [the severity of] overall punishment [for all types of crime] and murder and between overall punishment and suicide."[144] This study does not reveal whether legal punitiveness is a cause or a consequence of extreme self- and other-directed aggression, or whether all three are interrelated indicators of a highly pathogenic situation (which seems probable). But it at least strongly suggests that low punitiveness is not a guarantee of high crime.

Gurr also found no direct relationship between the size of military and police forces in relation to population, and the amount of civil disorders: a large coercive force does not by itself reduce turmoil.[145] Turmoil is inhibited, however, when size of coercive forces is combined with their degree of loyalty to the regime, and when the political system by which coercion is used is regarded by the population as legitimate. Thus legitimacy and certainty of punishment, not its severity, emerge as the effectively restraining aspects of punishment. While punitiveness does not by itself reduce (and may increase) aggressiveness, it tends to transfer aggression caused by agents within the group to outsiders[146] — a mechanism of

141 Gresham M. Sykes, *Crime and Society*, 2nd ed. (New York: Random House, 1967), p. 119.

142 Schur, *op. cit.*, pp. 205-223.

143 Nils Christie, "The Scandinavian Hangover," *Trans-Action*, 4 (January/February, 1967), p. 35.

144 Stuart Palmer, "Murder and Suicide in Forty Non-Literate Societies," *Journal of Criminal Law, Criminology, and Police Science*, 56 (1965), p. 324.

145 Ted Gurr, "Urban Disorder: Perspectives from the Comparative Study of Civil Strife," *American Behavioral Scientist*, 2, 4 (March-April, 1968), pp. 50-55.

146 George O. Wright, "Projection and Displacement: A Cross-Cultural Study of Folk Tale Aggression," *The Journal of Abnormal and Social Psychology*, 49 (1954), pp. 523-528.

considerable significance in the genesis of prejudice, domestic group violence, and war.

In contrast to punitiveness, the cultural commitment to a nonviolent restraining of the destructive behavior of members of the society and the prompt mobilization of a rescue organization for them may well reduce the prevalence of pathologies.[147] This "therapeutic" kind of social control appears frequently to have evolved further in premodern than in industrial societies,[148] perhaps because punishment seems less needed when a well-organized community system can be relied upon to participate in the rehabilitation of persons subject to pathological behavior. A narrowly "professional" ideology of therapy, however, which insists that the person who is defined as a "patient" be isolated from his community setting and dealt with in the aseptic environment of an agency specializing in the treatment of "his" type of pathology, may be a less effective approach than the one which permits the rehabilitative powers of ordinary community life to interact with professional intervention.[149] The community may also help to cause, as well as to heal, pathologies, and a certain measure of detachment from communal influences may be beneficial in the rehabilitation of some of the pathologically disturbed.[150]

It has been suggested that cathartic "safety valves," or institutionalized nondestructive modes of expression of tension, may be needed in the social control of pathological behavior. "The likelihood and magnitude of civil violence [and also probably of self-destructive behavior] tend to vary inversely with the availability of institutional mechanisms that permit the expression of nonviolent hostility."[151] While in traditional societies stable, ritualized occasions may have provided this opportunity, in industrial societies movements of dissent — not necessarily political ones — seem frequently to perform this function, while also pursuing other, more manifest, goals. (However, in the earlier stages of modernization such movements may themselves become carriers of what will be called, in the next section, secondary pathologies). There have been arguments that

[147] Raymond Firth, "Suicide and Risk-Taking in Tikopia Society," Psychiatry, 24 (1961), p. 17.

[148] A case of the "therapeutic" treatment of crime in the community is described in John Beattie, Bunyoro: An African Kingdom (New York: Holt, Rinehart & Winston, 1960), pp. 66-69.

[149] Mark G. Field, "Soviet and American Approaches to Mental Illness," in S. N. Eisenstadt, ed., Comparative Social Problems (New York: The Free Press, 1964), pp. 105-128.

[150] Philip L. Newman, " 'Wild Man' Behavior in a New Guinea Highlands Community," American Anthropologist, 66 (February, 1964), pp. 1-19; G. Morris Carstairs, "The Social Limits of Eccentricity: An English Study," in Opler, Culture and Mental Health, pp. 373-389.

[151] Gurr, op. cit., p. 269.

pornography may function more as a safety valve than as incitement to other-destructive sexual behavior.[152] But this may be true only for adults in well-organized, middle-class societies with strongly developed inner restraints on aggression, such as Denmark. The usual problem with safety valves is that in a situation in which a pathological disposition exists, they can provide a justification for pathological behavior. Experimental evidence suggests that cathartic release of aggressiveness does not reduce, but may in some cases actually increase, it.[153] Thus many types of safety valves are unsafe or useless.

Unproductive tension release is to be distinguished from creative sublimation of potentially pathogenic tendencies in the personality or society. Difficulties in fulfilling role obligations are associated not only with pathological behavior but also with stronger religious and artistic interests.[154] Periods of community disintegration have frequently been those of enhanced creativity in philosophy, religion, science, and art.[155] Cattell *et al.* have found, in a factor-analytical study of forty contemporary nations, a cluster of variables consisting of "large number of clashes with other countries," "large number of riots," and "frequent involvement in war," on the one hand, and "high creativity in science and philosophy," "high musical creativity," and "many Nobel prizes in Science, Literature and Peace," on the other.[156] A social setting which generates pathological responses in some persons subject to its influence may enhance the involvement with cultural systems and the capacity for culture creation in others (presumably because the creative imagination can provide some of the resources needed for coping with pathogenic conditions). The relative lack of accessibility to complex cultural systems in the urban lower class may be one of the reasons for its apparently higher rates of a variety of spontaneous pathological behavior.

When pathologies become highly prevalent in a society, measures of

152 "Copenhagen Police Chief Alex Haslund said that in 1966 there were 790 sex offenses in Copenhagen and 588 in 1967 after the censorship law on written pornography was revoked." "Denmark Sex Crimes Declining," *The Washington Post*, March, 22, 1968, p. 5. Apparently the purchases of pornography declined when it was legitimated, hence there might still be a *direct* relationship between its use and sex crimes.

153 Leonard Berkowitz, *Aggression: A Social Psychological Analysis* (New York: McGraw Hill Book Co., 1962), p. 207.

154 Argyle, *op. cit.*, pp. 145-154; Vytautas Kavolis, "A Role Theory of Artistic Interest," *Journal of Social Psychology*, 60 (1963), pp. 31-37.

155 Don Martindale, *Social Life and Cultural Change* (Princeton, N.J.: D. Van Nostrand Co., 1962); Vytautas Kavolis, "Community Dynamics and Artistic Creativity," *American Sociological Review*, 31 (1966), pp. 208-217.

156 R. B. Cattell, H. Breul, H. P. Hartman, "An Attempt at More Refined Definition of the Cultural Dimensions of Syntality in Modern Nations," *American Sociological Review*, 17 (1952), pp. 408-421.

control aimed at the individual prove to have been inadequate, and changes in the social and cultural order appear to become necessary. These changes can be undertaken as rationally devised *reforms* of particular aspects of the social order, executed, in modern societies, through the bureaucratic machinery of state administration. Or else the whole sociocultural configuration of a society may be reorganized by a *revitalization movement*, which is likely to transcend the bureaucratic apparatus and employ a high degree of appeal to mass emotions. Revitalization movements can be powerfully effective in solving outstanding social problems,[157] but they can themselves become foci of organized pathology, even while attempting to deal with conditions their members construe as pathological. Both the Nazi movement and, certainly in some of its phases, the Soviet Revolution have been more pathological than any of the conditions which they were intended to abolish. Religious revival movements have also frequently involved "psychopathology in a broad sense."[158] While reform is safer, it is weak in changing the informal, spontaneous, private behavior and modes of feeling and evaluation. It may also lack the thrust for changing pathogenic social conditions when powerful groups are interested in preserving them.

Social control of organized social pathologies (slavery, concentration camps, warfare) has usually depended heavily on coercive methods or the fear of retributive force but also on traditional, though nonenforceable, expectations of propriety. Effective nonpathological means of controlling organized pathologies sanctioned by a sovereign state have not yet evolved.[159]

5. PATHOLOGICAL RESPONSES TO PATHOLOGY

Attempts to control or reform conditions causing destructive or self-destructive behavior have more frequently than not entailed — and even generated — pathologies of their own, which may be designated as *secondary pathologies*. An illustration of this phenomenon is the use of violence to overcome existing pathological conditions. Both judicial cruelty and revolutionary violence are secondary pathologies — destructive modes of dealing with pathogenic conditions, when equally or more effective ways of dealing with these conditions do not appear to be available. Secondary pathologies may be more destructive in their effects than the path-

---

[157] Anthony F. C. Wallace, *Culture and Personality* (New York: Random House, 1961), pp. 143-156.

[158] Rosen, *op. cit.*, p. 224.

[159] On the social control of warfare, see Quincy Wright, *op. cit.*, and Richard A. Falk and Saul H. Mendlovitz, eds., *Toward A Theory of War Prevention*, 4 vols. (New York: World Law Fund, 1966).

ological behavior they are intended to control. When in eighteenth-century England 222 types of offenses, including "the shooting of a rabbit" and "the theft of a pocket-handkerchief," carried the capital punishment,[160] and in contemporary American society, when the individual who smokes his first marihuana cigarette may be subjected to a ten-year imprisonment, the punishment is clearly more pathological than the crime. (In both cases, however, the punishment has tended not to be enforced.)

Insofar as prisons are also, unintendedly, schools of crime, they constitute organized foci of secondary pathology, as do even defensive wars. Secondary pathologies are indeed so ubiquitous that effective control of pathological behavior presupposes an awareness of the potentially pathological nature of the means used to control primary pathologies.

Pathological responses to pathology seem most likely in periods of basic social transformation. The increases in judicial cruelty which occurred in Europe in the thirteenth century when the church justified the use of torture in judicial proceedings and in totalitarian societies in the twentieth century are associated with the emergence of new types of social organization — urban-commercial and industrial.[161] Internal political violence has been most frequent in the modernizing (rather than traditional or advanced industrial) societies,[162] although the contemporary American experience may yet upset this generalization. Certain psychological types (the "authoritarian personality") and certain past experiences (exposure to oppression)[163] appear to promote pathological responses to pathologies.

In this context, it is perhaps appropriate to introduce the theoretical notion of *society in a pathological state*. A society (or an international system of societies) may be said to be in a pathological state when it does not permit pathogenic conditions to be corrected by any but pathological means. Barrington Moore realized this when he "reluctantly" concluded that "the costs of moderation have been at least as atrocious as those of revolution, perhaps a great deal more."[164] It is, of course, the subjective perception of a pathological state — however empirically valid or invalid it may be — that generates the secondary pathology of destruction-to-get-rid-of-destruction. A pathological state which is not perceived

---

[160] George Ryley Scott, *The History of Capital Punishment, Including an Examination of the Case for and against the Death Penalty* (London: Torchstream Books, 1951), pp. 39-40.

[161] Sorokin, *Dynamics*, II, p. 592.

[162] Feierabend, *op. cit.*

[163] Grygier, *op. cit.*, p. 271.

[164] Barrington Moore, Jr., *Social Origins of Dictatorship and Democracy: Lord and Peasant in the Making of the Modern World* (Boston: Beacon Press, 1966), p. 277.

as such (but either as culturally "legitimate" or as "natural" and therefore not amenable to correction by any means) is more likely to produce
apathy, which is why oppression has not generally provoked social revolutions in premodern, largely illiterate societies. In many ways, however,
apathy — the slave state of mind[165] — may be regarded as a self-destructive form of behavior: it prevents action that might increase the chances
of life, health, and a sense of personal identity. The modern mind, in
many parts of the world, is no longer willing to buy stability at the cost
of self-destruction; it has frequently shown itself more inclined to try
secondary pathologies in situations *misperceived* as pathological states of
society. Therein lies the origin of some peculiarly modern social problems.

CONCLUSION

In a brief survey, it has been possible only to illustrate some substantive
findings and some theoretical perspectives drawn from the increasingly
numerous cross-cultural and (still rare) trans-historical studies of social
problems. It has not been possible to discuss the methodological issues
involved; however, the range of methodology is illustrated in the studies
presented in this volume. One qualification needs to be offered. The
causal factors contributing to the occurrence of pathological behavior
operate in complex sociohistorical settings and impinge on uniquely structured personalities. Hence they should not be regarded as sufficient explanations of any specific pathological behavior in a concrete society at a
particular moment of its history. The isolable causal chains in terms of
which destructive and self-destructive behavior are accounted for must be
seen as interacting within social systems of distinctive historical character
and working through countless life-histories, none identical with any
other.

[165] Stanley M. Elkins, *Slavery: A Problem in American Institutional and Intellectual Life* (Chicago: University of Chicago Press, 1959).

II

Interpretive Case Studies

Individual Pathology

In the genesis of an individual pathological response, the whole society is, in one way or another, implicated. The relationship between an individual's response and his society is two dimensional: (1) the organization of the society determines which occupants of the various social positions will feel the most strain — in Goode's terms, "felt difficulty in fulfilling role obligations"; and (2) the patterns of its cultural tradition affect the direction of response taken, by the individual occupying a particular social position, to the strain generated. Cultural tradition also shapes the reaction of the society to the pathological response exhibited by an individual. The society's reactions may be punishment oriented or rehabilitation oriented. The individual personality is another critical factor: it determines who, subjected to a stress-producing situation, will break down and who will not; who will help others to recover, who will punish, and who will stand aside; who will be able to recover and who will not. Newman's method of analysis of an individual's pathology in a preliterate society, presented in the following article, is also applicable to the study of case histories in a modern society.

"Wild Man" Behavior in a New Guinea Highlands Community[1]

Bizarre behavior patterns, variously referred to as "running amuck," "going berserk," or "madness," have been reported for New Guinea societies. While the specific form the behavior takes varies from one area in New Guinea to another it is generally stated that there is standardization of the pattern within a given area and that it represents "abnormal" or "deviant" behavior. Interpretations of these patterns usually point out their highly aggressive character and seek understanding of them as a mechanism for the release of tensions induced in the individual through psychic or social conflicts. Field observation in a New Guinea Highlands community of one of these patterns suggests that interpretations of this behavior must also take into account the community within which the individual displays the behavior, the effect this display may have on community opinion of the person, and the ideological background against which the behavior is played out. These are important factors, for in addition to providing an outlet for aggressive impulses, such behavior also serves as a means whereby the individual can forcefully and dramatically cause the community to revise its image of him in a manner whereby social pressures will be withdrawn without drastic loss of social support. Such a pattern can thus be viewed as instrumental behavior redefining the social situation of the person displaying it and depending for its success on community acceptance of the portrayal.

The particular pattern discussed here was observed among the Gururumba, a horticultural people living in the Upper Asaro valley in the Eastern Highlands of the Territory of New Guinea.[2] They refer to it as *ahaDe idzi Be*, "being (a) wild pig." Since they intend by this phrase to draw an analogy between the actions of a "wild" pig and a pattern of human action, the phrase will be translated figuratively as "wild man."

Reprinted by permission of the author and the American Anthropological Association from the *American Anthropologist*, Vol. 66 (February 1964), pp. 1-19.
[1] A shorter version of this paper was presented before the 61st annual meeting of the American Anthropological Association in Chicago, November 16, 1962.
[2] For a more detailed description of the Gururumba, see Newman 1962:1-39.

The meaning of the analogy is partly revealed in the fact that there are no pigs in this area of the Highlands that are wild in the sense of a group of non-domesticated animals roaming free in the forest or grassland unattended by humans. There are only pigs that have temporarily escaped their masters. The Gururumba do not pretend to know exactly what causes a pig to break away from the rather pampered life it leads in the company of man to run wildly about attacking people and other pigs, but they feel it is only a temporary lapse which will either run its course or will be corrected by capturing the pig and subjecting it to a reintegration ritual designed to curb any aggressive impulses that may be in the animal, thus making it again amenable to life under controlled conditions.

The wildness of a pig does not consist of its living outside the realm of human control, but consists of its breaking away from a set of imposed conditions. It is this quality that is at the base of the analogy, for this is also one of the important characteristics of a wild man. A description of the initial assumption and playing out of this pattern by one individual will be given in order to provide a background for the analysis to follow.

A WILD MAN IN ACTION

The person whose case is to be presented will be referred to as Gambiri. Gambiri was a man in his mid-thirties, married, with one small child and another on the way. Gambiri did not live in his own natal village, as is the usual pattern, but lived in the village of his wife. One day, in the late afternoon, I was sitting in the front door of our house talking to a group of children when Gambiri approached carrying a small bowl in one hand. When he stopped to listen, one of the children began asking him for food. Gambiri indicated he did not have any food, but as usual the child did not accept this first denial and snatched the bowl away to examine it for himself. There were further demands and further denials. Tempers rose and the child finally ran off with Gambiri's bowl with Gambiri chasing him.

A few minutes later Gambiri again appeared at the door. He was carrying a bow and a sheaf of arrows in one hand and a long-knife in the other. He ordered the children away from the door and came into the house. Although his manner seemed quite brusque I did not pay much attention to his action since children were frequently ordered about in this way when in our house. When he began rummaging about in our personal belongings, however, I asked what he was doing. He replied by demanding in a loud voice that I give back the bowl I had stolen from him. When I said I had not taken his bowl, he shouted "Maski," Neo-Melanesian for "no." Then he saw a plastic pot used as a toilet for one of our children and said in Neo-Melanesian, "There is my bowl. I can take it and throw it away in the forest. It is not heavy." By this time it was becoming clear that something was radically wrong. This was apparent from his aggressive behavior and from the agitated character of his actions. Some one said, "*Gambiri ahaDe idzi Be*" and someone else referred to him as "longlong," Neo-Melanesian for "crazy" or "insane."

Gambiri was gently guided outside by our cook who suggested that his missing bowl might be in the cook house. He found a bowl very similar to the one he had been carrying and picked it up as if to go away with it. The cook distracted him by offering a glass of sugared water which he consumed eagerly. He then went outside the cook house, without the bowl, and began trampling our small flower garden located nearby. This act was clearly one of defiance, as he not only stepped on the plants quite deliberately, but made a point of going back and forth across a low fence there as if to emphasize his trespass.

By this time a small crowd had gathered to watch and comment on his behavior. When Gambiri made threatening gestures toward them they ran off laughing or screaming in mock terror. He grabbed a young girl who did not run quite out of his reach on one of these sallies and took away her net carrying bag. With the net bag on his shoulder he rushed up to me demanding that I give him a piece of soap. My refusal brought on an emotional outburst, but the cook quieted him by suggesting that he look in his newly acquired net bag for soap. Gambiri sat down on the ground, removed the contents of the bag, found a piece of soap, which he gave to an onlooker, and a small knife, which he gave to me, saying that it had been given to him by an Australian Patrol Officer for being a good worker on the government road. After gathering up the contents of the bag he then made a series of demands on me, asking for a loin cloth, a tin of meat, and some tobacco. Each denial was answered with a shouted "Maski." If I had been cognizant of the pattern of wild man behavior I would have known that some of these demands should have been met. This particular episode was ended when he again accused me of stealing his bowl and was then told by an onlooker that a young boy who happened to be passing by at the moment had taken it. The onlooker also suggested that Gambiri ought to shoot the boy, a suggestion he took up with gusto as he put an arrow to his bow and ran after the intended victim.

Gambiri's departure from the limited area of our yard can be thought of as marking the end of an initial phase in the wild man pattern, the main function of which is to communicate assumption of the pattern. In a short period of time (about an hour) his actions became known to a wide audience. It was not more than ten minutes after Gambiri was recognized as "longlong" that men who happened to be on the scene began calling out to other villages informing them of what was happening. Within thirty minutes people from other villages began arriving to see exactly who was involved and to observe the behavior. The fact that the initial phase was played out at my house facilitated communication. First, the house was a focus of attention simply because of our presence in it and there were almost always people clustered around it. The village itself, by contrast, was usually empty except in the evening or on a special occasion. Second, the house was strategically located with reference to lines of communication. It was on a ridge top only a few yards from the spot where shouted messages were sent, and the government road and main native trail running through the clan territory were close by.

The communicative aspect of the initial phase is evident in other cases of this kind. In all cases gathered it is clear that the pattern was initially played out in a setting containing an audience.[3] Ceremonial and festive occasions or gatherings of people to discuss some matter of general import appear consistently as occasions when wild men make their appearance. In this highland environment with its areas of unoccupied grassland and forest it would be possible for a man to run wild in seclusion, but no one does.

The next phase of the wild man's behavior occupied, in this case, the evening of the day discussed above and the following day. During this period, Gambiri acted out the pattern throughout the territory of the subclan. He moved hurriedly from place to place, ending up wherever his attacks led him. Once in a place he would force his way into a house, demand some small item as his, stuff it into the stolen net bag, and engage in aggressive verbalizations or actions until diverted. He frequently made quick assertive moves as if to attack other persons, and although most of these forays were not consummated with blows, he did occasionally strike someone standing nearby or loose an arrow at some more distant person.

His coming was never a complete surprise to anyone, not only because it had become generally known that he had gone wild, but also because he was usually announced by the noise of the crowd that surrounded him. Some of the people in this crowd were simply curious onlookers, as were the children and young people who regarded Gambiri's performance as something of an occasion. They waited expectantly at a safe distance hoping something exciting would happen. If an attack were forthcoming it precipitated a noisy rush away from the wild man that was

---

[3] Two cases were observed in a single village within 12 months and material was collected on four others that had occurred in the recent past.

the reward for patient waiting. There were also others in the crowd who acted as gentle arbiters of Gambiri's behavior. They did not participate in the merriment of the occasion nor were they simply there out of curiosity. They remained quiet and watchful. Their function was to see that Gambiri did not harm anyone seriously and to guide him by gentle suggestion away from situations where his presence was becoming odious. In order to be effective, their guidance could not take the form of direct intervention since that would only have further aggravated the wild man. It therefore took the form of suggesting new targets for his attacks which would lead him away from a situation. Although the crowd around Gambiri was sometimes large and sometimes small these "watchers" were always discretely present. They were not always the same persons, for one group would, in effect, hand Gambiri off to another as he went from place to place.

By the end of this period the stolen net bag was bulging with loot. There were wooden arrow heads, skeins of wood fibre string, pieces of tobacco, bits of soap, odd pieces of food, short lengths of bark and cotton cloth, small tins saved for storage of personal items, knives, small drinking tubes, pig ropes, and an assortment of enameled bowls and plates. It was stated that a wild man might carry away a small pig or chicken, but, being aware of this, people were careful to hide such valuables if possible. On the other hand, there was an obligation to allow him to take something, so a few small items were always left in full view. Gambiri carried the loot with him wherever he went. At times he sat down, emptied the bag on the ground, and inspected its contents. He was not realistic in his appraisal of the worth of the objects in the bag so that a tobacco tin might be counted as a piece of Australian paper money; pieces of cloth or bits of string were treated with great care as if they were things of high value, and other items were said to have been given him by prestigeful and powerful persons such as an important clan leader or a white plantation owner. He would never relinquish an item if it were demanded that he do so, although he occasionally gave items away to bystanders.

On the third day, Gambiri began to widen the social context of his actions. Until this time his activity had been confined to the area of the clan where he resided. Now he began making forays into the territory of other clans. He seldom attempted to take anything in this context, but confined himself to chasing people in mock attack or appearing unexpectedly at a place with drawn bow as if he were going to shoot someone, then leaving abruptly after having caused some commotion. In one observed instance his attempt to enter a house and take items was severely rebuked.

On the evening of this day he ran into the forest and was not seen again until the next morning when he walked past the outer fringe of the village, without his net bag, and called to the men's house that he was going to a place on the other side of the Bismark mountains near Bundi, a journey of at least two days, to collect pandanus nuts. He spoke in the native language instead of Neo-Melanesian and did not exhibit any of the behavior characteristic of his actions on the three previous days. No one in the men's house made any comment to Gambiri except to indicate they had heard him.

Gambiri was not seen again for thirteen days. Then the Gururumba attended a funeral ceremony held in a nearby tribal group where he appeared briefly but took no direct part in the ceremony. On the sixteenth day his clan of residence was performing a dance as their part in a food distribution. Gambiri appeared in the village before the dance was to begin, but made no attempt to join the dancers and was obviously not prepared to join them. He was encouraged by others to join in, however, and they arranged his decoration from items not used by others. After this episode, Gambiri took up a regular routine of activity. To my knowledge no one ever spoke to him about his actions, although they were discussed by others. My own efforts to interview him concerning his actions were fruitless, as various people predicted they would be, for he disclaimed any knowledge of having done the things he did.

Gambiri took one of two possible modes of bringing the wild man pattern to an end. Disappearance into the forest with the bag of stolen articles is a constant element in the pattern. It is said that all wild men will do this and although no one knows exactly what he does with the things he collects, it is believed that he destroys them in the forest. Some people say he burns them, others that he throws them away piece by piece where they will never be found. After this he may go off to a distant place, as Gambiri did, or he may reappear in the village in his wild state but without his bulging bag. In the latter event he is captured and brought out of his wild state in a ceremony similar to a ceremony performed for pigs that have gone wild. The wild man is held over a smoking fire until he returns to a normal state. He is publicly rubbed all over with liquefied pig fat, and a small pig is killed in his name by a prominent person in his village, and he is presented with a sumptuous collection of cooked tubers and roots.

ELEMENTS IN THE WILD MAN PATTERN

The total behavior of the wild man can be broken down into a few elements selected because of their constant association with this behavior.

First there are the physical manifestations. Increase in the rate of the respiratory and circulatory systems, a drop in skin temperature, and sweating are notable somatic reactions. There is also a disturbance of motor activity. The wild man is hyper-active: he rushes about from place to place, gesticulates a great deal, attacks, shouts, scatters objects, and breaks into groups of people. In addition, he does not always appear to be in full control of his body, for he may fall down, bump into things inadvertently, and has difficulty in making small scale movements with his arms and legs. It was said that he also loses bowel and bladder control, but this was not observed.

Two other physical manifestations have been separated for special attention. Informants state that a wild man is unable to speak or hear. Indeed, the wild men that were observed seemed not to hear much that was going on around them. Children and adults frequently teased the wild man verbally by shouting at him without any visible response on his part. But, in *certain contexts* the wild man did hear and respond to the verbalizations of others when they suggested new targets for his attacks, or when certain things were said concerning objects in which he was interested. Similarly, there were some contexts in which the wild man did speak. He frequently shouted when attacking people, made denials of some statements made by others, and commented on the objects he had accumulated. The interesting point to consider here is that he always spoke in Neo-Melanesian. This *lingua franca* is not universally known in the Gururumba area and Gambiri's command of it was quite rudimentary. He seldom spoke it in the normal course of events, even to Europeans, but spoke it exclusively as a wild man. Informants regarded this as equivalent to a pre-contact pattern in which the wild man did not speak at all but used a simple system of hand signs and gestures to communicate the few things he wished to make known. I do not doubt that there is a marked reduction in the ability of a wild man to speak and hear, especially in the initial phases of the pattern, but the fact that there is not total loss of these functions and the fact that there are special forms and contexts of communication suggests that this reduction is not to be understood only in terms of physiological or psychological trauma.

The next important element in the behavior of a wild man is his treatment of, and attitude toward, material objects. A large part of his activity is directed toward acquiring objects from other people. Although objects are acquired in an aggressive manner, it is also true that people expect him to take things from them. Very valuable objects are secreted, if possible, but the wild man is allowed to take something. The actual value of these objects appears to matter very little to the wild man, for he puts his own value on them. One may find him referring to a piece of soap as a large amount of money or a tobacco leaf as a valuable Bird of Paradise plume. He may indicate that the stolen objects were given to him by a prestigeful or powerful person, or that they were rewards made to him for outstanding performance. Since he destroys the objects he collects, rather than hoarding them or distributing them, it is suggested that the value of the objects lies in the act of acquisition and destruction rather than in the material or social worth of the objects.

A third element to be considered is the fact that wild man behavior is limited by age and sex. It is an exclusively male pattern occurring only among men who are, approximately, 25 to 35 years old. Informants were quite explicit in their statements that no woman would exhibit this behavior. Informants could not provide any examples of its occurrence in a woman nor were any cases of this type observed. There are social factors which help explain the non-participation of women in this pattern and these will be discussed below along with those pertaining to the restriction of the pattern to a certain age group. It only needs pointing out at this juncture that the differential participation of the sexes in wild man behavior is consistent with their differential participation in other forms of publicly displayed expressive behavior.

Finally, attention should be drawn to the attitude of the community toward the wild man. A feeling of expectant excitement is observable in the community; the actions of the wild man take on the character of a public spectacle. When news of its occurrence spreads, people come in from their gardens, down from the forest, and from other villages simply to watch. Spectators are prone to keep their distance because of the potential danger, but at the same time the onlookers obviously enjoy the instances when the wild man suddenly turns on the group and chases one after another of them in erratic, and, seemingly, comic pursuit. In this respect the community responds to the wild man in much the same way they do to the comically frightening performances that are staged as entertainment in conjunction with large scale food distributions. Given this kind of attitude, the community can be regarded as an audience to a performance. This places the behavior described in a very different context than the amuck behavior described by Fortune among the Manus. There, the community reacts to protect itself by running away and hiding in the bush (Fortune 1932:54). It also contrasts with various kinds of armed and unarmed conflict that occasionally erupts within Gururumba villages. In these instances the play element is at a minimum, and there is little feeling of the enjoyment of a spectacle.

For the community at large to adopt this attitude is interesting in view of the fact that the wild man performs acts that in any other context would engender serious public disapproval and attempts to curtail the behavior. The amount of physical harm he can inflict on another person goes considerably beyond that tolerated in the usual course of events. Further, he is a man who has obviously lost control of himself and yet is allowed to remain in this state until control is restored spontaneously or until an action on his part (the destruction of the objects he has collected) signalizes the appropriate time for restorative action. The community does not display this same degree of tolerance for another behavior pattern called *afafaĭe*. This term designates what is probably an anxiety spell precipitated by physical trauma. The individual who is *afafaĭe* can neither speak nor hear and will viciously attack anyone at hand. Such persons are immediately restrained and an effort is made to restore them to their senses by blowing smoke in their faces or by holding them over a smoking fire. There is also the matter of the objects collected by the wild man. Within the clan and lineage, rights in personal property are closely guarded. Nothing can be taken without the owner's permission, and if permission is granted, it is usually only on condition of equivalent return or some other kind of reciprocation. When a wild man takes objects, it is an act that would be considered stealing in any other context. These examples indicate that the community not only accepts wild man behavior as a kind of exciting performance but also accepts a performance consisting of acts that are usually regarded as anti-social.

The extent of this permissive attitude is further indicated by the fact that when the wild man returns to normal, his aggressive and destructive acts are not held up to him nor is compensation for them demanded. This is noteworthy in a culture stressing strict reciprocity and balance in many areas of social interaction. Moreover, the community may hold a ceremony in which the former wild man is given gifts of special food. The speech made at the time of this food presentation appraises the former wild man of the quality of food given him as compared to what he was able to snatch up during his wild period and points out that his return to normalcy will enable him to participate again in such pleasurable activities as consuming special foods. It should be made clear that the intent of this speech is not subtle chastisement. Its purpose is to offer inducement to return to a regular pattern of activity and stems from the belief that a man may have had good cause for behaving in a bizarre manner. This belief, crucial to the understanding of wild man behavior, will be discussed below.

ANALYSIS

The analysis of the material presented above will be arranged in four parts. In the first three parts the focus will be on the social, psychological, and cultural determinants of the behavior as they can be understood from the available material. These first three parts will correspond to the model commonly found in current anthropological literature which sees human behavior as the product of one or some combination of these determinants. While such a model is useful, it does not allow us to explain all the facts presented in this case and it also seems deficient in so far as it makes behavior appear to be a rather automatic response to social pressures and psychological forces in terms of a pattern set by culture. Although it is accepted that culture must be regarded as a determinant of behavior, especially in the sense of a limiting factor, it is also felt that culture as a determinant can be emphasized to the point where we neglect to see man using his culture, and only see culture using man.

To put this in terms of the study at hand, it is possible to show that Gururumba culture is of such a nature that certain classes of individuals find themselves in social conditions productive of acute psychological tension. The wild man pattern is available as a mechanism for the release of such tension and it might be said that the existence of this pattern partially determines the behavior. The argument here is similar to that found in Kluckhohn's classic study of Navaho witchcraft. But witchcraft among the Navaho and wild man behavior among the Gururumba are not the only tension reducing mechanisms available in these cultures. This leaves unsolved the problem of demonstrating why one pattern is chosen over another. It is suggested here that one way of dealing with this problem is to accept the assumption that the behavior pattern an individual chooses is, in part at least, a function of the view he has of himself as a person and the view he wishes others to have of him. The fourth part of the analysis will utilize this assumption with respect to wild man behavior.

Social Determinants

Wild man behavior only occurs among young adult males of a restricted age group. It can be shown that men in this category are subject to unique kinds of social pressures and that wild man behavior is understandable as a response to these pressures.

As noted above, wild man behavior occurs among men who are, roughly, between 25 and 35 years of age. The exact age is not relevant, for the significant fact is that this category is defined in terms of its being a particular stage in the male life cycle. Men at this stage hold in common a social position marking them off from men in age groups above and below them; they are men who have just begun to establish their own families. Betrothal among the Gururumba occurs for males when they are in their late teens or early twenties. The betrothal period varies in length but usually covers a span of two to five years. During this period the betrothed pair are to avoid one another. In pre-contact times this was frequently accomplished by the male attaching himself to the men's house of another village where he was supported in ex-

change for his services as a warrior. Now, it is common for young men
to seek employment with Europeans. Because of the long betrothal
period, males are frequently in their mid-twenties before they begin active married life and may be well into their thirties before they have
established a family of two or three children. It is at this point that a
male begins to participate fully in adult life. It is the circumstances
connected with the establishment of a family and increased participation in adult male life that produce the social pressures related to wild
man behavior. These circumstances are primarily economic and fall into
four major categories: (a) the press of economic obligations incurred at
the time of betrothal and after marriage, (b) the instability of the
marriage situation with its consequent economic complications, (c)
involvement in group coordinated enterprises, (d) the importance of
successful economic manipulation for acquiring personal prestige and
power. Each of these will now be discussed in turn.

(a) The arrangement of marriages among the Gururumba is not
managed by the partners of the marriage but by their kinsmen and village-mates. Furthermore, and in common with other Highland New
Guinea groups, betrothal and marriage are accompanied by a complex
series of economic exchanges between the kinsmen and village-mates of
the marriage partners. On the surface these exchanges have the appearance of contractual arrangements between kin groups involving the
transfer of women. More than this is involved, however. The older men
who arrange the marriage of one of their younger kinsmen regard the
relationship established by the marriage as a base from which a wide
variety of exchange relationships can be derived. Involvement in exchange relationships is not only important because it is a means of
acquiring items or transforming one kind of item into another, but it
is also important because the successful manipulation of exchange relationships is a means of acquiring prestige and power.

The young man who has been newly married is thrust into a network
of economic obligations which he may find difficulty in dealing with.
These obligations take two distinct, but related, forms. The first stems
from the fact that he does not have sufficient resources to make bride
price payments or to put up the food and wealth given to affines in the
series of exchanges that take place after betrothal. These resources are
therefore provided by his kinsmen and village-mates, but after a marriage
has been consummated it is expected that all contributions made by
them will be repaid by the young man. A young man may make repayment by distributing to his debtors whatever resources come his way at
the time they are available, or by a debtor actively insisting on repayment by demanding contributions to his own debt payments. Both these
modes of repayment have their onerous aspects. The former sees almost

all incoming resources going out again in small dispersed amounts which limits the ability of the individual to make any large scale, dramatic re-payments, and the latter holds the possibility that a demand for repay-ment may be made at a time when payment from available resources is impossible. Failure to meet such a demand means loss of prestige, and borrowing to repay means further debt. Given the fact that a young married man has seldom had time to acquire many resources through the usual means of gardening or pig raising, has not been able to build potential resources by making others indebted to him, and has had little opportunity to develop his skills in the area of economic manipulation, it is understandable that he may soon find himself in a seemingly inex-tricable and personally frustrating situation with respect to demands made on him for debt repayment by his own kinsmen.

The second kind of obligation confronting the newly married man is the obligation he has to his kinsmen and village-mates to activate the relationship established with his wife's kinsmen after the marriage has been consummated. There are many standardized occasions on which a man can visit his affines or invite them to his village. These are not simply times for visiting and making new personal contacts; they are also situations when food and wealth objects are distributed in fulfill-ment of obligations attendant upon the affinal relationship. A young man is encouraged by his own village-mates to fulfill these obligations speedily and in style. If his own resources are not sufficient to the task, they will supply what is needed. They are motivated to help him because it enables them to establish or strengthen economic ties with his affines through participation in his affairs. The affinal ties of a man's village-mates are avenues others can exploit in their own economic ventures. Since the prestige and renown of a group is importantly determined by its successful manipulation of economic ties with other groups, and since these ties are, at base, the summation of individual ties between two groups, the young man who does not vigorously activate the relationship between himself and his affines is put in the position of barring others in his group from utilizing one of the avenues to individual and group renown.

(b) The circumstances discussed above may be further complicated because betrothal and the early years of marriage tend to be unstable in Gururumba society. The result can be additional economic complica-tions. For a variety of reasons, young women are often not amenable to the new life that comes with betrothal and marriage (Read 1954:868–869). They frequently react by running away, behaving so badly that they are sent away, or provoke their husbands to the point of beating them which gives them justification for leaving. The young husband may or may not be blamed for what happens, but in either case such a situation has its attendant economic difficulties. If the young woman has been harmed physically, then compensation for the injury must be paid. If the bride is behaving badly or runs away several times, quarrels and disputes between the bride's group and the groom's group may arise. Settlement of such disputes can be costly. Gifts may have to be exchanged or one side may have to feed the other when they come together for discussions. If the marriage is dissolved, the groom's group can demand that the bride price be returned, but this may be a complicated procedure since the bride's group will usually have distributed the bride wealth in order to fulfill its own commitments with the result that return is delayed, piecemeal, or, in some cases, less than the original amount given. Thus, even though a young man may not be directly blamed for the difficulty he has in retaining a bride, and even though he is not solely responsible for negotiating the return of the bride wealth, it is also true that dissolving a marriage does not always dissolve the economic obligations incurred at its inception. In fact, it can make them more difficult of resolution, since, without a wife, a young man is cut off from one of the important avenues of resource accumulation.

(c) As a man's family begins to develop and achieve some stability, he is increasingly drawn into group coordinated activities of an economic character. Some of these activities occur within the village. When a young man begins a garden, he puts in a patch of sugar cane which must be supported by poles. These poles are presented by a man's village-mates at the expense of a great deal of labor. This labor must be repaid in kind and by feeding all those who have contributed. Other activities are on an inter-village level. If the child of a man dies, mourners will come from many other villages in the clan. All these mourners must be fed and given gifts of food. All the men in the village where the death occurs are expected to contribute to this distribution. Still other activities are on an inter-clan level. A good sugar cane crop may be the basis of a large scale food presentation to another clan. All adult males are expected to contribute cane, as well as other food and wealth objects to the distribution. Again, this may represent a real drain on a young man's resources.

These are but illustrations of the many ways a young man becomes involved economically in the affairs of the various groups with which he is affiliated. The frequency of this kind of activity is indicated by the fact that in the 50 weeks for which accurate records were kept on a single village comprising some 45 adult males there were 110 occasions when most of them were directly involved in some kind of exchange activity. Older, well established men have no great difficulty in making contributions to these affairs, but younger men whose gardens are not yet in full production, whose pigs are not yet numerous, or whose resources in wealth objects are small will be hard pressed.

(d) The various economic entanglements a young man finds himself enmeshed in after marriage are not simply obligations to be fulfilled. They are, in addition, opportunities for acquiring prestige and power. The successful manipulation of these opportunities is the road to renown, and renown is an essential quality of the man or group having a following and the respect of others. Given the kind of society found among the Gururumba this means that renown can be translated into power. This translation is not only made on the individual level, but also on the group level. The differential distribution of renown gained through the skillful involvement in and management of economic affairs structures a wide range of relationships among groups and individuals. Therefore, the referent of success in manipulating the situations outlined above is not limited to the situations themselves, but is the much wider context of all the relationships, whether built on an economic base or not, between one individual and all others, and between the groups to which the individual belongs and all other groups. To make this point is to inform us that it is not only the successful fulfillment of obligations that is at stake for the individual; it is the nature of his total relationships with others.

These constitute the social pressures unique to the position of the young married man in Gururumba society. They are unique to this group in the sense that they begin to operate at this early stage in a man's life career and cease to operate, or operate with different effect, as he grows older. This cessation is in part due to the fact that some of these pressures no longer exist, as in the case of debts that are liquidated, and in part due to the individual's increased ability to handle these pressures as he develops skills and resources over the years. If one accepts the notion that the violent activity of a wild man is an institutionalized means for the reduction of tension, and if one accepts the situation discussed above as one productive of tensions, then the occurrence of wild man behavior among young men in this situation becomes explicable. The wild man pattern can be viewed as a positively sanctioned role in which the individual can actively relieve tensions induced by commonly recurring social pressures. The Gururumba themselves make the same connection between the elements of the observed correlation that is suggested here. One of the ways they will answer questions concerning the cause of wild man behavior in a specific individual is by detailing the way social pressures have played on him. In the case of Gambiri, for example, they pointed out that: he had not paid back his bride price and he was past the age when this should have been done; his wife was pregnant

with a second child which meant he would soon be faced with the prospect of paying his affines for the child (one of the standard obligations
to affines); he had only one pig; he was living in his wife's village in
order to utilize garden land to which his wife had access because his own
garden had been unproductive, but even in the new setting his plants
were not flourishing; his natal kinsmen regarded him as a member of his
wife's village and were not prone to help him economically.

This explanation can be extended to interpret the form taken by some
of the wild man's actions. The accumulation and destruction of objects
becomes an understandable outlet for a man beset by difficulties arising
from his inability to effectively control objects. The excessively high
value the wild man places on objects of little real worth also becomes
understandable in these terms as well as his forceful extraction of objects
from others.

Cultural Determinants

The remarks immediately preceding anticipate a discussion of the cultural determinants of wild man behavior. They indicate a correspondence
between the form of the pattern and the function it serves. The form
of the pattern provides a partial resolution of the frustrations faced
by young men in this culture by allowing them to engage in actions
directly expressive of those frustrations. Culture becomes a determinant
of behavior in that it supplies a pattern of action suited by its form to
the individual's needs.

There is also another sense in which culture is a determinant of wild
man behavior. It will be remembered that no concerted action on the
part of the community is developed to stop the actions of a wild man
even though he performs acts that would be negatively sanctioned in any
other context. Wild man behavior is allowed behavior and to speak of
its cultural determinants is to speak of standard beliefs making the behavior understandable and acceptable to others.

The immediate cause of wild man behavior as the Gururumba see it is
an attack on the individual by a ghost. As an initial response to questions asking what makes a wild man wild, most informants will answer
either that he has been "bitten" by a ghost or that he is, temporarily, a
ghost. Both answers have the same basic meaning, for they convey the
idea that a wild man is acting like a ghost, i.e., in an aggressive and
malevolent manner (Newman 1962:285–293). Neither answer implies
that the wild man is possessed. He may have been "bitten" by a ghost
and the ghost may have gotten inside him, but a wild man is not simply
an empty human vessel filled and animated by a ghost. Rather, the
ghost enters the body of the person and bites the liver and other
internal organs which releases within him certain pre-existent forces. It

is the nature of these internal forces rather than the nature of the external cause which produces wild man behavior. The character of these forces is to be found in the people's characterization of their own inner nature and in their beliefs concerning ghosts and ancestors.

Ghosts (*foroso*) and ancestors (*aBwafo*) are thought of as entities motivated almost completely by what is referred to in the common parlance of our own culture as "the baser instincts." They give free reign to aggressive impulses and are not checked by socially imposed restraints. Ghosts are viewed as malevolent, destructive entities who attack the living for no apparent reason or for selfish reasons, as when they feel they are being forgotten. Ghosts are the recently dead, the dead whose names are remembered, while ancestors are the long-dead, those whose names have been forgotten. Furthermore, ancestors are considered to be the progenitors of the race and to have lived at a time in the distant past when men did not live as they do now. They can be referred to as primeval men since the Gururumba consider that they lived in a time when men were without advanced culture. This means, on the one hand, that in that time men did not have the technological knowledge they now have. Fire, houses, and domesticated plants and animals were unknown. On the other hand, it means that they were not bound by the rules of society as the Gururumba now know them. These primeval men did not live in social groups, share food, exchange wealth, make bride price payments, or practice any of the formalized social arrangements characteristic of contemporary Gururumba life. Furthermore, they attacked others on a whim, stole food regularly, and were inveterate rapists.

These notions are not of interest because they are beliefs the Gururumba hold about supernatural entities; they are of interest because they are beliefs they hold about themselves. The Gururumba believe they have the same basic nature as do ghosts and primeval men. As one male informant put it after giving an account of primeval men, "That is what we are really like, we are really like that, but now we understand (now we have advanced culture). If there were no villages or no headmen we would be like that." This same sentiment is echoed in the assertion made by informants that men as well as ghosts are "like pigs," or would be "like pigs" if they did not have rules imposed upon them. The uncontrolled, voracious pig who will eat its own children if not watched is equated with basic human nature.[4]

These statements illustrate two points and lead to a third. First, they make clear that the Gururumba are aware of selfishness, destructiveness, and aggressiveness within them. These are the forces released in a wild

[4] Marie Reay collected almost identical statements from the Kuma. See Reay 1962:459.

man when a ghost bites him. Second, they indicate an awareness that
such impulses are in some measure kept in check by submission to
society and its rules. Finally, when the Gururumba respond to questions
about the reasons for wild man behavior by detailing the frustrating
social circumstances a man finds himself in, it indicates that they know
the course of events may take such a turn that it is no longer possible
for an individual to hold these tendencies in check. If this happens,
then the man must be allowed his outlet; his actions are not to be interfered with because it is understood they are partially induced by society.
The proper stance for society is to draw back, let the action run its
course, and then attempt to reintegrate the individual.[5]

The cultural determinants of wild man behavior become a known
pattern of behavior available in the cultural inventory suitable by its
form as a response of an individual to a socially generated situation, and
other beliefs productive of attitudes on the part of the community make
activation of the pattern possible.

Psychological Determinants

Not much can be said here about the psychological determinants of wild
man behavior. The investigator was not equipped, either in terms of
testing materials or training, to make the relevant observations in the
field and does not feel confident about making detailed psychological
interpretations of the material that is available. However, since one
of the important tasks of this essay is an illustration of method, we can
at least suggest the form this part of the analysis might take.

The material at hand suggests at least two lines of inquiry concerning
the psychological determinants of wild man behavior. First, drawing on
psychoanalytic theory, it would appear reasonable to suppose that wild
man behavior is a form of anxiety hysteria. This is suggested by such
observed phenomena as the suddenness of its onset, somatic and motor
disturbances, sensory blocking (speech and hearing), the irrationality of
the outbreak in terms of the precipitating event, the histrionic character
of the action, and mendacity (Fenichel 1945:194, 527).

A thorough analysis in psychoanalytic terms would seek to discover
the neurotic conflict represented in the hysteric reaction. This could be
done, in part, by attempting to identify the source of the anxiety through
an examination of the situation with which the hysteria is connected.
In this case it would be noted that the hysteric reaction centers on
material objects: the wild man aggressively collects, then destroys, the
possessions of others. Since adequate control over material objects is an

[5] These beliefs and attitudes suggest that the frustration-aggression hypothesis
is not a unique product of the Western world's social science.

important means of gaining the satisfactions to be derived from social relationships in this culture, it would follow that there is the possibility of the individual experiencing deprivation if his control of objects is inadequate. Such deprivation might be experienced by an adult as the equivalent of an infantile deprivation such as loss of love. If this were demonstrated, then wild man behavior could be seen as a hysteric reaction focused on objects and representing conflict between the instinctual demand to retain love (symbolized by the collection of objects, because objects bring satisfaction) and the instinctual demand of self-preservation (symbolized by the destruction of objects because objects are experienced as sources of deprivation).

A second line of inquiry could be developed using personality studies for the purpose of discovering whether or not there are personality characteristics, or types, unique to the individuals who actually manifest wild man behavior. One asks the question, "Why do some young men react to the pressures of their situation by becoming wild men while others do not?" The answer may lie, in part, in situational factors, i.e., fortuitous circumstances may create greater pressures for some than for others. But, it may also be that some men do not have the kind of personality that can withstand pressures as well as others, or that wild man behavior is just an extreme form of behavior typical of a personality type commonly found in this culture. In the case of Gambiri, for example, the former may be indicated, for it seems clear on impressionistic grounds that he was not as self-confident or as self-assertive as the more successful males in his age group. Since these are not only valued male characteristics in this culture, but are also necessary traits enabling the individual to "make out" successfully in this society, it would seem that their lack might be viewed as a causative factor in wild man behavior.

Explanations of this behavior in psychological terms would view it (a) as the outcome of psychogenic processes or (b) the characteristics of a certain personality type. Psychological determinants could be joined with the cultural and social determinants in a more comprehensive explanatory scheme by pointing to the way the particular psychological factors operative in this case are emphasized, selected, and developed by the unique sociocultural context in which they occur.

The Individual as Determinant

The three major classes of determinants in the preceding sections reflect the main ways anthropologists have of understanding a given behavior pattern in a particular culture. There are, of course, variations on each of these methodological themes, but there is also a consistency in all of them; they engender a very mechanical view of human behavior. This is not without its advantages and it does bring a certain kind of understanding. But, the kind of understanding it brings excludes consideration of the individual and the manner in which he is a determinant of his own behavior. Unless we are to assume that humans are only capable of *reacting to* situations instead of *acting in* situations, or can only react in terms of patterns set by culture and psychological forces, such an exclusion appears unwarranted. It makes man appear to act without self-awareness, and without awareness of the appearance he makes or wishes to make to others. The social psychologists have long been appraising us of the importance of not making this exclusion.

Nowhere in the above discussion has consideration been included of what people think about a man after he has gone wild, or what a wild man thinks of himself. Such data would not have served any obvious purpose had it been included, for the above model is not built to utilize it. If it is included, however, a different and more complete understanding of wild man behavior can be achieved and a different model suggested.

There are no recriminations against a wild man after he has gone wild, and no one in his clan or village will mention the episode to him. They do talk about it among themselves, however. It is evident from these conversations that after the wild man episode they do not think of him as the same kind of person he was formerly thought to be. Formerly he was thought of as a man with essentially the same capacities and capabilities as any other man. It is probably more accurate to say that formerly no one gave much thought to his capacities and capabilities, but that his actions as a wild man generate such thought. As indicated in the section on cultural determinants, the Gururumba are aware of the kinds of pressures social life imposes on them. When a man goes wild they also become aware of the fact that this particular individual is not as capable as others of withstanding those pressures. This awareness is reflected in their treatment of an individual after a wild man episode. Specifically, there is an observable reduction in the expectation others have of the degree he will participate in exchange transactions and a corresponding reduction in the intensity of demands made on him: He may still have debts, but repayment is not pressed aggressively; he still has obligations to affines, but others seldom attempt to further their own ends by encouraging their participation in the fulfillment of his obligations; he still contributes to group sponsored food distributions, but no attempt is made to extract a prior commitment from him as to how much he will contribute; he knows he can still call on his village-mates to help him in work projects, but his village-mates know that their compensation will be in the form of return labor rather than a share in a food distribution. The outcome of wild man behavior is thus a reduction of demands made without loss of social support. The wild man does not become an outcast or deviant in the eyes of others; he becomes a man now known to be incapable of, or unwilling to participate in, certain affairs with the same degree of intensity as others, but still a man who can participate to some degree.

This new assessment made by others is in accord with the way a wild man feels about himself. This can be seen in the way such an individual contrasts with two other kinds of persons. On the one hand, he contrasts with men who remain apart from the general life of the community. Such men are rare, but they exist. They live away from the village; they do not stay in the men's house, except occasionally; they seldom attend any village gathering; they only infrequently call upon others for aid. They do not appear rebellious but neither are they committed. On the other hand, the wild man contrasts with those individuals who will occasionally become so angry with some life circumstance that they give the appearance of renouncing all social ties. They threaten to leave the community or to withdraw their support by some other means. These outbursts are usually only temporary and such persons are mollified in most cases. Unlike the first kind of person, the wild man sees himself as committed to economic involvement but comes to realize that there must be limits to his commitment. Unlike the second kind of person, the wild man sees himself as one who cannot make clear to others the limits of his commitment by threatening an open breach when those limits have been taxed. All this suggests that the men who become wild see themselves as persons who will never succeed brilliantly but who also see themselves as doing better than failing miserably.

The real problem for such a man consists of letting others know what kind of person he is. In order to maintain the position he sees as congenial to himself, he must make others realize his willingness to "play the game" but with less intensity than others "play" it. This is difficult because he gives the appearance of being committed with the result that others press demands, and if demands are not met, others explain this in terms of his youth, his inexperience, or temporary situational difficulties. They assume he will eventually live up to expectations, but he thinks of the expectations as being too high. It is difficult to communicate this because he does not want to do or say things that might indicate he is either "giving up the game" or issuing threats so the game will be made to run his way. Wild man behavior can be seen as a solution to the individual's problem of closing the gap between what he thinks of himself and what others think of him.

How is it that wild man behavior has this effect? The answer given here is speculative but, I feel, reasonable. The wild man is not directly

presenting himself to those who view him; he is presenting his view of
the way the everyday actions of others look to him. His aggressive collection of the belongings of others, his excessive valuation of objects having
small worth, his refusal to hear objections to his acts, his refusal to speak
about his acts, and his disregard for the way his acts may affect others
(as in his destruction of their belongings or forced entry into their
houses) are dramatic expressions of the way certain patterns of everyday
life appear to him. Although Gururumba beliefs portray human nature
as highly aggressive, people do not habitually act as if it mattered to
them. By forcefully calling attention to this aggressiveness the performance of the wild man makes it clear that he is an individual who cannot
fully accept it. What others know about this man — his current situation, his past performance, his character — is seen in a new light and
given a new interpretation.

Revision of opinion by others occurs only in cases where the community can in fact review the individual's past life and find justification
for believing this person is as he now presents himself to be. There are
three kinds of situations where review does not occur. In them no revision of opinion is made nor is the individual allowed to carry out
the wild man pattern. This occurs when young unmarried men attempt
to present themselves as wild men. People laugh at them and accuse
them of fakery or interpret the behavior as something other than wild
man behavior. Being too young there is not enough in their life histories
to warrant an assumption that they are different from others. It also
occurs when a wild man wanders into the villages of other clans. In this
situation he may be accused of faking, and his actions may be physically
resisted. Being from another place these people are not as intimately
acquainted with the details of the wild man's life as those who live in
daily contact with him. Finally, it occurs in the case of the behavior
called *afafaʲe* mentioned above. This looks, superficially, very much like
wild man behavior except that it does not involve the taking of objects.
It occurs, primarily, in older men and is brought to a swift conclusion
by physically restraining the person and holding him over a smoking
fire until he returns to normal. These older men are firmly established
and there is no reason for the community to believe they are now any
different than they have always appeared to be. The fact that a person
can be accused of faking a wild man performance clearly indicates that
a judgment of legitimacy is made by the community. If wild man behavior were simply a tension reduction mechanism, legitimacy would rest
only on whether or not the performance remained within the bounds of
the allowed pattern. In wild man behavior, however, legitimacy rests
equally on the judgment that the performance reveals something about
the performer. The performance can be seen as occasioning the reorgani-

zation of what people know about a person, but it must also be seen that the reorganization does not take place unless the community can find substantiation for it in the past behavior of the person.

REFERENCES

Fenichel, Otto. The psychoanalytic theory of neurosis. New York, W. W. Norton and Company, Inc., 1945.

Fortune, Reo F. Sorcerers of Dobu: The social anthropology of the Dobu islanders of the Western Pacific. New York, E. P. Dutton and Company, Inc., 1932.

Newman, Philip L. Supernaturalism and ritual among the Gururumba. Unpublished doctoral dissertation, University of Washington, 1962.

Read, Kenneth E. Marriage among the Gahuku-Gama of Eastern Central Highlands, New Guinea. South Pacific 7:864-870, 1954.

Reay, Marie. The sweet witchcraft of Kuma dream experience. Mankind 5:459-463, 1962.

Collective Pathology

In the following selection, Parsons' inquiry into the social context of the rise of Fascism demonstrates, like Newman's, the causal relationship between social strain and social pathology. There are several differences, however. In New Guinea, the strain has been experienced by an individual in a relatively stable, well-organized, "traditional" society; in Europe, by a large population in a rapidly changing, "progressive," modern society. Pathological phenomena are promoted in the first case by stability (an individual's inability to modify the social situation which tradition has shaped for him), in the second case by the rapidity of change and its varying rates in different parts of the social order. Another critical difference is that the reaction of the "primitive" society to what was perceived as pathology was mainly rehabilitative, and of the "advanced" society, punitive. And while the wild man of New Guinea is presumably advancing, at the end of his case history, to a personally more gratifying mode of existence, his European counterparts have met their end amidst the rubble of the nations they had wanted to lead to recovery by pathological means.

TALCOTT PARSONS

Some Sociological Aspects of the Fascist Movements

The older type, especially of European, social theory was, very largely, oriented to the understanding, in broad terms, of the social situation of the writer's own time. Whatever was sound in these older attempts, as of a Comte, a Spencer or a Marx, tended to be so intimately bound up with scientifically dubious elements of grandiose speculative construction and methodological assumption and dogma that the whole genus of analysis has tended to become discredited as a result of the general reaction against speculative theories.

In the course of such reactions it is not uncommon for the baby to be thrown out with the bath, for elements of sound insight and analysis to be lost sight of through their seemingly inseparable involvement with these other elements. Perhaps in the last few years more strongly than at any other time have there been signs that warrant the hope of an ability in the social sciences to apply generalized theoretical analysis to such problems in a thoroughly empirical, tentative spirit which will make possible a cumulative development of understanding, relatively unmarred by scientifically irrelevant or untenable elements. The very breadth of the problem of diagnosis of the state of a great civilization creates a strong demand for such a method.

Perhaps the most dramatic single development in the society of the Western world in its most recent phase has been the emergence of the great political movements usually referred to as "Fascist." In spite of their uneven incidence, with Germany and Italy by far the most prominent centers, and their varying character in different countries, there is sufficient similarity to justify the hypothesis that the broad phenomenon is deeply rooted in the structure of Western society as a whole and its internal strains and conflicts. However much my own approach may turn out to differ from the Marxian, this much must certainly be granted the latter — that it does relate Fascism to fundamental and generalized aspects of Western society.

As a starting point for the present analysis perhaps the common formula of characterization as the "radicalism of the right" is as satisfactory as any. It has at least the virtue of calling attention to two important points. In the first place Fascism is not "old conservatism" of the sort especially familiar before 1914, although elements which were once conservative in that sense have often been drawn into the Fascist movements. Secondly, it is definitely of the "right" in that it is specifically oriented in opposition to the political movements of the "left," notably of course communism.

Perhaps the most important reason why we are justified in speaking of "radicalism" lies in the existence of a popular mass movement in which large masses of the "common people" have become imbued with a highly emotional, indeed often fanatical, zeal for a cause. These mass movements, which are in an important sense revolutionary movements, are above all what distinguishes Fascism from ordinary conservatism. They are movements which, though their primary orientation is political, have many features in common with great religious movements in history, a fact which may serve as a guide to the sociological analysis of their origins and character.

A second important feature is the role played by privileged elite groups, groups with a "vested interest" in their position. While from some points of view the combination of these two elements in the same movement is paradoxical, it will be argued here that it is of the very essence of the phenomenon and perhaps more than anything else throws light on the social forces at work.

It has come to be a well-known fact that movements of religious proselytism tend to develop in situations involving a certain type of social disorganization, primarily that early though only roughly characterized by Durkheim as "anomie." Anomie may perhaps most briefly be characterized as the state where large numbers of individuals are to a serious degree lacking in the kind of integration with stable institutional patterns which is essential to their own personal stability and to the smooth functioning of the social system. Of this there are in turn perhaps two principal aspects. In the first place there seems to be a deep-seated need for a relative stability of the expectations to which action is oriented. The aspect of this on which Durkheim lays primary stress is the sufficiently clear definition of the goals of action — there can, he says, be no sense of achievement in progress toward the realization of an infinite goal. But goals are, to a very large extent defined by institutionalized expectations. This Durkheim illustrated by the inability of indefinite increase of wealth, once cut loose from definite standards, to satisfy ambition.

Similar considerations apply to other aspects of conduct. Expectations cannot be stable if the standards with which conformity is demanded are left so vague as not to be a real guide, or if the individual is subjected, in the same situation, to two or more conflicting expectations each of which advances claims to legitimacy which cannot be ignored.

The second, it would seem somewhat more difficult and complex aspect, lies in the need for a sufficiently concrete and stable system of symbols around which the sentiments of the individual can crystallize. In many different aspects of life highly concrete associations are formed which perhaps in many cases have no great intrinsic importance in themselves, but in that they become stabilized and perpetuated through a living social tradition perform a highly important function in integrating social groups and in stabilizing the orientation of individuals within them.

The general character of the typical reaction of the individual to anomie is that usually referred to in psychological terms as a state of insecurity. The personality is not stably organized about a coherent system of values, goals, and expectations. Attitudes tend to vacillate between indecision which paralyzes action — and all manner of scruples and inhibitions — and on the other hand compulsively "overdetermined" reactions which endow particular goals and symbols with an excess of hatred, devotion or enthusiasm over what is appropriate to the given situation. Generalized insecurity is commonly associated with high levels of anxiety and aggression, both of which are to an important extent "free-floating" in that they are not merely aroused in appropriate form and intensity by fear or anger-provoking situations but may be displaced onto situations or symbols only remotely connected with their original sources.

The present formulation of the psychological correlates of anomie has consciously adhered to the level closest to the more general character of social situations — lack of definition of goals and standards, conflicting expectations, inadequately concrete and stable symbolization. I am well aware that many psychologists find the deepest sources of insecurity to lie in the relations of the individual to his parents and others in the family in early childhood. The two approaches are by no means necessarily in conflict. There is much evidence that insecurity developed in adults from the sources here indicated affects their relations to their children and in turn the character formation of the latter, so that a cumulative vicious circle may work itself out.

An increase in anomie may be a consequence of almost any change in the social situation which upsets previous established definitions of the situation, or routines of life, or symbolic associations. To be sure, the members of some societies have average character types which are better able to withstand and adapt to rapid changes than are others — but in any case there is a limit to the extent and rapidity of change which can take place without engendering anomie on a large scale. There is ample evidence that the period immediately preceding our own time was, throughout the Western world, one of such rapid and fundamental change as to make this inevitable.

It was, in the first place, the period of the Industrial Revolution which, though going much farther back in history, tended cumulatively to gain in force throughout the nineteenth century and well into the twentieth. Though in widely differing degrees, most Western countries changed from predominantly agricultural to industrial and commercial societies, a change impinging not only on occupation but on the life of very large numbers of the population in many different aspects, especially in the tremendous growth of cities and the continual introduction of new elements into the standard of living.

Secondly, and intimately connected with this, the society has been subjected to many other influences adversely affecting situational stability. Migration of population from the rural areas to the growing urban concentrations has been only one phase of a tremendous and complex migration process which has necessitated the complex process of adaptation to new social environments — sometimes, as in the great bulk of immigration into the United States, assimilation to a drastically different cultural tradition with exposure to conflicting expectations and discrimination on ethnic lines. A somewhat different source of strain lies in the instability of the new economy — the exposure to cyclical fluctuations with unemployment and rapid and drastic changes in the standard of living. Inflation and many of the social and economic effects of war fit into the same general pattern.

Though it is perhaps more significant as a consequence of than as a causal factor in anomie, the fact is relevant that not only in women's dress but in any number of other fields our society is to a very high degree subject to rapid and violent changes of fad and fashion. No sooner have we become attached to a pattern than its social prestige melts away leaving the necessity to form a new orientation. This is especially true in the recreational and other expressional fields, but applies also to political and cultural ideas, and to many fields of consumption patterns.

Finally, the cultural development of the period has been preeminently one to undermine simplicity and stability of orientation. It has been to an extraordinary extent a period of the "debunking" of traditional values and ideas, and one in which for previously stable cultural patterns in such fields as religion, ethics, and philosophy, no comparably stable substitutes have appeared — rather a conspicuously unstable factionalism and tendency to faddistic fluctuation. Part of the situation is an inevitable consequence of the enormous development of popular education, and of the development of mass means of communication so that cultural influences which in an earlier time reached only relatively small "sophisticated" minorities now impinge upon a very large proportion of the total population.

Returning for a moment to the psychological level of consideration, one of the most conspicuous features of the present situation lies in the extent to which patterns of orientation which the individual can be expected to take completely for granted have disappeared. The complexity of the influences which impinge upon him has increased enormously, in many or most situations the society does not provide him with only one socially sanctioned definition of the situation and approved pattern of behavior but with a considerable number of possible alternatives, the order of preference between which is by no means clear. The "burden of decision" is enormously great. In such a situation it is not surprising that large numbers of people should, to quote a recent unpublished study,[1] be attracted to movements which can offer them "membership in a group with a vigorous *esprit de corps* with submission to some strong authority and rigid system of belief, the individual thus finding a measure of escape from painful perplexities or from a situation of *anomie*."

Thus the large-scale incidence of anomie in Western society in recent times is hardly open to doubt. This fact alone, however, demonstrates only susceptibility to the appeal of movements of the general sociological type of fascism but it is far from being adequate to the explanation of the actual appearance of such movements or above all the specific patterns in terms of which they have become structured. It is this latter problem which must next be approached.

The state of anomie in Western society is not primarily a consequence of the impingement on it of structurally fortuitous disorganizing forces though these have certainly contributed. It has, rather, involved a very central dynamic process of its own about which a crucially important complex of factors of change may be grouped, what, following Max Weber, may be called the "process of rationalization." The main outline of its character and influence is too familiar to need to be discussed in detail — but it must be kept clearly in mind as a basis for the subsequent analysis.

[1] Theodore W. Sprague, "Jehova's Witnesses: a Study in Group Integration." Dissertation, Harvard University, 1942.

Undoubtedly the most convenient single point of reference is to be found in the patterns of science. The development of science is of course inherently dynamic and has a certain immediate effect in progressively modifying traditional conceptions of the empirical world. It is, however, its application in technology which provides the most striking source of cumulative social change, profoundly affecting the concrete circumstances of men's lives in a multitude of ways. Again it is not only that the explicit formal content of occupational roles is affected — this is the center from which many complex ramifications of change radiate into the informal and symbolic areas of men's working lives, and into their private lives through changes in their patterns of consumption, recreation, etc. Whatever the positive value of the changes, they always involve an abandonment of traditional orientation patterns, circumstances and definitions of the situation which necessitates a process of readjustment.

Though by no means simply an aspect of science and its application in technology a second dynamic complex is intimately related to it. It may be characterized as the treatment of a wide range of action patterns and contexts of human relationship in terms of orientation to relatively specific and limited goals. Perhaps the classic center of the complex is the field of "contractual" relationships, and its formulation at the hands of such theorists as Spencer and Tönnies provides the classic sociological characterization. Contractualism overlaps widely with the use of money and the wide extension of market relationships. This involves the enormous extension of the mobility of elements essential to coordinated human action and the extension of the possibility of focussing elements from many sources on the realization of a single goal. Codification and systematization of personal rights and individual liberties is another essential aspect as is the clear development of the modern institution of ownership in the sphere of property. The question of where ownership is lodged is not the primary issue — but rather the concentration of the various rights which taken together we call ownership into a single bundle rather than their dispersion; and by the same token their segregation from the other elements of the status of their holder.

By no means the least important element of this complex is the patterning of functional roles primarily about their functional content itself with clear segregation from other elements of the total social status of the individual — in kinship, local ties, even to a considerable extent social class and ethnic adherence. Though prominent in the case of independent roles such as those of private professional practice, this patterning of functional roles is most prominent in the field of large-scale organization, indeed without it the latter as we know it would scarcely be conceivable at all.

The interdependence between the complex of science and technology on the one hand, and that just discussed on the other is exceedingly close. Some schools of thought, as of Veblen and Ogburn, give the former unquestioned primacy. This is at least open to serious question since it is only in relatively highly developed stages of the patterning of functionally specialized roles that the most favorable situation for the functioning of scientific investigation and technological application is attained. Less directly the mobility of resources through property and market relations, and the institutions of personal freedom all greatly facilitate the influence of science on social life.

Finally, science itself is a central part of the cultural tradition of our society. As such it is perhaps the most conspicuous embodiment of the more general pattern which may be called that of "critical rationality," differing from others primarily in the place accorded to the canons of empirical observation and verification. This same spirit of critical rationality has to an increasing extent ramified into many or even most other areas of the cultural tradition.

Notably of course it has permeated philosophical thought and the religious traditions of the various branches of Christianity. In this direction two consequences above all have appeared — the questioning of the cognitive status of the "non-empirical" elements of philosophical and religious thought, and the tendency to eliminate patterns and entities of primarily symbolic significance. The use of the categories of "ignorance" and "superstition" as sufficient characterizations of all thought not in conformity with the particular rational or pseudo-rational standards of the moment is an indication of the basic attitude.

The present concern is not whether the patterns of rationality in these different areas are in some sense superior to those they have tended to supplant, but rather the relation of their relatively rapid process of development to the functioning of the social system. It should be clear that their development is in itself perhaps the most important single source of anomie. Its significance in this respect is by no means simple and cannot be adequately analyzed here. It is partly a matter of the sheer rapidity of the process, which does not provide an opportunity for stable reorientation. Another aspect is the unevenness and incompleteness of its incidence so that it engenders conflicts in the social pressures impinging on the same groups and as between different groups. There is also the question whether, to balance its undermining effect on traditional patterns and values, it succeeds in providing even for the groups most thoroughly permeated, functionally adequate substitutes.

But beyond the significance as a source of temporary or permanent anomie, the process of rationalization has a further significance of crucial interest here. It is to it that we must look for the primary explanation of the structuring of attitudes and social organization so far as it can be treated as a response to the generalized condition of anomie. This question will have to be discussed on two primary levels, first that of the cognitive definition of the situation, second that of the differential affective appeal of the competing definitions of the situation which have come to be available.

The process of rationalization would scarcely have been of profound social importance if it had not affected large numbers of people in the immediate circumstances of their daily lives. But as an essential part of the same general cultural movement there has developed a tradition of "social thought" which, in a sufficiently broad perspective, can be seen to be highly distinctive in spite of its internal complexity. It has provided, above all, two interrelated things, a diagnosis of the status of the society — particularly in relation to the traditional patterns and structures with which the process of rationalization has stood in conflict, and a frame of reference for determining the proper attitudes of "reasonable" men toward the social problems of the day. Its functioning as the "ideology" of social and political movements is a natural consequence. In a very broad sense it is the ideological patterns of the movements of the "left" which are in question.

Such a tradition of thought is inevitably compounded of various different elements which today we find it convenient to distinguish. In the first place, there are certain elements of genuine scientific insight which by contrast with previous stages may be considered new. Undoubtedly the "utilitarian" pattern of analysis of the division of labor and exchange and the corresponding analysis of the functioning of a system of competitive market relationships — in short the "classical economics" — is largely in this category. With the shift on this level from "economic individualism" in the direction of socialism, especially Marxism, certain changes of emphasis on different factors have occurred but a fundamental constancy of cognitive pattern, the "utilitarian," has remained.

From the perspective of a later vantage point we can now see that in spite of the undoubtedly sound elements there have from a scientific point of view been certain shortcomings in this scheme of thought. Attention has been concentrated on one sector of the total structure of a social system — that of contract, exchange, monetary transactions — and others such as family life have been neglected. But even within the area of focussed attention the "fallacy of misplaced concreteness" has, understandably enough, played a prominent role. The prominent patterns of thought have, that is, been inadequately placed in perspective and integrated with other elements of a total social system.

The scientifically relevant element has, at the same time, been closely related to certain patterns of value orientation — with both a positive and a negative aspect. In one connection the new social thought expressed a revolt against the old order and a rationalization or justification of the changes introduced by the process of rationalization. Its primary targets of attack have been traditionally established statuses of prestige, authority and privilege and the traditionalized patterns themselves which have been integrated with these. Positively, the rights of the individual both as against other human agencies and as against tradition itself have provided the main focus. A fundamental trend toward egalitarianism has also been prominent. Broadly the pattern can be described as one of "emancipation" from the control of forces without rational sanction, from unjust authority, from monopoly and competitive privilege, from the "tyranny" of ignorance and superstition.

Finally, apart both from questions of science and of ethical value the tendency has, it has been noted, been to extend patterns of rationality into the metaphysical realm. Science has been taken as the prototype of all sound cognitive orientation and all elements of tradition not scientifically defensive have tended to be "debunked." Here of course traditional religion has been the primary object of attack.

In the earlier phases of its development this scheme of thought overwhelmingly embodied positive value attitudes. It defined the situation for the emergence and establishment of a new and magnificent social order, for freedom against tyranny, for enlightenment against ignorance and superstition, for equality and justice against privilege, for free enterprise against monopoly and the irrational restrictions of custom.

Gradually, however, with the growing ascendancy of the associated patterns, in certain directions certain elements of the scheme of thought have with altered emphasis and formulation come to be built into a pattern embodying quite different value attitudes. This has centered primarily on the developed system of emancipated and rationalized economic organization. The liberation of free enterprise from the tyranny of monopoly and custom has, it is said, led only to the system of capitalistic exploitation. The "profit motive" has become the object of deep reproach. Inequality, unemployment, and new forms of unjust privilege have been brought into the lime-light. Political liberation from the tyrannical Bourbons has led only to a new enslavement under the "executive Committee of the Bourgeoisie."

This new negative orientation to certain primary aspects of the maturing modern social order has above all centered on the symbol of "capitalism," which in certain circles has come to be considered as all-embracing a key to the understanding of all human ills as Original Sin once was. But it is important to note that the main intellectual movements within which this has developed have retained, even in an extreme form, the rationalized patterns in other connections, particularly in attitudes toward ignorance and superstition — lurking behind which economic interests are often seen — and many other symbolic and unrationalized patterns of thought and social behavior. What in terms of the recent situation is "leftist" social thought is overwhelmingly "positivistic" as well as utilitarian.

With the wisdom of hindsight, it can now be clearly seen that this rationalistic scheme of thought has not been adequate to provide a stably institutionalized diagnosis of even a "modern" social system as a whole, nor has it been adequate to formulate all of the important values of our society, nor its cognitive orientation to the world. It has been guilty of the fallacy of misplaced concreteness in neglecting or underestimating the role of what Pareto has called the "non-logical" aspects of human behavior in society, of the sentiments and traditions of family and informal social relationships, of the refinements of social stratification, of the peculiarities of regional, ethnic or national culture — perhaps above all of religion. On this level it has indeed helped to provoke a most important "anti-intellectualist" reaction.

On another level it has "debunked" many of the older values of our cultural tradition, and above all the cognitive patterns of religion, to a point well beyond that to which common values and symbols in the society had moved. Even apart from questions of its metaphysical validity it cannot be said adequately to have expressed the common orientations of the members of the society.

But on top of these inherent strains a crucial role has been played by the emergence within the rationalized cultural tradition itself of a definition of the situation which has thoroughly "debunked" many of the institutionalized products of the process of rationalization itself. Surely the stage was set for a combination of this definition of the situation with a reassertion of all the patterns which the utilitarian scheme had omitted or slighted — an acceptance of its own indictment but a generalization of the diagnosis to make "capitalism" appear a logical outcome of the whole process of rationalization itself, not merely of its perversion, and the fact that in certain directions it had not been carried far enough. By the same token it is possible to treat both capitalism and its leftist antagonists, especially communism, not as genuine antagonists but as brothers under the skin, the common enemy. The Jew serves as a convenient symbolic link between them.

This reaction against the "ideology" of the rationalization of society is one principal aspect at least of the ideology of fascism. It characteristically accepts in essentials the socialist indictment of the existing order described as capitalism, but extends it to include leftist radicalism and the whole penumbra of scientific and philosophical rationalism.[2]

The ideological definition of the situation in terms of which the orientation of a social movement becomes structured is of great importance but it never stands alone. It is necessarily in the closest interdependence with the psychological states and the social situations of the people to whom it appeals. We must now turn to the analysis of certain effects of the process of rationalization on this level.

The fundamental fact is that the incidence of the process within the social structure is highly uneven — different elements of a population become "rationalized" in different degrees, at different rates, and in different aspects of their personalities and orientations.

It may be said that both traditional and rationalized patterns are, to a high degree, genuinely institutionalized in our society. Indeed the distinction is itself largely relative and dynamic rather than absolute, and both are functionally essential to an even relatively stable society. Some elements of the population are relatively securely integrated but with varying emphasis in one direction or the other. Thus the best integrated professional groups would lean in the rational direction, certain rural elements in the traditional.

This difference of incidence has important consequences on both the structural and the psychological levels. Structurally it differentiates the social system broadly along a continuum of variation from the most highly traditionalized areas which have been least touched by the more recent phases of the process of rationalization to the most "emancipated" areas which tend at least partly to institutionalize the most "advanced" of the rationalized patterns or those which are otherwise most thoroughly emancipated from the traditional background.

For these and other reasons certain areas of the social structure have come to stand out conspicuously. In the first place is the area of "intellectualism" emancipated from the patterns and symbols of traditional thought, secondly of urbanism particularly on the metropolitan scale with its freedom from particularistic controls, its cosmopolitanism and general disrespect for traditional ties. Third is the area of economic, technological, and administrative rationalization in the market system and large-scale organization, especially toward the top, with its responsiveness to *ad hoc* situations and its relation to conflicting codes. Fourth is the area of "cultural" emancipation in literature and the arts with its high susceptibility to unstable faddism, and its association with bo-

---

[2] I am aware of the importance of other aspects of the total fascist pattern such as its romanticism and a tendency to ethical nihilism, but cannot stop to analyze them here.

hemianism. Finally there is the moral emancipation of "Society" with
its partial permeation of the upper middle class, the adoption of man-
ners and folkways not in keeping with various traditional canons of
respectability, all the way from women smoking to polite adultery.

The uneven incidence of these various forms of emancipation results
in an imperfect structural integration with latent or overt elements of
conflict and antagonism. These conflicts in turn readily become associated with the tensions involved in other structural strains in the society.
In particular may be mentioned here first, the difficult competitive position of the lower middle class, near enough to the realization of success
goals to feel their attraction keenly but the great majority, by the sheer
relation of their numbers to the relatively few prizes, doomed to frustration. Secondly, the particular strains in the situation of youth engendered by the necessity of emancipation from the family of orientation
and exposure to the insecurities of competitive occupational adjustment
at about the same stage of the life cycle, and third, the insecurity of the
adult feminine role in our urban society.[3]

An element of at least latent antagonism between relatively emancipated and relatively traditionalized elements of the society would exist
even if all its members were perfectly integrated with institutional
patterns, if there were no anomie. But we have seen that anomie exists
on a large scale. In relation to the above discussion, however, two principal foci, each with a tendency to a different structuring of attitudes
need to be distinguished. On the one hand certain of the population
elements involved in the spearheads of the processes of emancipation
and rationalization are subject to a high incidence of it with its attendant insecurity. These elements tend to find the main points of reference
of their orientations in the relatively well institutionalized rational and
emancipated patterns — in science, liberalism, democracy, humanitarian-
ism, individual freedom. But being insecure they tend to "overreact" and
both positively and negatively to be susceptible to symbolizations and
definitions of the situation which are more or less distorted caricatures
of reality and which are overloaded with affect. Thus negatively the
traditional order from which emancipation has been taking place is
characterized overwhelmingly as embodying ignorance, superstition, nar-
row-mindedness, privilege, or in the later stages, acquisitive capitalistic
exploitation. On the positive side there has been not only a marked

[3] A colleague (E. Y. Hartshorne in an unpublished paper) has noted that in
Germany the most conspicuous support of the Nazis came from the lower middle
class, from youth, and from women. On the two latter factors see the author's
paper "Age and Sex in the Social Structure of the United States," (*American
Sociological Review*, Vol. 7, October, 1942) reprinted in this volume [*Essays in
Sociological Theory*].

abstractness but also some form of naive rationalistic utopianism. The pattern tends to bear conspicuous marks of the psychology of compulsion. It is held that if only certain symbolic sources of evil, superstition, or privilege or capitalism were removed "everything would be all right" automatically and for all time. Indeed there is every reason to believe that the psychology of this type of insecurity has had much to do with the cognitive biases and inadequacies of utilitarian thought as sketched above. It has contributed largely to the currency of a definition of the situation which contains conspicuous elements of utopianism and of distorted caricature.

The other type of reaction has been prominent in those areas of the society where traditional elements have formed the institutionalized points of reference for orientation. There the principal sources of anomie have often been derived from situational factors such as technological change, mobility and ethnic assimilation with relatively little direct relation to rationalized ideological patterns. There insecurity has tended to be structured in terms of a felt threat to the traditionalized values. The typical reaction has been of an over-determined "fundamentalist" type. Aggression has turned toward symbols of the rationalizing and emancipated areas which are felt to be "subversive" of the value. Naturally there has at the same time been an exaggerated assertion of and loyalty to those traditional values. The availability of ready-made caricatured definitions of the situation and extreme symbols has of course greatly facilitated this structuring. The use of such slogans as "capitalism," has made it possible to exaggerate the "rottenness" of the whole modern society so far as it has departed from the good old values.

In the complex process of interaction in Western society between imperfectly integrated institutional structures, ideological definitions of the situation, and the psychological reaction patterns typical of anomie, at a certain stage in the dynamic process of its development this new structured mass movement has come upon the scene and at certain points in the Western world has gained ascendancy. It is perhaps safe to conclude from the above analysis that its possibility is at least as deeply rooted in the social structure and dynamics of our society as was socialism at an earlier stage.

Before turning to another phase of the problem a word may be said about the role of nationalism in the present context. Though not, in terms of the "old regime," itself strictly a traditional value, the complex of sentiments focussing on national cultures has involved many of these traditionalistic elements — varying in specific content from one case to another. Ever since the French Revolution a functional relationship between the rise of nationalism and the process of rationalization has been evident — they have developed concurrently.

For a variety of reasons nationalistic sentiment has been perhaps the readiest channel for the fundamentalist reaction to flow into. The national state assumed great actual importance. The actual or potential enemy in the power system of states, differing in national tradition, has formed a convenient target for the projection of many aggressive affects. At the same time many of the emancipated areas of the social structure have been defined as "international" and could be regarded as subversive of national interest, honor, and solidarity. Finally, nationalism has been a kind of lowest common denominator of traditionalistic sentiments. Above all, the humblest insecure citizen, whatever his frustrations in other connections, could not be deprived of his sense of "belonging" to the great national community.

Undoubtedly one of the most important reasons for the different degrees of success of the fascist movement in different countries has lain in the differing degrees in which national traditions and with them pride and honor, have been integrated with the symbols of the rationalized patterns of Western culture. In the United States, on the one hand, the great national tradition stems from the Enlightenment of the eighteenth century — liberty, democracy, the rights of the individual are our great slogans. A radically fundamentalist revolt would have to overcome the enormous power of these symbols. In Germany on the other hand the political symbols of a liberal democratic regime could be treated as having been ruthlessly imposed on a defeated and humiliated Germany by the alien enemy. National sentiments instead of being closely integrated with the existing regime could readily be mobilized against it.

The second important element of the fascist movements, that of "vested interests" can be much more briefly treated. It is one of the most fundamental theorems of the theory of institutions that in proportion to the institutionalization of any pattern a self-interest in conformity with it develops. Self-interest and moral sentiments are not necessarily antithetical, but may, and often do, motivate conduct in the same direction. Though this is true generally, it has a particularly important application to statuses involving prestige and authority in the social system. There, on top of the broader meaning of an interest in conformity, there is an interest in defending higher status and its perquisites against challenge from less privileged elements. For this reason the reaction of privileged elements to insecurity is almost inevitably structured in the direction of an attitude of defense of their privileges against challenge. For the same reason any movement which undermines the legitimacy of an established order tends to become particularly structured about an overt or implied challenge to the legitimacy of privileged statuses within it.

Western society has in all its recent history been relatively highly stratified, involving institutionalized positions of power, privilege, and prestige for certain elements. In the nature of the case the sentiments and symbols associated with these prestige elements have been integrated with those institutionalized in the society as a whole. In so far, then, as the process of rationalization and other disorganizing forces have undermined the security of traditional patterns the status and the bases of the legitimacy of privileged elements have inevitably been involved. But in addition to this they have been affected by threats to the legitimacy and security of their own position in the social structure. This situation tends to be particularly acute since the process of more general change is regularly accompanied by a process of the "circulation of the elite."

It is in the nature of a highly differentiated social structure that such privileged elements should be in a position to exercise influence on the power relations of the society through channels other than those open to the masses, through political intrigue, financial influence, and so on. Hence, with the progressive increase in the acuteness of a generalized state of anomie it is to be expected that such elements, which have been privileged in relation to a traditional social order should, within the limits provided by the particular situation, develop forms of activity, sometimes approaching conspiratorial patterns, which in these terms may be regarded as a defense of their vested interests. Exactly what groups are involved in this phenomenon is a matter of the particular structural situation in the society in question.

The general phenomenon would seem to be clear enough. It is also not difficult to understand the tendency for elite elements whose main patterns go far back into the older traditional society to become susceptible to the fascist type of appeal — such as the landed nobility and higher clergy in Spain, or the Junker class in Germany. But there is a further complication which requires some comment.

The process of institutional change in the recent history of our society has brought to the fore elite elements whose position has been institutionalized primarily about the newer rationalized patterns. The most important are the business and professional elites. The latter are, except where radical fascist movements have immediately threatened to gain the ascendancy, perhaps the securest elite elements in the modern West.

The position of the business elite has, however, been much more complex. It gained for a time a position of great ascendancy, but for various reasons this rested on insecure foundations. With the "leftward" turn in the movement of ideology its position came under strong attack as the key element of capitalism. With its position thus threatened by the leftward sweep of the process of rationalization the legitimacy, the moral validity of its position was under attack, and its actual vested interests became less and less secure. From this point of view Fascism has constituted in one respect a continuation, even an intensification of the same threat. The threat has been made concrete by the rise to power of a new political elite with the means in hand to implement their threat.

At the same time fascism has seemed to stand, in the logic of the sentiments, for "sound" traditional values and to constitute a bulwark against subversive radicalism. Very concretely it has been instrumental in breaking the power of organized labor. At the same time on the level of power politics there has been a distinct area of potential mutual usefulness as between a political movement of the fascist type and entrenched business interests. This has been especially true because of the fascist tendency immediately to mobilize the economy in preparation for war.

The relation between fascism and vested interests in general may thus be regarded as a constant. In the case of the older traditional interests it is relatively unequivocal, but in that of business it is highly ambivalent. Especially where, as in Germany, business interests have not been closely integrated with strong liberal institutions the relationship has tended to be very close. But even there the movement can by no means be considered a simple expression of these vested interests and there are elements in the Nazi movement which may, in a certain state of the internal balance of power, turn out to be highly subversive of business.

In such brief space it has been possible to analyze only a few aspects of the very complex sociological problem presented by the fascist movement — the analysis is in no sense complete. But perhaps it will serve in a humble way to illustrate a direction in which it seems possible to utilize the conceptual tools of sociology in orienting ourselves, at least intellectually, to some of the larger aspects of the tragic social world we live in. To consider the possibility of going farther, of predicting the probable social consequences, of possible outcomes of the war and considering what we can do about fascism in other than a strictly military sense would raise such complex issues even on the scientific level, that it is better not even to attempt to touch upon them here.

III

Self-Destructive Behavior

Drunkenness

An exhaustive investigation of a case history reveals the complex interaction among the variables involved in social pathogenesis but does not disclose to what extent the relationships are general (operative in all situations of a similar type) and to what extent they are "accidental" (peculiar only to the situation at hand). To deal with this question, the statistical technique of comparing a sample of societies along a single dimension of their organization and relating this dimension to a type of pathological behavior has been developed. When the sample consists of preliterate societies, a further question arises: whether the findings can be applied to modern (advanced industrial) societies. If, for example, Field (in the article that follows) finds that the kinship system is more important than the political order in the genesis of drunkenness in preliterate societies, will this finding hold in modern societies in which the structural importance of the political order — the state — has increased and that of the kinship system declined in comparison with preliterate societies? Until parallel studies on a sample of modern societies are made, the relevance of preliterate studies to modern societies would seem to lie in the general causal mechanisms suggested and not in the specific structural correlates of pathology revealed (many of which have disappeared in the course of social evolution).

78

A New Cross-Cultural Study
of Drunkenness

The cross-cultural method has several important potential advantages for extending our knowledge of drinking behavior. First, this technique examines relations between variables across a number of tribes at once, while the typical anthropological report is restricted to just a single tribe. Furthermore, the method deals simultaneously with a great range of modal drinking patterns — from abstention in some tribes to periodic bouts of extreme drunkenness in others. Finally, the tribes that are included are separated from each other and also from Western industrial society, so that relationships emerging across a sample of tribes cannot be attributed to the widespread influence of a small number of cultural heritages. This method is therefore a potentially valuable tool in the development of general explanations of wide scope and applicability concerning drunkenness. These generalizations may in turn advance our knowledge of alcoholism in modern society.

PREVIOUS CROSS-CULTURAL RESEARCH
ON DRUNKENNESS

Cross-cultural research of this kind depends upon the development of valid rating categories for assessing the extent of drunkenness and their successful application to the available anthropological literature on primitive societies. After this, the anthropological reports for each society must also be scored on other theoretically relevant variables which may then be related to the index of drunkenness. This has been done only once in the past — in the classic cross-cultural research of Horton (6).

To explain his results, Horton presented an anxiety theory of drunkenness. He proposed that a major factor determining the degree of drunkenness in a society is the level of anxiety or fear among the individual

From "A New Cross-Cultural Study of Drunkenness" by Peter B. Field in *Society, Culture and Drinking Patterns*, David J. Pittman and Charles R. Snyder, eds. Reprinted in abridged form by permission of the author, the editors, and John Wiley & Sons, Inc., Publishers.

members. Drunkenness, however, can be inhibited as well as produced by anxiety. Consequently, according to Horton, the level of drunkenness in a society is a resultant of a complex interaction of anxiety-reduction and anxiety-induction. He states, for instance, that the ". . . strength of the drinking response in any society tends to vary directly with the level of anxiety in that society." However, since the ". . . drinking of alcohol tends to be accompanied by the release of sexual and aggressive impulses," and since sexual and aggressive impulses are often punished, drinking will be weaker where these responses lead to anxiety about punishment — that is, the ". . . strength of the drinking response tends to vary inversely with the strength of the counteranxiety elicited by painful experiences during and after drinking" (6, p. 230).

Horton's study was one of a series of research reports directly influenced by the efforts of Hull and his collaborators to integrate behavior theory and psychoanalysis. A hallmark of this approach was the explanation of complex socio-cultural phenomena in terms of individual drives — especially frustration or anxiety. Prior to Horton's work, for example, two members of Hull's school of thought reported an inverse relation between the price of cotton and the number of lynchings per year in the Deep South, and explained this in terms of frustration and aggression (7). In view of theoretical precedents of this kind, it is not surprising that Horton should have interpreted the level of drunkenness in a society as an expression of the level of fear or anxiety in the society. His research is, however, one of the very few reporting an important relation of any kind between the level of anxiety in a society and any aspect of alcohol use. Indeed, it is the only social research cited in a recent review of the most important research evidence that alcohol reduces fear (3).

Not all of Horton's results support his own theory unequivocally, and those which appear to do so vary greatly in quality. The most convincing support comes from his finding that aggressive and sexual responses are often released at drinking bouts, suggesting that there is ordinarily an inhibiting force which holds these responses in check. This fear-like force is temporarily weakened at drinking bouts. However, his two major indices of the social anxiety level — that is, an insecure food supply and acculturation by contact with Western civilization — are very indirect and questionable measures of fear. Furthermore, as Lemert (8, p. 370) has pointed out, Horton failed ". . . to include a well-defined variable of social organization. Correlating such things as the technological level of a society or the amount of its wealth or the death rate of its population with a psychological reaction such as anxiety can only partially reveal the dynamics behind primitive drinking, because these non-sociological facts always take on variable meaning and impact for the members of societies through the media of social organization." Several authors have also made the very important point that a simple anxiety theory of alcoholism and drunkenness is inadequate because it does not explain why other modes of reducing anxiety instead of drinking are not used (e.g., 9). Why does a society develop drunkenness in response to food shortages rather than, say, ritual magic aimed at inducing a reluctant god to supply food? Why, moreover, does a psychoneurotic become an alcoholic instead of developing a different form of anxiety-reducing personality disorder?

Since Horton wrote the above-cited paper, a number of studies of primitive drinking have been reported, but these have not unequivocally supported his position. As a case in point, Lemert (8) found that the greatest drunkenness among the Indians of the American Northwest occurred when they were enriched by the fur trade; it is hard to understand why this might have been associated with fear. For his part, Lemert identified a number of other factors — including cultural conservatism, anomie, and interclan rivalry — affecting drunkenness on the Northwest Coast. Other studies of individual tribes, such as Heath's study of the Camba . . . have suggested social disorganization or social isolation as important causal variables in drunkenness.

METHODS AND PROCEDURES

The re-examination of Horton's theory which is an integral part of the present study was made possible by the development of new cross-cultural scales which were not available to him. This re-examination was begun by assembling a group of scales on the basis of their theoretical relevance to alcohol problems.[1] These scales were originally developed by many different raters for a wide variety of purposes and vary widely in degree of reliability. Some, such as Horton's drunkenness measure or Murdock's (14) social structure ratings, have been scored by only one judge so that their interscorer reliability cannot be directly estimated (although we know from the magnitude of the correlations with other variables that it must be substantial). In certain other instances where reliability can be estimated, the measures are reliable enough to indicate the presence of a non-chance relationship but are too crude for more accurate prediction.

The most important scale in the tables to follow is Horton's measure of "strong vs. moderate and slight degrees of insobriety" (6, pp. 265–266). Tribes with "strong" insobriety were described by ethnographers as drinking to unconsciousness, drinking for many hours or days, or getting "excessively" drunk. The last category probably indicates

[1] The source of each scale used in the tables to follow is given in the reference list at the end of this chapter.

extreme functional impairment. Tribes with "slight" or "moderate" in-sobriety either did not get drunk, or, if they did, did not drink for days and did not drink to unconsciousness. This scale measures degree of drunkenness at periodic drinking bouts and not, of course, the number of alcoholics in the society or the death rate from alcoholism.[2]

After the scales were assembled, Horton's fifty-six tribes were divided into two subsamples of roughly equal size. The first subsample consisted of all of Horton's tribes that had also been rated by Whiting and Child (29). Preliminary correlations were examined using only this subsample. While only a few of the Whiting and Child child-rearing ratings showed promising relationships, a group of highly suggestive relationships appeared using Murdock's social structure ratings (14). These relationships were checked in the second subsample. As a rule, the preliminary relationships emerged just as clearly in the second sample, and for no important relation did an association reverse or change markedly between the samples. This strongly indicates that the relations found between drunkenness and social structure are not the result of capitalization upon chance associations. For this reason the subsamples were combined for ease of presentation. Finally, unpublished social-structure ratings on six additional tribes were kindly provided by George P. Murdock in a personal communication, and were added to the two subsamples to complete the final sample.

Unless otherwise indicated, scales were dichotomized at the median. Associations were tested for statistical significance by chi-square corrected for continuity with one degree of freedom. Tetrachoric correlation coefficients for each association were estimated by the method given in (27). All probability values reported in this chapter are based on a conservative two-tailed criterion. Any association based on less than fifty-six cases indicates that either an ethnographer or a rater omitted relevant information on one or more of Horton's tribes.

RESULTS AND DISCUSSION

1. Drunkenness, Fear, and Subsistence Insecurity

The first section of Table 1 shows the relations between Horton's measure of drunkenness and the best available measures of fear (4a, 29).

---

[2] The scale also excludes solitary drinking and drinking by women. The few societies without available alcohol were excluded, and so were the societies with no satisfactory ethnographic information about drunkenness. Societies similar to a neighboring society already in the sample were excluded. The societies that were included come from all over the world, with a number of representatives in each major culture area. Horton excluded the Moslem societies of North Africa, since they have a religious taboo on alcohol; this was a questionable decision, but it probably affects neither his general conclusions nor mine.

None of these relationships is statistically significant and no clear positive or negative trend appears. The first five measures of fear are drawn from beliefs concerning the causation of illness. Fear of spirits, for example, means that the society attributes illness to malevolent spirits. The last rating is an even more direct measure of fear based on records of direct statements of fear of ghosts at funerals. All of these scales of fear have shown significant relations to other measures such as sex anxiety or severe child rearing (28, 29), *which suggests that they are genuine measures of fear*.[3] They are all reliable enough to show significant relations to Horton's drunkenness score, if they existed. Horton himself was unable to find a relation between degree of drunkenness and sorcery, but the reason for this was not clear. The consistent negative evidence in Table 1 suggests that, *within the limits of these measures*, variation in the level of fear is not related to the extent of drunkenness in primitive tribes.

TABLE 1. THE RELATIONS OF DEGREE OF DRUNKENNESS TO INDICES OF FEAR

	x^2	r_{tet}
Fear of sorcerers	0.00	−.06
Fear of spirits	0.00	.07
Fear of others (sorcerers and spirits combined)	0.00	.06
Fear of ghosts	0.34	.29
Fear of animal spirits	0.91	−.39
Fear of ghosts at funerals[a]	0.00	.08

[a] N = 30; 27 for the other measures.

The data in the first column of Table 2 clearly confirm Horton's finding that tribes with very primitive hunting and gathering economies tend to have more drunkenness than tribes with more advanced herding and agricultural economies. The second column in Table 2 shows a very strong relation between Horton's measure of an insecure food supply and the absence of agriculture; indeed, this relation is so strong that it is perhaps justifiable to assume that Horton's "subsistence insecurity" is more of an indication of the lack of a stable agricultural basis for society than of the level of fear.

The implications of this latter, alternative assumption are far reaching. We know that the social organization of a hunting tribe is quite different in some ways from the social organization of a tribe with an

---

[3] A few other measures of anxiety given by Whiting and Child also showed no significant relation to drunkenness, but these either were based on such small numbers or were so unclear, theoretically, that they are not presented here.

Table 2. The Relations of Type of Subsistence Economy to Degree of Drunkenness and Insecure Food Supply[a]

Subsistence Economy	Drunkenness		Insecure Food Supply	
	χ^2	$r$tet	χ^2	$r$tet
Predominance of herding and agriculture over hunting and fishing (4)	4.14[b]	−.50	1.45	−.41
Agriculture	3.24	−.47	12.32[c]	−.85
Animal husbandry	1.34	−.32	0.02	−.13
Fishing and marine hunting	3.86[b]	.49	2.64	.49
Hunting and gathering	5.71[b]	.57	2.42	.48

[a] For all insecure food supply correlations, $N = 37$; N is either 49 or 50 for the other correlations. The Murdock (14) scales on economy were divided at "important" versus "present but unimportant."
[b] $P < .05$.
[c] $P < .001$.

advanced herding and agricultural subsistence economy. Tribes that live by hunting are frequently nomadic but agriculture requires a settled, stable community. With the development of agriculture and herding, it is also possible to support larger concentrated populations which would starve under a hunting economy (13, pp. 80–81). When such a population is present in one place over several generations, community divisions will be formed, occupational specialization will be more obvious, and social stratification and centralized political authority become possible. At the same time complex corporate-kin structures may emerge with the addition of a unilocal rule of marital residence and the development of unilinear descent. Thus with the transition from the hunting band to the compact village, formalized social control over the individual's behavior may well become more diffuse and pervasive. Parallel psychological differences may also appear. For instance, Barry, Child, and Bacon (2) have shown that herding and agricultural tribes expect obedience and responsibility from their children, while hunting and fishing societies demand independence, achievement, and self-assertion instead.

2. Drunkenness and Social Organization

These results and speculations suggest that something other than fear, perhaps a social variable, explains primitive drunkenness. Perhaps this variable can be detected by examining the primitive drinking bout.

Horton has described the sequence of behavior in drinking bouts in this way: first there is gaiety, laughter, friendliness, lewd jokes, jollity, and loquacity. After this, sexual behavior, verbal quarrels, and fights are often observed. In the tribes Horton classifies as extremely drunken, this goes on for many hours or days, extreme functional impairment is usual, and the bouts end with most of the participants unconscious.

Although anxiety is certainly being reduced, something more important is happening. Respect and reserve are giving way to friendly equality. Usually inhibited aggressive and sexual impulses are emerging. Behavior is directed at momentary personal pleasure and self-indulgence rather than duty, responsibility, and task performance. There is loosely organized companionship rather than formal execution of institutionalized obligations. In one sense the group is clearly becoming disorganized, since its members eventually withdraw into unconsciousness; but this disorganization is the final outcome of informal tension release in a companionship setting. In summary, a personal, informal organization has replaced a formal, well-structured organization: alcohol has facilitated informal, personal interaction by temporary removal of social inhibitions; and it has disorganized precisely controlled behavior, making difficult the performance of duties, labor, respect and avoidance, ceremonials and rituals, and other legalized obligations requiring inhibition of impulses.

In tribes with a great deal of this kind of informal, friendly, loosely controlled behavior at drinking bouts, there is a strong possibility that ordinary social relationships are also informal, personally organized, and based on friendly equality. Marriages may be primarily unions of individuals for companionship and mutual support, rather than socially extended alliances designed to fulfill broader economic or social functions, such as inheritance and lineage continuity. Formal alignments of kinsmen with clearly formulated mutual rights and obligations may be weak or absent. Social solidarity may be stronger between individuals of the same generation than between adjacent generations — that is, the drunken tribes may have a wide-ranging kinship system emphasizing friendly solidarity among siblings, cousins, and spouses, rather than hierarchical, lineal solidarity between parents and children. This in turn might mean that the drunken tribes place less importance on the conservation and transmission across generations of an elaborate social tradition.

In these tribes the organization of tribesmen to attain common objectives may be weak and informal. That is, in these tribes functions such as ceremonials, military operations, and transmission of property from one generation to another may be carried on by individuals or informal groups rather than assigned to specialists such as priests, a warrior caste, or a land-owning group. In the informally-structured tribes with primitive hunting and gathering economies there may be few differentiated structures serving well-defined social purposes.

Another possibility suggested by this line of reasoning is that there may be a general weakness of extreme power, respect, or reserve differentials between individuals in the extremely drunken tribes. If a society is highly organized, prestige and power will be vested in a few individuals rather than diffused throughout the tribe. This may happen both in political organization and in the family. The leader of a South American band of hunters has little power, but an African monarch wields a great deal. Similarly, in the drunken tribes there should be no great differences between husband and wife in centralized power and in control of the family, and therefore polygyny should not be important. This informal equality may be reflected in the child-rearing practices: we would not expect a great deal of pressure for submission and obedience on the part of children in the drunken tribes.

Form of Kin Group. Preliminary evidence for the relevance of social organization in explaining drunkenness among primitive peoples is presented in Table 3. The following facts will help to clarify the meaning of this table. Tribes with kin groups organized into units tracing descent through males are called "patrilineal"; those organized into units tracing descent through females are called "matrilineal"; while tribes with both these forms of kin group are referred to as having "double" descent. In contrast, tribes lacking kin groups organized into special corporate units (tribes which, for this reason, are more loosely organized and might be expected to exhibit more drunkenness) are referred to as "bilateral," which means that kinship is traced through males and females without formal distinction.

TABLE 3. THE RELATION OF DEGREE OF DRUNKENNESS TO TYPE OF KIN GROUP

Degree of Drunkenness	Type of Kin Group			
	Bilateral	Matrilineal	Patrilineal	Double
Extreme	19	5	9	1
Moderate or slight	2	3	12	4

Thus in Table 3, although patrilineal tribes appear to have somewhat less drunkenness than matrilineal tribes, the outstanding fact is the striking association of drunkenness with bilateral descent — in other words, its association with the absence of patrilineal or matrilineal kin groups of a corporate nature. Since, according to Murdock (13), kin groups based upon patrilineal and matrilineal descent parallel one another almost exactly, it seems permissible for statistical purposes to classify these together with double descent groups in a single category of "unilineal" groups. Viewed in relation to the presence or absence of unilineal kin groups so defined, degree of drunkenness yields a strong negative correlation of −.67 which is highly significant.[4]

A major distinction between the bilateral kindred, the most widespread and characteristic form of arrangement of kin in a bilateral society, and unilineal kin group is this: a unilineal kin group is a "corporate" group while the bilateral kindred is not. The term "corporate" means that unilineal kin groups are structured groups with ". . . perpetuity through time, collective ownership of property, and unified activity as a legal individual" (19, p. 200). An individual and his kindred die, but unilineal kin groups, like tribes, extend indefinitely into the past and the future.

Murdock (13, p. 61) points out that since the kindred is not a group except from the point of view of one individual and since it has no temporal continuity, it ". . . can rarely act as a collectivity. One kindred cannot, for example, take blood vengeance against another if the two happen to have members in common. Moreover, a kindred cannot hold land or other property. . . ." Murdock notes further that a member of a bilateral kindred may be involved in conflicting or incompatible obligations, while these conflicts cannot arise under unilineal descent. He also states that unilineal kin groups are discrete social units, automatically defining the role of every participant in a ceremonial activity or every bystander in a dispute (13, p. 62). By contrast, according to Pehrson (19), bilateral societies have often been called "amorphous," "unstructured," "loosely organized," or "infinitely complex" — the latter term being synonymous with fragmented. He suggests, however, that bilateral tribes are not truly disorganized; they have a flexible, noncorporate organization featuring a network of horizontal ties uniting individuals of the same generation.

Similarly Davenport (4, p. 569) concludes that the kindred structure ". . . occurs where collective and corporate control is absent or minimal." Davenport also points out that in addition to kindreds, some bilateral tribes have nonunilineal descent groups which have some corporate functions. However, affiliation with them is not as well institutionalized as it is in unilineal societies: an individual's affiliation is usually determined by choice, not by birth as it is in unilineal tribes; he may move from one group to another during his lifetime; and his claim to membership in a group may depend on his decision to perform actions maintaining reciprocal ties with the group, or on performance of some

---

[4] $\chi^2 = 9.94$, 1 df; $< .01$; $N = 55$. The degree of drunkenness was dichotomized at "extreme" versus "moderate or slight" in accordance with Horton's definitions noted above.

specialized technique for validating membership, such as giving a pot-latch.

In a later article Pehrson (20) points out that the bilateral Lappish band has flexible, variable structure permitting the individual a wide range of alternative courses of action. The structure of the band, he re-ports, is a wide-ranging alliance of sibling groups held together — some-times loosely — by conjugal ties. Devices such as the extension of sibling terminology to cousins increase the solidarity between members of the same generation. Sahlins (22) points out that in other bilateral tribes friendly relations between tribesmen may be secured at the expense of marital ties, as in Eskimo wife lending; in the most primitive tribes similar friendly relations are secured by the continuous circulation of food and other goods among individuals — a kind of mutual sharing that has also been noted in drinking groups. Finally, Wolf (30) reports that in open or non-corporate peasant communities, social, economic, and political arrangements are based on informal, personal ties between indi-viduals and families.

Since there are several different kinds of unilinear kin groups, the non-bilateral societies in Table 3 were re-examined for evidence of possible differences in drunkenness in each type of group. The association of unilinearity with little drunkenness was most marked for societies seg-mented into unilineal sibs: only seven of the twenty-one societies below the median on drunkenness did not have sibs. Of the twenty-two so-cieties with this structure, fourteen were below the median on drunken-ness. (Societies that had more inclusive structures — moieties or phra-tries — in addition to sibs were excluded from this tabulation and con-sidered below.) According to Murdock (13, p. 73), ". . . the sib is associated with totemism and ceremonial, acts as a unit in life crisis situa-tions, and regulates marriage and inheritance." In other words, it is associated with the most central symbols of formal solidarity, and regu-lates the individual's most important links to other individuals. Normally a sib is composed of several lineages, differentiating it internally. With sib exogamy, members of one sex marry into other sibs, thus forming collateral ties in the community. These tribes, then, have complex webs of formal kin affiliations spreading temporally and spatially throughout the entire society.

There were four tribes divided into unilineal moieties, or half-tribes, and all were above the median on drunkenness. Lowie (11, p. 247) points out that such moiety divisions are "fluid" and are not often found in tribes with large populations (p. 245). These indirect relations may well explain this result. On the other hand, there may be a failure to create strong solidarity by overinclusion of members, since the solidarity of all kin groups necessitates the exclusion of some tribesmen. In any event, if these four tribes with moiety divisions had been classified empirically with the bilateral groups, the already high correlation between drunkenness and form of kin group would have been still higher ($r = -.78$, $P < .001$). (There were only two tribes with phratries — one drunk and one sober — so no generalization is possible here.)

These results indicating the importance of social disorganization in primitive drunkenness also suggest a new explanation of Horton's findings on acculturation. His best predictor of drunkenness was severity of acculturation by contact with Western civilization. He examined the possibility that this might have been caused simply by the introduction of distilled liquors, and concluded that while there was some relationship, it was not an important one. He concluded that anxiety was produced during acculturation, and this caused drunkenness. However, it is not obvious that acculturation always increases anxiety, although it certainly may do so in special instances. Acculturation may in fact reduce anxiety by diminishing supernatural fears, or by providing rational solutions for anxiety-arousing cultural problems. It is very clear, however, that prolonged, intensive contact with Western civilization eventually disorganizes and destroys the social structure of a tribe. It also seems likely that rapid, far-reaching acculturative changes will be facilitated by an originally loose tribal social organization. For these reasons, it seems reasonable to suppose that Horton's relation between drunkenness and acculturation indicates an underlying process of loosening of a traditional social organization, not increased anxiety.

The general conclusion indicated by the findings to this point is: drunkenness in primitive societies is determined less by the level of fear in a society than by the absence of corporate kin groups with stability, permanence, formal structure, and well-defined functions.

Marital Residence. Table 4 shows that there is a strong relation between degree of drunkenness and the form of marital residence. "Bilocal" residence means that the newlyweds customarily make a decision at marriage as to whether they will reside near the bridegroom's parents or near the bride's parents; "neolocal" residence means that they reside in a new location. All 11 tribes with bilocal or neolocal residence are above the median on degree of drunkenness. The five tribes with "uxoripatrilocal" residence, in which residence with the bridegroom's family follows a period of residence with the bride's family, are also uniformly above the median of drunkenness. The large number of societies in which the bride leaves her home and lives with the groom near his family, which is called "patrilocal" residence, includes, on the other hand, most of the tribes below the median on drunkenness. Tribes with "matrilocal" or "avunculocal" residence (in which the newlyweds live in the first case with the wife's family, and in the second with the groom's mother's

Table 4. The Relation of Degree of Drunkenness to Form of Marital Residence

	Form of Residence				
Degree of Drunkenness	Bilocal or Neolocal	Uxoripatri-local	Matri-local	Avuncu-local	Patri-local
Extreme	11	5	8	1	9
Moderate or slight	0	0	4	2	15

brother) are harder to place. The former seems to show the extreme drunkenness pattern while the latter seems to be much closer to the sober patrilocal pattern.

Since two of the avunculocal tribes have residence shifts partially similar to the uxoripatrilocal tribes, they have been classified with the non-patrilocal tribes, following conservative procedure. If, on the other hand, the crucial variable here is immediate residence with a male exercising authority over the groom, and if avunculocal tribes are therefore grouped with patrilocal tribes, the relation between residence and drunkenness will be still stronger ($r = .71$, $\chi^2 = 11.81$, $P < .001$, $N = 55$).

The correlation between non-patrilocal residence and drunkenness ($r = .64$) is almost as high as the correlation between bilateral descent and drunkenness.[5] There is a correlation of .67 between non-patrilocal residence and bilateral descent. While these two predictor variables are importantly related to each other, each predicts some independent portion of the total variance in drunkenness scores. The multiple correlation using these two variables as joint predictors of drunkenness is .72. This means that the degree of dependence of drunkenness on form of residence and kin group is so strong that its level can be predicted with moderate accuracy in individual tribes from just these two variables alone. If the tribes with unilineal moieties had been grouped with the bilateral tribes, and the avunculocal with the patrilocal tribes, the multiple correlation would have been considerably higher.

The extreme drunkenness of the neolocal and bilocal tribes appears to reflect the fact that it is difficult for a society to develop extended lineal kinship structures if independent choice of residence is permitted the newlyweds. It is also probable that if the married couple is permitted to choose its residence, it will not be constrained by lineal and corporate rules in many other areas. There seems to be an intimate relationship between drunkenness and personal choice, absence of institutionalized constraints, and isolation of both the nuclear family and the individual from corporate kin structures.

[5] For patrilocal versus all other rules of residence, $\chi^2 = 8.92$, 1 df; $P < .01$; $N = 55$.

Absence of drunkenness, on the other hand, appears to be associated with male dominance reflected in patrilocal and perhaps avunculocal residence. We know that the father or the paternal grandfather usually wields authority in the household (13, p. 39) but we also know that he loses some of his power to his wife in matrilocal societies (24, pp. 507–508; 37). There are several reasons for this. In husband-wife conflicts, the wife will be supported by her own kinsmen, who are close at hand under matrilocal residence. Furthermore, since the man does not own land or the household in these tribes, his ties to his wife's home are weaker. Moreover, since the mother's brother can take on child-rearing duties, the father will be loosely attached to the nuclear family. He may divide his time between his sister's household and his wife's household, with both his authority and his obligations divided between them. For reasons such as these, Linton (17) concludes that marriage is particularly unstable in matrilineal societies.

By contrast, according to Linton, in patrilineal societies the woman is integrated into her husband's lineage by a series of marriage-stabilizing devices motivated by the interest of the husband's family in the children. With patrilocal residence, which means that the wife's kinsmen are at a distance and cannot support her, the father's formal and de facto authority grow. With increased centralization of familial power and the formation of hierarchical chains of command in the family, extreme drunkenness diminishes.

The tribes with uxoripatrilocal residence are significantly more drunken than the patrilocal tribes. In these five tribes, as in many of the matrilocal tribes, the bridegroom is required to serve as a hired hand for his wife's family, and must often undergo trials to determine his suitability for the marriage. It is only after this that he acquires full marital rights or, with uxoripatrilocal residence, permission to remove the bride from her own family. One implication of this' custom is that the husband's authority over his wife develops only gradually and is not clearly reinforced by external social influences. A second implication follows from the fact that there are at least two shifts of marital residence in these tribes, and that authority over a man is not consistently held by a single person, but is successively taken by his father and father-in-law. This means the attenuation of lineal structures and so, perhaps, more drunkenness.

While sobriety is obviously associated with a father-centered family, the crucial factors mediating this relationship are not entirely clear. One possibility is that there is a general increase in respect, reserve, and self-control in these tribesmen, because most of their interpersonal relations are organized hierarchically. Another possibility is that with patrilocal residence there is decreased mobility on the part of the heads of the households; therefore there will be a greater opportunity for the formation of formalized social ties in the community, and this in turn implies that there will be strong pressure exerted against interpersonal aggression, informal self-indulgence, and related individualistic behavior prominent at drinking bouts.

Still another possibility is that there may be a general stabilization of the society's interpersonal relationships when the authority of the father in any society is legitimized and extended by supporting rules of residence and descent; that is, in societies where internal power struggles by individuals or groups are minimized in normal interpersonal relationships, prolonged drinking bouts with their inevitable changing, transient coalitions, and conflicts will also be minimized. Certainly these factors are not mutually exclusive. In fact, each to some extent implies the other.

One further possible stabilizing influence might be role differentiation and specialization within the family; with a highly stable power structure it would often be possible for the father to delegate increased authority to his wife in defined areas such as child rearing and routine household management, while he specializes for example in ceremonial or political activities. This role differentiation would in turn make husband and wife more interdependent, minimize conflicts over allocation of rights and privileges, make the family a more closely cooperating unit pursuing mutually accepted goals, and therefore suppress highly personal, individualistic drinking behavior. Quite a different result would be expected, on the other hand, in modern urban society where corporate division of labor means that the average worker is minimally involved in company goals, has relatively little commitment to his co-workers and supervisor, is free after work hours, and can change jobs at will. . . . These conditions have little in common with those just discussed as prevailing in father-centered tribes, and may have opposite effects on drunkenness.

To summarize, drunkenness increases markedly if the authority of the man in the household is lessened or diffused, and if the nuclear family is less integrated into larger kin structures through bilocal or neolocal residence.

.   .   .

Household Type and Settlement Pattern. The absence in our data of any important relation between household type and drunkenness was unexpected, especially since household type tends to predict a number of important psychological phenomena, including child-rearing practices (15, 28). The correlation between household type and drunkenness is empirically maximized by testing nuclear and polygynous households against extended and mother-child households. Even so, it is still an insignificant and unimpressive .36, and this combination of household types is hard to rationalize theoretically. No other combinations of household type yield a significant or nearly significant relation to drunkenness. Nuclear household tested alone against other household types (Table 5) correlates only .25.

There is, however, a significant relation between drunkenness and patterns of settlement, as rated by Murdock (14).[6] Since it was not possible to order his categories confidently with respect to degree of community organization, a correlation coefficient based upon a dichotomization would not be very meaningful. However, Murdock's two extreme categories — "nomadic bands" versus "complex villages and towns" — show a significant difference in degree of insobriety. All nine nomadic tribes are characterized by extreme drunkenness, while thirteen of twenty-seven tribes with compact villages or towns exhibit this pattern. It seems likely that factors of the sort already mentioned explain these relations, since tribes with very small population wandering over an extensive territory would have little chance of elaborating the kind of social organization apparently conducive to sobriety. There may well be an independent stabilizing influence exerted by the small village, however. The only two bilateral tribes that were relatively sober (Macusi and Taulipang) had a village settlement pattern.

Social Stratification and Political Integration. The final aspects of social organization investigated in this study in relation to degree of drunkenness were extent of social stratification (including the presence of slavery) and degree of political integration into units transcending the local community. While the elaboration of these aspects of social organization signifies population growth and complexity in social arrangements relative to small nomadic tribes, they are not of the same order in the structuring of social relations as is the development of corporate kin groups. Indeed, stratification and political integration may, in the course of social evolution, proceed at the expense of corporate kin groups and with consequences other than sobriety. . . .

Hence it is not surprising, but nevertheless important, that none of the measures considered in this connection yielded a significant relation with degree of drunkenness. Within the range of complexity of social organization represented by our sample, there was a tendency for political integration and, to a lesser extent, stratification to be negatively correlated with drunkenness, but not significantly so. The lack of very strong relationships using these variables implies that kin group and residence factors may be the important causal elements, since they do not appear

[6] $\chi^2 = 11.03$, 4 df; $P < .05$, $N = 55$.

to influence drunkenness indirectly by mutual correlation with stratification or political factors.

3. Tests of Some Social-psychological Variables

In a study of this kind it is important to explore variables other than those which obviously reflect social organization. Since this study is re-examining many of the hypotheses of Horton — hypotheses which were essentially psychological in conception — it is necessary to pursue their implications in the light of all available new evidence. Moreover, the social-psychological and clinical literature contains a number of points of view on drunkenness and alcoholism testable by the cross-cultural method. The recent proliferation of cross-cultural indices not only makes tests of alternative hypotheses possible, but also permits a crude comparison of the power of variables of social organization with other kinds of variables in explaining drunkenness in primitive societies.

Aggression Anxiety. An important feature of Horton's theory attributes the relative absence of drunkenness to fear concerning the expression of previously punished aggressive impulses. Yet in point of fact, all but one of Whiting and Child's (29) measures of aggression training or aggression in fantasy failed to relate significantly to Horton's drunkenness score. The single exception is shown in Table 5: there is a barely significant inverse relation between drunkenness and punishment for aggression in childhood, supporting this aspect of Horton's theory. However, the inverse relation between drunkenness and general pressure for responsible performance of duties and obedience is slightly stronger, suggesting that drunkenness is correlated with generalized lack of discipline instead of with permissive aggression training alone.

TABLE 5. THE RELATION OF DEGREE OF DRUNKENNESS TO SELECTED
CHILD-REARING MEASURES[a]

Child-rearing Measures	N	χ^2	z	r_{tet}
Aggression socialization anxiety	26	1.39	1.97[b]	—.47
Pressure for obedience and responsibility rather than self-reliance and achievement (from 5 to 12 years) (4)	20	3.23	2.76[c]	—.71
Indulgence during childhood (from 5 to 12 years)	25	6.74[c]	1.66	.81
Indulgence of the infant	25	2.06	1.00	.55

[a] χ^2 was computed at 1 df; z was estimated by the Mann-Whitney test for rank-ordered data.
[b] $P < .05$.
[c] $P < .01$.

This interpretation seems to be supported by the other results in Table 5 which show that indulgence during childhood correlates significantly with drunkenness. Childhood indulgence is defined as a function of: protection from environmental discomforts; amount of overt affection shown the child; degree, immediacy, and consistency of drive reduction; constancy of presence and absence of pain inflicted by the nurturant agent; and lowness of degree of socialization demanded (Barry, Bacon, and Child, unpublished). (There were only a few tribes that were exceptions to this relationship — that is, that were both sober and indulgent to their children, or drunken and severe to their children — but these exceptions were quite marked. Since a rank test reflects the degree of exception as well as the presence of an exception, the association drops from high significance with a median division to borderline significance using a rank test.) Indulgence of the infant shows a similar trend to indulgence of the child, but is not statistically reliable.[7]

Wright (31) has previously shown that societies which punish aggression severely do not thereby eliminate aggressive responses; instead the object of aggression is changed. In societies with high aggression socialization anxiety, agents and objects of aggression in folktales are likely to be strangers, signifying displacement along a scale of similarity-dissimilarity to the hero and his family. My interpretation of these results is that in the sober societies aggression is displaced toward, and expected from, an out-group, which is a logical corollary of the proposition that little drunkenness is found in societies segmented into a number of internally solidary lineal units. A reasonable general conclusion suggested by these facts is that fear of aggression directed against close relatives at drinking bouts is a more genuine causal influence diminishing drunkenness than is generalized fear of aggression, and that generalized pressure for strict obedience and self-control is still more important.

Wright (31) has also shown that acts of fantasy aggression are *less* intense in tribes which allow their children freedom to express aggression — that is, in the drunken tribes. This suggests, on the one hand, that the drunken tribes do not express aggression against distant or inappropriate objects; in other words, they are neither unusually conflicted about aggression nor "unconsciously hostile" in the psychiatric sense. On the other hand, the aggression of the drunken tribes will be much more obvious against family members and friends, because the psychological mechanisms enforcing submissiveness and respect are weak. While interpersonal relations seem to be stronger and more lasting in the sober tribes, this is achieved only at the cost of repression of aggression. The superficially strong interpersonal ties in the sober tribes are much more

[7] It is probably relevant in this connection that Parker (18) has found fifteen articles reporting a close mother-son attachment in alcoholics; and several authors have reported that youngest children in a family are both relatively indulged and overrepresented among alcoholics (16).

ambivalent than the loose, informal relations in the drunken tribes. This tentative formulation of drunken aggression needs further testing, on the other hand, in view of the lack of relation between drunkenness and the indices of projected aggression in Table 1.

.   .   .

4. A Note on Ethnic Differences in Rates of Alcoholism

Caution is necessary in applying these results on primitive drunkenness directly to national or ethnic variations in alcoholism, since these phenomena have important differences as well as similarities. But it is a fact that some father-centered ethnic groups with a high degree of lineal social solidarity — such as the Jews and Chinese (25) — have very low rates of alcoholism and drunkenness, as the conclusions reported in this chapter would predict. These cross-cultural findings also suggest a highly speculative possibility that might be worth checking: that some patri-centered Western countries with a highly traditional, lineal social organization (such as Italy) have developed preferences for wine or beer rather than distilled liquors in part *because* of their social structure, which should discourage extreme drunkenness.

The Irish present a different problem. They are the group most over-represented among American alcoholics, and yet they seem on the surface to be a traditional father-dominated group. The most prominent current hypothesis concerning Irish drunkenness was proposed by Bales (1), based in part on Horton's anxiety theory. Bales noted instances of anxiety in Irish life and, following Horton, suggested that high anxiety played a causal role in Irish drunkenness. However, some of the anxiety-arousing conditions he mentioned, such as absentee landlordship and penal restrictions on Irish industry, can be explained just as well as indices of the alienation of the Catholic majority from the controlling jural, formal aspects of their own society (the imposed legal, governmental, and economic systems, and the established Protestant church).

One writer on Ireland, in fact, uses the phrase "disorganized social system" (21, p. 46) to describe the wholesale evictions and the general loosening of ties to the land in the 18th and 19th Centuries. Furthermore, the authority of the Irish father in the home does not seem to be as impressive as paternal authority in southern Europe. Bales, for example, comments that the Irish-American father ". . . in many cases seems to have dropped into a role of impotence and insignificance . . ." Bales also noted a close mother-son attachment in many of his Irish alcoholics, and Opler and Singer (17) found a very close, dependent relation of the Irish son to his mother, who keeps him a "boy and a burden." These authors also call the Irish father "shadowy and evanescent." Factors such as these have been shown to be associated with drunkenness in primitive tribes in the present study. These suggestions underscore the need for a more extensive treatment of Irish drinking patterns in the light of these new cross-cultural findings. . . .

SUMMARY

This chapter has reported an extensive re-examination of Horton's cross-cultural study of the functions of alcohol in primitive tribes. The most important single conclusion was that the degree of drunkenness at periodic communal drinking bouts is related to variables indicating a personal (or informal) rather than a corporate (or formal) organization, but is substantially unrelated to the level of anxiety in the society.

Following are some of the variables found to be positively correlated with relative *sobriety* in primitive tribes: (*a*) corporate kin groups with continuity over time, collective ownership of property, and unified action as a legal individual; (*b*) patrilocal residence at marriage; (*c*) approach to a clan-community organization;[8] (*d*) presence of a bride-price;[8] (*e*) a village settlement pattern (rather than nomadism). It was suggested that societies with these features are likely to be well organized, to have a high degree of lineal social solidarity, and to have interpersonal relationships structured along hierarchical or respect lines. It was hypothesized that these factors in turn controlled extremely informal, friendly, and loosely structured behavior at drinking bouts. This interpretation was supported by the fact that the sober tribes were shown to control aggression severely in their children, while the drunken tribes are relatively indulgent with their children and permit disobedience and self-assertion.

No indices of fear were found that correlated significantly with drunkenness, and it was concluded that Horton's measures of an insecure food supply and acculturation indicated a loose social organization rather than fear. Indices suggested by psychoanalytic hypotheses about alcoholism (oral fixations, latent homosexuality, and drives toward self-injury) did not predict primitive drunkenness.[8]

REFERENCES

1. Bales, Robert Freed, "Cultural Differences in Rates of Alcoholism," *Quart. J. Stud. Alc.*, 6:480-499, 1946.
2. Barry, Herbert, III, Irvin L. Child, and Margaret K. Bacon, "Relation of Child Training to Subsistence Economy," *Amer. Anthrop.*, 61:51-63, 1959.
3. Conger, John J., "Alcoholism: Theory, Problem, and Challenge, II: Rein-

8 Omitted in this abridgment. [Ed.]

forcement Theory and the Dynamics of Alcoholism," *Quart. J. Stud. Alc.*, 17:296-305, 1956.

4. Davenport, William, "Nonunilinear Descent and Descent Groups," *Amer. Anthrop.*, 61:557-572, 1959.

4a. Friendly, Joan P., *A Cross-Cultural Study of Ascetic Mourning Behavior*, unpublished undergraduate honors thesis, Radcliffe College, 1956.

5. Heath, Dwight B., "Drinking Patterns of the Bolivian Camba," *Quart. J. Stud. Alc.*, 19:491-508, 1958.

6. Horton, Donald, "The Functions of Alcohol in Primitive Societies: A Cross-Cultural Study," *Quart. J. Stud. Alc.*, 4:199-320, 1943.

7. Hovland, Carl Iver, and Robert R. Sears, "Minor Studies of Aggression, VI: Correlation of Lynchings With Economic Indices," *J. Psychol.*, 9:301-310, 1940.

8. Lemert, Edwin M., "Alcohol and the Northwest Coast Indians," *Univ. Calif. Publ. in Culture and Society*, 2:303-406, 1954.

9. ———, "Alcoholism: Theory, Problem, and Challenge, III. Alcoholism and the Sociocultural Situation," *Quart. J. Stud. Alc.*, 17:306-317, 1956.

10. Linton, Ralph, "The Natural History of the Family," *in* Ruth Nanda Anshen (Ed.), *The Family: Its Function and Destiny*, New York: Harper and Brothers, 1949.

11. Lowie, Robert H., *Social Organization*, New York: Holt, Rinehart, and Winston, 1948.

12. Murdock, George Peter, "Family Stability in Non-European Cultures," *Ann. Amer. Acad. Pol. Soc. Sci.*, 272:195-201, 1950.

13. ———, *Social Structure*, New York: The Macmillan Company; 1949.

14. ———, "World Ethnographic Sample," *Amer. Anthrop.* 59:664-687, 1957.

15. ———, and John W. M. Whiting, "Cultural Determination of Parental Attitudes: The Relationship Between the Social Structure, Particularly Family Structure, and Parental Behavior," *in* M. J. E. Senn (Ed.), *Problems of Infancy and Childhood*, New York: Josiah Macy Foundation, 1951.

16. Navratil, L. "On the Etiology of Alcoholism," *Quart. J. Stud. Alc.*, 20:236-244, 1959.

17. Opler, Marvin K., and Jerome L. Singer, "Ethnic Differences in Behavior and Psychopathology: Italian and Irish," *Int. J. Soc. Psychiat.*, 2:11-23, 1956.

18. Parker, Frederick B., "A Comparison of the Sex Temperament of Alcoholics and Moderate Drinkers," *Amer. Sociol. Rev.*, 24:366-374, 1959.

19. Pehrson, Robert N., "Bilateral Kin Groupings as a Structural Type: A Preliminary Statement," *J. East Asiatic Studies*, 3:199-202, 1954.

20. ———, "The Bilateral Network of Social Relations in Könkämä Lapp District" (Publication Three of the Indiana University Research Center in Anthropology, Folklore, and Linguistics), *Int. J. Amer. Linguist.*, 23:(Part) 2, 1957.

21. Potter, George, *To the Golden Door: The Story of the Irish in Ireland and America*, Boston: Little, Brown and Company, 1960.

22. Sahlins, Marshall D., "The Origin of Society," *Sci. American*, 203:76-87, 1960.

23. Schneider, David M., "A Note on Bridewealth and the Stability of Marriage," *Man*, 53:55-57, 1953.
24. Simmons, Leo W., "Statistical Correlations in the Science of Society," *in* George Peter Murdock (Ed.), *Studies in the Science of Society*, New Haven: Yale University Press, 1937.
25. Snyder, Charles R., *Alcohol and the Jews*, Glencoe, Ill.: The Free Press, 1958.
26. Strodtbeck, Fred L., "Husband-Wife Interaction Over Revealed Differences," *Amer. Sociol. Rev.*, 16:468-473, 1951.
27. Wert, James E., Charles O. Neidt, and J. Stanley Ahmann, *Statistical Methods in Educational and Psychological Research*, New York: Appleton-Century-Crofts, 1954.
28. Whiting, John W. M., "Sorcery, Sin, and the Superego: A Cross-Cultural Study of Some Mechanisms of Social Control," *in* M. R. Jones (Ed.), *Nebraska Symposium on Motivation*, Lincoln: University of Nebraska Press, 1959.
29. ———, and Irvin L. Child, *Child Training and Personality: A Cross-Cultural Study*, New Haven: Yale University Press, 1953.
30. Wolf, Eric R., "Types of Latin American Peasantry: A Preliminary Discussion," *Amer. Anthrop.*, 57:452-471, 1955.
31. Wright, George O., "Projection and Displacement: A Cross-Cultural Study of Folk-Tale Aggression," *J. Abnorm. Soc. Psychol.*, 49:523-528, 1954.

Psychiatric Impairments

While drunkenness, considered as a form of self-destructive behavior, may be regarded ·as a partly voluntaristic pathology, psychiatric symptoms arise independently of an individual's conscious choice. (The sick person unconsciously "prefers" the symptoms common to the cultural tradition in which he has developed or is functioning, but this is a kind of choosing in which the conscious mind does not participate.) Consequently, if the occupancy of particular social positions is associated with high rates of psychiatric symptoms, the causation of the pathology must be sought in the characteristics of the social system within which these positions are located. Langner's article deals with the effects of structurally imposed deprivation of social esteem on the psychophysical condition of the individual. He takes a hypothesis formulated in one society, with regard to one dimension of differential distribution of social esteem (class), and tests it in another society, on another di-

mension of distribution of esteem (sex). The verification of a causal hypothesis in a second social setting and with another measure of the independent variable greatly increases our confidence in the general validity of the hypothesis.

5   THOMAS S. LANGNER

Psychophysiological Symptoms and the Status of Women in Two Mexican Communities

. . . In initiating this work, it seemed to me that persons of low status would tend to exhibit a negative self-image, while those of high status would be more likely to have a positive self-image. Self-image was, in turn, assumed to be indicative of ego-strength. Without love, attention, and status, the processes of adaptation and planning would be abandoned. Instead withdrawal, resignation, fatalism, physical violence, alcoholism, and addiction would be utilized as ways of meeting life stresses.

An initial assumption (which later proved false) was that people project their individual self-images onto persons of their age-sex position in general. For example, I assumed that a woman who does not hold herself in high esteem will agree that "men are more intelligent than women" or that "women's place is in the home."

As mentioned above, evidence has already been gathered indicating that low socioeconomic status and low age status tend to be associated with increased psychiatric impairment and the multiplication of psychophysiological symptoms. Perhaps this is related to the low *prestige* of older people and of the poor who are uneducated and employed in manual labor. A logical further step was to investigate the low prestige of women to see whether it related to symptomatology and some measure of self-image. If a group of women could be found whose prestige status was equal to that of men, they could be compared in terms of symptoms and self-image with a group of women in a community where women had low status.

From "Psychophysiological Symptoms and the Status of Women in Two Mexican Communities" by Thomas Langner in *Approaches to Cross-Cultural Psychiatry,* Jane M. Murphy and Alexander H. Leighton, eds. Copyright © 1965 by Cornell University Press. Reprinted in abridged form by permission of the author and publisher.

This hypothesis about sexual status is a corollary of the general hypothesis that low status is associated with increased psychiatric disturbance and a negative self-image. An opportunity for research came into view when I read Miguel Covarrubias's book, *Mexico South*.[1] This describes the community of Tehuantepec, where there is a remarkable equality between women (Tehuanas) and men (Tehuanos). Would these women with high status in their society exhibit fewer symptoms *in relation to men* of the same community than the more typical lower-status women of a "control" community such as Mexico City? Would the Tehuanas also have a better "self-image"? Thus Tehuantepec and Mexico City were chosen as contrasting communities in which these hypotheses could be tested.

STATUS OF WOMEN IN MEXICO

In Mexico City there prevails a pattern of women's status typical of countries with a history of Spanish colonization. The woman is sheltered during adolescence. She is placed on a pedestal and courted, her "honor" defended at any cost by her brothers and father. After this brief period in the limelight, she marries and is then expected to take responsibility for a household. She undertakes the education and religious training of the children and often contributes full or partial economic support of the family. Extramarital activity on her part is strongly condemned by the society and might expose her to physical punishment by her husband.

The man, on the other hand, is not condemned for having extramarital affairs. He may even have a *casa chica*, that is, a second family composed of a mistress and her children, whom he supports. The plight of women in Mexico City has been described by Rogelio Díaz-Guerrero, a Mexican psychiatrist and psychologist.[2] He conducted a survey of symptoms among residents of Mexico City, and concluded that the women had many more symptoms than men because of their low position in Mexican society.

While the role of "asexual drudge" is a relatively common one among the married women of Mexico City, quite the opposite is true of the women of Tehuantepec. Their independence is well known. The anthropologist-artist Covarrubias reports:

> The relations between the sexes are natural and uninhibited, free of the puritanical outlook on sex of the Indians of the highlands, and of the Spanish feudal concept of the inferior position of women, so characteristic of other parts of Mexico. . . .
> The frankness of Zapotec women, their rather loose use of strong

[1] M. Covarrubias, *Mexico South* (New York: Alfred A. Knopf, 1954).
[2] R. Díaz-Guerrero, "Neurosis and the Mexican Family Structure," *American Journal of Psychiatry*, vol. 112 (Dec. 1955), pp. 411-417.

language, and their social and economic independence give them a position of equality with men, and a self-reliance that is unique in Mexico.[3]

My own experience with the Tehuanas, while limited, reaffirmed this picture. They had no apprehension at being interviewed or observed by a strange man, even though husbands and sons were away in the fields. In addition to this independence, women seemed to be the "social cynosures" of the community. For example, during the daylight hours of a two-day fiesta there were few men available to dance with the women. While the men were working in the fields, Tehuanas danced in pairs and drank beer and native liquors. The festivities did not stop simply because many men were absent. The older men played in the band, while the few younger men and children clapped their hands in rhythm. The ladies then formed a chain, each placing her hands on the waist of the woman in front of her. They danced in this fashion for the rest of the afternoon, making colorful patterns in their embroidered velveteen dresses.

An anthropologist's observations and my own brief impressions indicate that the position of women in Tehuantepec is higher than the position of women in Mexico City. The main hypothesis to be tested is that this position, or sexual status, is related to a particular range of mental disorder as measured by psychophysiological symptoms. Presumably, the women of Tehauntepec, having higher sexual status than the women of Mexico City, would report fewer symptoms on the average.

It would be ideal if the average number of symptoms reported by the Tehuanas could be compared directly with the average for women in Mexico City. This would be a comparison of the absolute (as opposed to the relative) levels of symptomatology. Such a direct comparison, however, makes an assumption about the comparability of women in a complex metropolis and a rural town. Such an assumption is called into question by many factors, not the least of which is that one location has a heterogeneous culture while the other has a consistent tradition. In addition we are actually interested in comparing the status of women relative to men in each community. We should therefore also compare the sex difference in the average number of symptoms in Tehuantepec with the sex difference in the average number of symptoms in Mexico City. Put in operational terms this means finding the difference between the average number of symptoms of men and women in Tehuantepec, then doing the same for residents of Mexico City. After that, the difference between those two differences is calculated, thus providing a

[3] M. Covarrubias, *op. cit.*, pp. 338-339.

statistical comparison of the relative sex differences in symptomatology in the two cities.

TWO CITIES

Mexico City lies in a great basin surrounded by mountains except to the north. It is 7,349 feet above sea level, and the climate is temperate. The rainy season lasts from June through September.

The population of this cosmopolitan manufacturing center is now about 4,000,000. The people are almost all Catholics. With the exception of some North Americans and Europeans, the population is descended from Indians and their Spanish conquerors. While the national language of Mexico is Spanish, many Indian tongues are still spoken. The city is a complex of parks and boulevards. Architecture varies from old Spanish structures to radically modern buildings. Transportation by bus, streetcar, and taxi is available. Hotels, elegant restaurants, museums, opera, and theater make Mexico City the Latin-American equivalent of Paris.

Tehuantepec, in the state of Oaxaca, is small by contrast. In comparison to many other Mexican communities, however, it is sizable. It is located fifteen kilometers from the Pacific coast, several hundred miles southwest of Mexico City in a jungle area called the Isthmus of Tehuantepec. Tehuantepec is one of three main towns on the Isthmus and has a population of about 14,000. It is situated on the Pan American Highway at a bend in the wide river named Rio Tehuantepec. The surrounding area is covered with lush tropical growth, much of it under cultivation. Coconut palms and fruit trees grow in great profusion. By contrast the rest of the Isthmus is either desert or jungle.

Although Spanish is spoken, the native tongue called Zapotec is still in common use. Traditional customs are preserved, and in each of the twelve wards or *barrios* there is a constant round of fiestas, elaborate wedding ceremonies, and Saints' days. The *barrio* fiestas are promoted mainly by the women, who vie for leadership. Husbands generally comply or are shamed into complying.

The Tehuantepec houses are small and mostly made of adobe brick. They have back yards surrounded by tightly woven stick fences and covered with a loose palm thatching. These areas are cool during the intense midday heat but light enough to permit work. A few buildings and churches are of Spanish architecture. Being practically at sea level, the city is extremely hot and the rainfall is even greater than in Mexico City. There are, however, long dry spells, which threaten corn, fruit, and other crops. The precariousness of life under these circumstances may partially account for the group solidarity and reciprocity exhibited by these agricultural communities.

THE QUESTIONNAIRE

An interview to be conducted in the home of each respondent was chosen as a practical method of gathering data on sex differences in symptomatology. The limited time available for field work was a major consideration in choosing the questionnaire survey method. This procedure yields data that are comparable between individuals and appropriate for statistical treatment. The survey used a five-page questionnaire. The questions were precoded for IBM analysis so that the interviewer, in most instances, needed only to circle the code number next to the answer coinciding with that given by the respondent.

The questionnaire consists of four major sections: (1) demographic or "background" variables; (2) psychophysiological symptoms comprising the Twenty-two Item Score; (3) miscellaneous psychophysiological and psychoneurotic symptoms; (4) attitude questions concerning male dominance and the family.

The questionnaire survey was introduced as a study of health in the community. Following this, questions were asked concerning age, schooling, family income, type of work, and marital status. The interview then shifted to questions about health. These were the twenty-two questions about psychophysiological symptoms often associated with psychoneurosis.

These questions had been tested during the Midtown Study on 139 hospitalized and clinic psychiatric patients and on a screened "well" group of 72 persons, each of whom had been interviewed for half an hour by a psychiatrist. Of approximately 120 items so tested in the Midtown [Manhattan] Study, these 22 had the highest validity (distinguished best between known sick and known well). The items and their ability to discriminate between patients and "wells" are given in Table 1.

It seemed pertinent to include ten additional questions which had already been used in a survey of residents of Mexico City by Díaz-Guerrero.[4] These covered various other psychoneurotic and psychophysiological symptoms.

A group of questions pertaining to the Mexican family and attitudes toward male dominance had also been used by Díaz-Guerrero. These were modified somewhat and incorporated into the questionnaire. Disagreement with a "male dominance" statement such as "men are more intelligent than women" was considered to indicate an attitude of "female equality." Attitudes of "female equality" were assumed to be a measure of each woman's individual self-esteem. The assumption was made that a positive correlation existed between a woman's individual

[4] R. Díaz-Guerrero, *op. cit.*

TABLE 1. TWENTY-TWO ITEM SCORE

Item	r	V.V.	CR
1. Feel weak all over	.76	2.46	10.00
2. Can't get going	.66	2.21	13.33
3. Low and very low spirits	.76	1.88	6.94
4. Hot all over	.47	1.70	8.70
5. Heart beats hard often	.63	1.61	6.05
6. Appetite poor	.75	1.51	5.00
7. Restlessness	.57	1.51	13.08
8. Worrying type	.52	1.42	8.62
9. Shortness of breath often	.75	1.40	5.00
10. Nervous often	.79	1.38	7.65
11. Fainting (more than a few times)	.74	1.38	7.65
12. Trouble getting to sleep often	.65	1.23	7.09
13. Sour stomach	.52	1.16	6.04
14. Memory not all right	.65	1.14	3.93
15. Cold sweats often	.60	1.14	3.93
16. Hands tremble often	.50	1.14	3.93
17. Clogging in nose	.49	1.14	5.53
18. Personal worries get me down physically	.67	1.02	6.03
19. Feel somewhat apart even among friends	.41	.95	5.54
20. Nothing turns out right	.56	.87	4.17
21. Headaches often	.54	.60	2.68
22. Wonder anything worthwhile, agree	.52	.48	2.65

From Thomas S. Langner, "A Twenty-Two Item Screening Score of Psychiatric Symptoms Indicating Impairment," *Journal of Health and Human Behavior*, vol. 3 (Winter 1962), p. 273; by permission of The American Sociological Association. Criteria for selection of items: r = tetrachoric correlation of item with the Mental Health Impairment Rating assigned independently by two psychiatrists to each of 1,660 respondents; V.V. = validity value based on comparison of 139 sick and 72 screened well; CR = t test of significance (Critical Ratio) of difference between the percentage of 139 sick and 72 psychiatrically screened "well" giving the pathognomonic answer. All items are at .01 confidence level or better.

self-esteem and her opinion of the status of women in general. Presumably, the woman who felt men were no more intelligent than women would hold her own intelligence in good esteem. If she also felt that women's place was not in the home, and that men shouldn't "wear the pants" in the family, then she would have a generally more positive self-image than women who agreed with such statements. Women with a positive self-image (as measured by the "female equality" items) were expected to exhibit fewer psychophysiological symptoms.

The interview contained a total of forty-nine questions, and was conducted in Spanish. Its administration averaged one-half hour per person. Explanations of items not clearly understood were made in Spanish in Mexico City and in Spanish or Zapotec in Tehuantepec. There were three revisions of the Spanish translation of the questionnaire prior to the field trip, and a team of interviewers with a survey supervisor was organized.[5]

Some changes were necessary in listing categories of demographic data. An intimate knowledge of the social structure is required to define meaningful levels of schooling, occupation, and different marital statuses. For example, the number of families abandoned is so large that a category for this circumstance was added to the list of marital statuses in order to avoid including them under "divorced and separated." The categories of literate and illiterate were added to the levels of schooling. A fair proportion of people, particularly in rural areas, have had no schooling but can read and write. These were labeled *alfabeta*. Another sizable group have had no schooling, and in addition cannot read or write. They were labeled *analfabeta*.

SAMPLING

The sample in Mexico City is based on "place name" neighborhoods. The neighborhoods were sampled to assure a wide socioeconomic range of respondents. Ideally, a random sample of city blocks would have been chosen, and respondents selected randomly from these blocks. In view of limitations of time, and the lack of adequate block statistics, a sample of neighborhoods was substituted. No recent data were available on the exact socioeconomic distribution of Mexico City by city blocks. Developing this would have been a major project in itself. As an alternative a large number of "lower class," "middle class," and "upper class" areas of Mexico City were marked on a block map. In order to categorize an area as lower, middle, or upper class, all four interviewers had to agree on the socioeconomic level.[6] If there was disagreement, as in two or three instances, the area was not covered. The interviews were to be distributed equally among the three socioeconomic levels. The apportionment of interviews to areas within each level was left to the discretion of the interviewer supervisor. In each block chosen, an approximate

[5] In Mexico City a psychoanalyst, Dr. Ramón Parres, and a psychologist, Professor Sara Zendejas, recommended seven interviewers. A graduate student in anthropology, Miss Susan Drucker, filled the role of survey supervisor. With her help and with suggestions by three other interviewers (there were seven interviewers in Mexico City, only four of whom attended the initial meeting, during which the questionnaire was revised and the sampling design planned), final revisions in questionnaire wording were made. Spanish-speaking professionals (a librarian, a psychiatrist, and a pathologist), who were of course also fluent in English and were acquainted with medical and psychiatric terminology, aided in these initial versions. Grateful acknowledgment for their assistance is made to Miss Miranda and Dr. Borelli of Payne Whitney Clinic and Dr. García of St. Vincent's Hospital.

[6] Only four interviewers made judgments of the class level of different areas of the city. Three were native to the city, one a resident.

sampling *n* was used so that all sides of the block would be covered. . . .

Within each dwelling unit the respondent was chosen by means of a table of random numbers, from persons aged twenty to fifty-nine in the household. Thus the interviewer had no choice as to the sex, age, or personality characteristics of the respondent. The only exception was that all "foreigners" (Germans, Italians, North Americans, and so on) not born in Mexico were excluded. This was done in an attempt to get a homogeneous sample suited to testing the main hypothesis of the study. The latter rests on the assumption that in Mexico City the traditional Spanish-Colonial attitude toward women is maintained. Northern European and North American attitudes might vary somewhat from this pattern. After selection of the appropriate respondent, the interview was conducted in the home.

The sampling in Tehuantepec was conducted in much the same manner.[7] However, the areas of the city (*barrios* or wards) were ignored, and a sampling *n* of every twelfth dwelling unit chosen. At this time it was expected that 200 interviews could be collected. Thus every twelfth dwelling unit would properly have covered the entire city. An average of six persons to a dwelling unit was estimated. With a population of 14,000, approximately 2,400 dwelling units needed to be sampled. Owing to the voluntary status of the interviewers, the press of their duties in the Public Health Clinic, and the short time available for data collection, only fifty-nine interviews were completed. These interviews did, however, constitute a random sample adequate for statistical comparison, even though somewhat smaller than originally planned.

Streets were marked out on a map radiating from the Public Health Clinic, which was the work place of the two Public Health nurses who did the interviewing. Seven of the fifty-nine interviews were conducted in my presence during a two-day training period. The same random number chart (as in Mexico City) was used to select respondents within the dwelling units. Every twelfth unit (counting both sides of the street) was enumerated, and a random person between twenty and fifty-nine years of age selected. If no age-eligibles lived in the unit, the eleventh and thirteenth units were enumerated until an age-eligible respondent was selected. Owing to the large number of people residing in each house, only one or two households had no age-eligibles.

[7] Establishing relationships with the authorities prior to the sampling was more complex in the case of Tehuantepec. Through Dr. Manuel Martínez-Baez and Dr. Varela of the School of Public Health and Tropical Diseases in Mexico City I received an introduction to Dr. Castellanos, Chief of Public Health in the State of Oaxaca. He in turn gave me a letter to Dr. Ernesto Medina Ruíz, Director of the Health Department of the Isthmus. Dr. Medina's nurses, Mrs. Mariscal the chief nurse, and Miss Delaizuno volunteered their services as interviewers.

The final samples drawn from both cities show some bias in favor of women (see Table 2). While women actually out-number men, the sample exaggerates this fact.[8] The prolonged absence of men as itinerant workers and, in rural Tehuantepec, their work in the fields during the entire day may have contributed to the bias. In addition, it is possible that some of the interviewers misunderstood the random number selection chart, while others might not have desired to return late at night in order to interview the man of the family.

The average age of the men and women in Tehuantepec and Mexico City does not vary radically. It ranges between thirty-two and thirty-nine years. Only one category is radically deficient in the sample. This is Tehuanos in their twenties. Despite a somewhat exaggerated sex ratio, the age distribution of the sample is fairly even (see Table 2).

TABLE 2. SAMPLE CHARACTERISTICS: AGE AND EDUCATION BY SEX, INCOME, AND RESIDENCE (IN PER CENT)

| | Tehuantepec | | Mexico City | | | |
| | | | Low Income | | High Income | |
Variables	Male N = 18	Female N = 41	Male N = 38	Female N = 97	Male N = 67	Female N = 100
Age						
20-29	5.6	39.0	23.7	32.0	46.3	21.0
30-39	50.0	31.7	28.9	35.1	20.9	40.0
40-49	22.2	12.2	26.3	13.4	19.4	25.0
50-59	16.6	12.2	21.1	19.5	13.4	14.0
No answer	5.6	4.9	0.0	0.0	0.0	0.0
Average Age[a]	(38.0)	(32.4)	(39.5)	(36.8)	(34.7)	(37.6)
Education[b]						
Illiterate	33.3	51.2	18.4	27.8	0.0	1.0
Literate	61.1	46.4	31.6	45.4	7.5	6.0
Primary	5.6	0.0	34.2	18.6	23.9	34.0
Secondary	0.0	2.4	15.8	8.2	68.6	59.0

[a] The average is based on frequencies in the full eight age categories, each of five years' span.

[b] Illiterate (analfabeta); Literate (alfabeta), but no schooling; Primary (primaria completa), up to 2 years of high school; Secondary (escuela superior), includes 3 years of high school or more; all secondary, preparatory, college, and professional schooling.

[8] Other studies show a predominance of women in household samples. In a tenement in Mexico City, housing working-class (but not destitute) families, Oscar Lewis found that 58 per cent of married people were women. This does not compare with the 68 per cent of all persons aged 20 to 59 who were women in the Tehuantepec sample, nor the 72 per cent among low-income Mexico City dwellers, but it is identical with the 58 per cent among those of "high" income in Mexico City. The inclusion of unmarried women and men would probably raise Lewis' proportion of women further, since the young unmarried men would more likely be itinerant farm workers, or braceros.

The educational distribution of the sample shows marked differences by sex, residence, and income. Men, residents of Mexico City, and those of high income show more years of education and less illiteracy.

FINDINGS

1. *In a community where women's prestige status approaches that of men, women report slightly more symptoms than men. In a community where women's status is low, women report considerably more symptoms than men.*

The average number of complaints reported (that is, from among the symptoms listed in the Twenty-two Item Score) was calculated according to sex, residence, and income. This information is presented in Table 3.

TABLE 3. AVERAGE NUMBER OF SYMPTOMS (TWENTY-TWO ITEM SCORE) ACCORDING TO SEX, RESIDENCE, AND INCOME

	Average No. of Symptoms		No. Interviewed	
	Men	Women	Men	Women
Tehuantepec (all income is under $32 per week)[a]	3.56	4.70	18	41
Mexico City, low income (under $32 per week)	5.18	7.27	38	97
Mexico City, high income ($32 per week or more)	3.66	4.80	67	100
Mexico City, total	(4.21)	(6.06)	(105)	(192)
Midtown, low income[b] (under $50 per week)	3.84	4.06	49	145
Midtown, high income ($50 per week or more)	2.27	2.93	622	777
Midtown, total	(2.38)	(3.11)	(671[c])	(922[c])

[a] The modal family-income bracket in Tehuantepec was 100-109 pesos, with a midpoint of 104.50 pesos, or $8.36 per week. The range was from 50 to 799 pesos, or $4.00 to $63.92 per week. There was only one family with this top income, *all others* receiving $24.72 or less. The $32 figure is used as an approximation for making comparisons with Mexico City.

[b] Only 32 people had a "family income" of under $25 per week in Midtown. While this group would have been more comparable to the Mexico City low-income group and the Tehuantepec sample, only six men were involved, too few for calculating an average score. The radical differences in income range between the cities could not be completely corrected. For example, the proportion with income under $25 per week was 1.9 per cent in Midtown, 45.7 per cent in Mexico City, and 100.0 per cent in Tehuantepec. The "under $50" group, the next available category, comprising 12.1 per cent of the Midtown sample, was therefore chosen for comparative purposes.

[c] Sixty-seven people did not know or would not reveal their income (2.8 per cent of the women and 4.9 per cent of the men).

A low-income group in Mexico City (with a "family income" under $32 per week) was selected to match the range of income in Tehuantepec. Women in Tehuantepec (4.70) are closer in their average number of symptoms to men of Tehuantepec (3.56) than comparable low-income women of Mexico City (7.27) are to low-income men of Mexico City (5.18). The mean difference between men and women in Tehuantepec is 1.14 symptoms, while in Mexico City it is 2.09 symptoms. While the difference between these mean differences is not quite statistically significant at the 5 per cent level, this was due to the small number of cases in Tehuantepec. The direction of the data is clear and supports the original hypothesis. The Tehuanas are about twice as close to the level of male symptomatology as the women of Mexico City. The Tehuanas are one symptom "worse off" than the Tehuanos, while the women of Mexico City are two symptoms "worse off" than the men of Mexico City.

The mere counting of symptoms (without regard for their patterning) may seem highly oversimplified as a method of assessing psychiatric impairment. The reader is reminded, however, that in the studies mentioned previously, people who reported more symptoms exhibited more impairment when examined individually by psychiatrists. The number of symptoms, then, is a crude but helpful index of impairment.

Do women report fewer symptoms in cultures where they command respect? It is my impression that the women of Midtown and other areas of New York City enjoy much greater status than the women of other countries I have visited. It is in line with the status hypothesis that although women of Midtown report a larger number of psychophysiological symptoms than Midtown men, they are closer to men in their level of symptomatology (men 2.38, women 3.11) than is the case in the Mexican metropolis (men 4.21, women 6.06).[9]

[9] While women reported a greater number of psychophysiological symptoms than men in the Midtown Study, there were no sex differences found in impairment rates of men and women. It should be noted that the impairment ratings were made on the basis of psychophysiological symptoms, behavioral and social symptoms, such as withdrawal and "acting-out," and upon the individual's total role functioning in the marital, parental, and occupational spheres. The psychophysiological symptoms, then, formed only one criterion of the overall mental health rating. Men typically were judged more heavily on their job performance, since unemployment or possession of a job not befitting their education was taken as a clear-cut indication of their impairment. It is not surprising then that women, even though they had more psychophysiological complaints, were not given more severe mental health ratings than the men. It was more difficult to judge their role performance, for, as many authors have pointed out, women's roles are often vague or contradictory in the United States. For example, they were less likely to be downgraded for unemployment. It is also possible that their complaints were often discounted by the psychiatrists, just as managerial persons

2. *The lower the income level, the greater the average number of symptoms reported.*

Several findings relative to the Twenty-two Item Score are of interest though they are tangential to the main hypothesis. First, at higher income levels the average number of symptoms was considerably less than at lower income levels. For example, within Mexico City, women of high income averaged 4.80 symptoms, and women of low income averaged 7.27 symptoms. Similarly, men of high income had fewer symptoms (3.66) on the average than men of low income (5.18) (see Table 3). It can also be seen that the high-income group in Mexico City averages about the same number of symptoms as the Tehuantepec sample, which is much lower in income level.[10]

The Midtown data also show this trend. Midtowners of high income average fewer symptoms than Midtowners of low income. If the Midtown income distribution had been divided in half (instead of into the lowest one-eighth against the other seven-eighths) the differences between income groups might have been even larger.

3. *Cross-cultural comparisons of symptomatology are difficult to interpret.*

The Tehuantepec respondents report approximately the same average number of symptoms as the low-income group in Midtown.[11] Even though their weekly income level is roughly comparable (under $32 and under $50), the meaning of identical income is quite different in the two communities. There are two reasons for this. First, there is the problem of relative income. Since almost every Tehuantepec family earns under $32 a week, no one is considered poor simply by virtue of being within that income range. Where Midtowners are concerned, only one-eighth of the sample has a family income of under $50 a week. This segment of the metropolitan population is quite poor relative to its geographic neighbors who constitute a reference group. Second, it is questionable to utilize cash income as an index of wealth when comparing a rural and an urban area. Cash income does not indicate overall

---

are more likely to accept women employees' medical excuses for short absences, such as headaches, colds, or menstrual cramps, as legitimate, that is, nonpsychiatric.

[10] The variations due to sex, residence, and income are all of the same general order of magnitude. Analysis of variance shows, for example, that the variation in mean number of symptoms due to sex is almost identical with variation due to residence (Tehuantepec versus Mexico City).

[11] The Tehuanas report somewhat more symptoms than low-income Midtown women, but the difference is not noteworthy.

access to goods in a rural agricultural area, where many people raise and eat their crops and livestock. Barter rather than cash may be the predominant form of exchange. Kinship may determine access to goods rather than the open market. Thus $32 in Tehuantepec is easily the equivalent of $50 in Mexico City.

As a whole, Mexico City residents report about two more psychophysiological symptoms than their fellow metropolitans in Midtown. Actually, the *lowest eighth* income group of Mid-towners is on a par with the *higher half* income group of Mexico City dwellers in number of symptoms. Several problems arise in the comparison of Mexico City and Midtown. The first of these may be called the problem of "symptom choice." It should be recalled that the Twenty-two Item Score constitutes a partial measure of only one form or expression of mental disturbance. Do people in Mexico City express mental disturbance through psychophysiological symptoms to the same degree that Midtowners do, or do they utilize other avenues of expression in greater proportion? If psychophysiological symptoms are as good an indicator of overall psychiatric impairment in Mexico as they are in the United States, then we can more confidently make direct comparisons. In order to determine whether this is true or not the symptom checklist would need to be standardized in both cultures against clinical cases and random samples of nonpatients in the community. No effort was made to do this in the present pilot study.

The degree to which psychophysiological symptoms actually reduce role functioning in different nations or environmental settings is also a problem in making direct comparisons. Roles involving manual labor will probably be more affected than those involving interpersonal skills. The predominantly manual labor force of Mexico will perhaps suffer more impairment per given psychophysiological symptom than the more heavily managerial, sales, and clerical labor force of the United States. This may be an oversimplification, however, for a back pain may impair the day laborer, while a headache might reduce the productivity of the executive.

4. Women generally report more psychophysiological symptoms.

Women consistently have more aches and complaints than men. This is true even though, as has been shown, there is definite variation in the degree to which the number of symptoms for women exceeds that of men (for example, Tehuantepec compared with Mexico City). The results of surveys in Stirling County and Midtown as well as in Mexico bear this out. Our data show women reporting more complaints than men regardless of income levels in Tehuantepec, Mexico City, and Midtown. This is conveyed in both Table 3 and Table 4.

TABLE 4. COMPLAINTS REPORTED ON TWENTY-TWO ITEM SCORE BY SEX AND CITY (IN PER CENT)

| | Tehuantepec | | Mexico City | | | |
| | | | Low Income | | High Income | |
Symptoms	Male N = 18	Female N = 41	Male N = 38	Female N = 97	Male N = 67	Female N = 100
Feel weak all over	11.1	22.0	15.8	38.1	4.5	7.0
Can't get going	22.2	39.0	44.7	75.3	34.3	46.0
Low and very low spirits	11.1	14.6	15.8	37.1	4.5	15.0
Hot all over	11.1	26.8	36.8	44.3	29.9	28.0
Heart beats hard often	0.0	9.7	2.6	11.3	3.0	3.0
Appetite poor	5.6	4.9	2.6	8.2	0.0	3.0
Restlessness	22.2	31.7	39.5	41.2	37.3	32.0
Worrying type	66.7	68.3	63.2	73.2	44.8	68.0
Shortness of breath often	0.0	4.9	2.6	10.3	0.0	3.0
Nervous often	5.6	12.2	21.1	22.7	11.9	20.0
Fainting (more than a few times)	0.0	0.0	5.3	6.2	0.0	4.0
Trouble getting to sleep often	16.7	12.2	10.5	10.3	7.5	8.0
Sour stomach	5.6	31.7	26.3	39.2	29.9	26.0
Memory not all right	0.0	22.0	26.3	27.8	9.0	22.0
Cold sweats often	16.7	14.6	31.6	19.6	11.9	9.0
Hands tremble often	0.0	0.0	5.3	11.3	7.5	4.0
Clogging in nose	16.7	24.3	15.8	48.5	17.9	27.0
Personal worries get me down physically	33.3	26.8	26.3	43.3	10.4	29.0
Feel somewhat apart even among friends	16.7	17.1	13.2	29.9	11.9	16.0
Nothing turns out right	38.9	36.6	36.8	46.4	22.4	25.0
Headaches often	5.6	2.4	2.6	26.8	4.5	15.0
Wonder anything worthwhile, agree	50.0	48.8	73.7	64.9	61.2	61.0

These figures suggest a striking consistency in sex differences across nationalities, social strata, and in country and city. The finding that women report more psychophysiological and psychoneurotic symptoms than men is a good example of the cumulative effect of a series of epidemiological studies. The existence of a genuine sex difference in symptoms is given credence when supported by findings from studies of several contrasting cultural groups and when such findings are consistent despite the different techniques of gathering the information, different personnel, translation problems, the variation in meanings of symptoms, and the contrasting cultural modes of expressing mental disturbances.

The repeated finding of such relationships in cross-cultural epidemiological studies may thus lead to the development of more universal theories of behavior applicable to a broad range of human types.

There is also evidence, supported by medical study, of basic differences between men and women in *all* types of illness. Hinkle found that women have more complaints (higher morbidity) while men have higher death rates (mortality).[12] In a sample of telephone company employees, more episodes of acute respiratory and gastrointestinal illness, more days of disability, and more visits to the doctor were found among women. Men, on the other hand, had more days of disability for chronic illness though they had fewer total days of disability.

If women tend to have more minor ailments, it is not surprising that they also have more psychophysiological complaints. There may well be a physiological basis for the female proneness to these psychophysiological disturbances. Men, however, seem prone to choose psychiatric symptoms which can roughly be described as "acting-out." More men than women are alcoholics. More men are involved in assault and battery, gang fights, homicide, stealing, and other antisocial behavior. There is some evidence from the Midtown survey that men are also more prone to character disorders, such as suspiciousness and rigidity. While the Midtown survey found no sex differences in overall psychiatric impairment, there were marked differences between men and women in the types of disorders exhibited.

The fact that women have a larger average number of psychophysiological complaints does not automatically mean, then, that their overall mental health is worse than that of men. Since the Twenty-two Item Score is largely composed of this type of item, we can only say that women, more than men, tend to report these symptoms. Perhaps it is that women react to stress particularly through these symptoms.

5. Women's attitudes favoring sexual equality are not related to their sexual status or to the number of their symptoms.

The prestige status of women is high in Tehuantepec. It was originally expected that this high status would be reflected by or conducive to a "positive self-image." I assumed that positive self-image of each woman could be assessed by her attitudes toward women in general, which were thought to be a projective measure of her attitudes toward herself. Statements concerning female equality were therefore taken to indicate a positive self-image.

12 L. E. Hinkle, Jr., R. Redmont, N. Plummer, and H. G. Wolff, "An Examination of the Relations Between Symptoms, Disability and Serious Illness in Two Homogeneous Groups of Men and Women," *American Journal of Public Health*, vol. 50 (1960).

Moreover, I also hypothesized that women with a more positive self-image (or attitudes favoring female equality) would report fewer symptoms. A positive self-image was assumed to be indicative of ego-strength. Affection and prestige status were mentioned as two important requisites for building and maintaining ego-strength. Ego-strength was broadly defined as ability to resist stress, to adapt, to plan for survival, and to develop conscious control over the self and the environment. Since women with higher prestige status would have a more positive self-image and hence greater ego-strength, it was postulated that they would be more resistant to environmental stress and report fewer symptoms. Thus women with a positive self-image, as evidenced by attitudes favoring female equality, would also report fewer symptoms.

The data turned out contrary to both hypotheses. The women of Mexico City, particularly those of high socioeconomic status, tended to voice equalitarian attitudes. This was in contrast to the Tehuanas. With minor exceptions, the proportion of equalitarian attitudes increased from provincial Tehuantepec to the low-income group in Mexico City, and from low to high income within Mexico City.[13] This can be seen in Table 5.

The proportion of women who believe it is proper for an unmarried woman to go out alone with a man increases from 2.4 per cent in Tehuantepec to 18.6 per cent and 46.0 per cent among women of low and high income in Mexico City. Many factors may be involved in this trend. For one, the degree of sophistication and education may account for the increase. Attitudes of "emancipation," however, may not accurately reflect the true status of women. Often with emancipation, as in urban and especially higher income Mexican families, the woman actually loses power and status as she ceases to provide income for the family. Lewis observed that the *casa chica* pattern (which rests on masculine dominance and the cult of *machismo*, or masculinity) is weaker in rural areas than in the cities, and weaker among the lower classes than the middle or upper classes.[14] This may be a function of the proportion of women in the labor force. Almost all the rural Tehuanas are breadwinners. This is less true in the big city, and even less characteristic of the high-income group. The proportion of women favoring equality with men may thus increase as the actual status and prestige of women decrease.

[13] The exception was that about 85 per cent of *all* the Mexican women interviewed did not think it natural for married men to have lovers, indicating a rejection of the *casa chica*.

[14] O. Lewis, *Five Families* (New York: Basic Books, 1959), p. 17. The relative unanimity of all the women on the *casa chica* issue seems to call Lewis' impressions into question, however.

TABLE 5. ATTITUDES TOWARD FEMALE EQUALITY BY RESIDENCE, INCOME, AND SEX (IN PER CENT)

	Women			Men		
Attitudes[a]	T[b] N = 41	MCLo[c] N = 97	MCHi[d] N = 100	T[a] N = 18	MCLo[b] N = 38	MCHi[c] N = 67
Do you believe it is proper for an unmarried woman to go out alone with a man? Yes	2.4	18.6	46.0	0.0	35.1	59.7
Do you believe the place for women is the home? No	9.7	2.6	15.0	5.6	2.6	14.9
Do you believe that men should "wear the pants" in the family? No	7.3	7.2	24.0	11.1	7.9	31.3
Do you believe that men are more intelligent than women? No	36.5	49.5	70.2	11.1	56.7	80.6
Do you think it is natural for married men to have lovers? No	83.0	80.4	88.0	55.6	81.0	80.6

[a] Attitude questions from Díaz-Guerrero, "Neurosis and the Mexican Family Structure," American Journal of Psychiatry, vol. 112 (Dec. 1955), pp. 411-417.
[b] Tehuantepec.
[c] Mexico City low income.
[d] Mexico City high income.

It is also of interest that there does not appear to be a relationship between attitudes favoring equality and the number of psychophysiological symptoms reported by women. No single attitude showed a consistent relationship to the average number of symptoms except: "Men are more intelligent than women." Women who disagreed with this statement averaged fewer symptoms. Why did the data fail to support the hypothesis? Perhaps these social attitudes are somewhat superficial and are not closely related to the personality structure or the symptomatology of the Mexican women. They probably do not measure the "self-image" of the individual woman but rather a stereotyped social image of women in general. In other words, the social attitudes reflected in these questions seem to be more a function of traditional versus modern cultural patterns than of personality dynamics. Hence the statements are probably not as "projective" as they were meant to be. If they had tapped the self-image of each woman, they would presumably have been highly correlated with the amount of symptomatology. . . .

Suicide

Each distinctive cultural tradition structures the individual experiences of its members in specific ways. Some of these culturally imposed patterns appear to be more conducive to specific kinds of pathological behaviors than others. While it cannot be presupposed, without adequate research, that a set of cultural patterns which contributes to one kind of pathology is generally pathogenic, eventually it may be possible to determine which sets of values and attitudes in a cultural tradition are likely to have a more adverse effect on human welfare. Hendin's studies of suicide in Scandinavia illuminate the contribution of intense psychoanalytic study of individual cases in a cross-cultural perspective to an understanding of the sources of social pathology in culturally accepted (rather than deviant) beliefs, values, and attitudes. Cultural values, of course, affect the forms of social interaction. It seems possible that, as advanced industrial society increasingly solves its organizational problems (as Sweden has done to a high degree), the role of structural constraints (such as objective class position) will be of declining importance, and the role of cultural attitudes, of increasing significance, in the social causation of pathological behavior.

6   HERBERT HENDIN

Suicide in Sweden

. . . The Swedish suicidal rate of about 18.5 per 100,000 is the sixth highest in the world. But nowadays being sixth highest in anything would ordinarily be no claim to distinction. Largely because Sweden has been managing so well with so many of the economic problems that

Excerpted from the *Psychiatric Quarterly*, Vol. 36, No. 1 (Utica, N.Y.: State Hospitals Press, 1962), pp. 1-28. The article later appeared in a slightly different form in the author's *Suicide and Scandinavia* (New York: Grune & Stratton, 1964) published in a paperback edition by Anchor Books, 1965. Reprinted by permission of the author and publishers. The case studies on which Hendin's conclusions are based have been omitted for this printing.

plague the rest of the world, it is felt by many that her people have no right to the Swedish suicide rate. Also those, in or out of Sweden, who dislike the degree of economic planning or social welfare measures present in that country, have sought to explain the suicide rate as the consequence of character defects produced by these measures. I would only note in this regard that we have known for over a hundred years that countries with a great deal of poverty have low suicide rates, yet no one will suggest planned-poverty as a cure for suicide. This situation proves only that economic problems and problems of survival can suppress other psychological ones. It is only as countries begin to solve reasonably well the problem of survival that they are even in a position to become aware of the psychosocial tensions and conflicts within their cultures.

It must also be kept in mind that suicide is only one barometer of social tension. Crime, alcoholism, homosexuality and neurosis are also such barometers. One such index cannot be consulted without reference to all the others. For example, while her suicide rate is high, the Swedish homicide rate is only one-tenth that of the United States.

The Scandinavian countries have markedly different suicide rates. The Danish rate averaging 22 per 100,000 and the Swedish rate of 18.5 per 100,000 are among the world's highest and are over twice the strikingly low Norwegian rate of 7.5. (The rates in the United States and England are about 10.5 to 11 per 100,000.) While as I indicated before, the basic focus of this work was on reasons and not rates and on problems rather than possibilities, nevertheless, since so much is said about it, a word about suicide statistics is necessary.

In addition to the welfare state, bad weather and good statistical bureaus have been blamed for the high Danish and Swedish suicide rates. Norway's low rate would seem to be an answer to all three points since it has equally developed social welfare measures, similar bad weather and a statistical bureau with a history of accuracy that is even older than those of Sweden and Denmark. The writer has discussed the statistical question in detail with the persons in charge of suicide statistics in each of the three countries. We could find no evidence that would support a statistical explanation.

However, it is easier for suicide to go unreported in the rural areas of all countries, and countries vary in percentage of rural population. For this reason, it was found useful to compare the suicide rates in such major cities as Copenhagen, Stockholm, Oslo and New York. This has the added advantage that in all four cities a doctor must see the deceased person. The rates for all these cities are higher than for their respective countries, but the information obtained by comparing them is the same as that revealed by a comparison of the four countries. The Stockholm rate is well over twice the Oslo rate, as the Swedish rate is well over twice the Norwegian rate. The Copenhagen rate is almost three times the Oslo rate, just as the Danish rate is almost three times the Norwegian. New York City is in the same relation to the three other cities cited as the United States is to the three countries.

There remains the possibility that even in these major cities only the Danish and Swedish doctors are reporting "honestly," because of a lesser social need to conceal suicide. The writer has begun informally interviewing doctors in the four countries, over the past couple of years, concerning their practice in this regard. While as to practices in the rural districts, the writer cannot yet say, he is so far, not persuaded that any significant difference exists in the practices of the doctors in the major cities.

What is more important and not generally understood is that in a country with a strong religious or moral prohibition against suicide there is likely to be more concealment of suicide, but there is equally likely to be less suicide. Thus, even the doctors' attitude toward suicide is largely a reflection of their society's attitude toward suicide, and their society's attitude toward suicide has an important bearing on the suicide rate.

In this particular study, almost all the suicidal patients were seen at one hospital — Södersjukhuset in Stockholm. They were seen following their admission to at least the emergency ward of the hospital because of attempted suicide. They were interviewed shortly after their suicide attempts. My experience has been that the preoccupations and dreams of patients seen shortly after suicide attempts are very revealing about their suicidal motivations. If they are seen six months later the whole episode may be well covered up. Most of the patients were then seen during their stay in the hospital although half a dozen who were not admitted to the hospital were seen on repeated subsequent visits as outpatients. I saw the patients as many times as I felt were necessary to get an adequate psychodynamic picture of them, and this would vary from between five and 25 sessions. Half of them were interviewed in Swedish and half in English. There was no difference in the findings between these two groups. Psychological tests — Rorschach and TAT — were done on almost all the patients, and I had the benefit of comparing my clinical findings with the findings of the psychologist doing the tests. Twenty-five suicidal patients were studied in this manner in addition to others who were seen less intensively. In addition, half a dozen non-patient nurses were interviewed at Långbro Hospital, and about a dozen other non-suicidal patients in both hospitals for the sake of comparison.

Since Swedish reserve is generally accepted even by the Swedes as a national characteristic, I was prepared for more difficulty than was experienced in Denmark in establishing initial contacts with the patients. And they did, in fact, show greater reserve about dealing with emotional problems than had the Danish patients. It would often take four or five hours to get both the amount of information and emotional response that the Danish patient gave in two.

A common reaction on the part of the Swedish women on seeing me for the second or third time was to express embarrassment at having revealed so much about themselves. This contrasted with the Danish women who so often said that after their first interview they had thought of so many things they should have said and wanted to say, but forgot to, and were now anxious to tell in the second interview. The Swedish women, both patients and nurses, blush — and by blush I mean a full facial reddening from the top of the forehead right down to the neck — strikingly more frequently than do women in America. The blush could come whenever in the course of the interview inner feelings were exposed, and the blush was a reaction to this exposure rather than to any one specific subject area. The blushing was indicative both of the desire to reveal feelings, and of the embarrassment about doing so.

The men were somewhat harder to reach emotionally. On any probing into their feelings, they were often defensive. Very often, when most co-operative, they co-operated with an attitude of intellectual curiosity rather than with emotional involvement. They were markedly status conscious and were deferential to a somewhat exaggerated degree toward doctors in a way that interfered with easy emotional expression. However, when one got past these initial barriers the men also turned out to be in much poorer contact with their own feelings than were the women. They would often have obvious emotional reactions to wives, parents, employers and friends, but have little or no awareness of these reactions on their part. Particularly difficult for them was the direct expression of anger, or even open criticism of anyone in their immediate environments.

Early in my work, I was impressed with the preoccupation with performance and success shown by the Swedish male patients and with how related these concerns were to their suicide attempts. The Swede's striving to get ahead and his intensive pursuit of money and material goods seemed as strong as anything seen in the United States. His concern with his success in these matters tends to make an American psychiatrist feel quite at home. However, the intimate relationship between ambition, anxiety about success and attempted suicide was in sharp contrast to what I had seen in Denmark. The Danish men, both old and young, although occasionally presenting work as a problem, turned out to be much more concerned with the loss of some love object than they were with work or performance. In Sweden, some of the young men (35 and under), like young men in Denmark or the United States, were reacting to the loss of women. But it is the older men rather than the younger ones who are the heart of the suicide problem in any country. The men in Sweden of 35 and over are generally not committing suicide over women but over frustration caused by failure to live up to very rigidly maintained high expectations of themselves.

Their attitudes would quickly dispel the idea that the social welfare state had destroyed individual initiative and ambition. Some of the psychological roots of the Swede's performance anxiety and competitive concerns will be taken up later. Economically speaking, it must be stressed that added work or added ambition and determination can pay off in Sweden. Despite all the high taxes which may make new accumulation of great wealth very difficult, added work or a wife working in addition to her husband can result, for the majority of working and middle class people, in significantly more money; and there are plenty of things for the money to buy — houses, cars, clothes and TV sets. The country is wealthy and has important natural resources (water power, timber and iron) that are lacking in Denmark. Thus there are incentives for the Swede's ambition, and this fact is bound to play a role in determining his competitive and acquisitive attitudes.

In the Swedish suicidal men, out-and-out anxiety was more striking than depression, and the depression which existed was often secondary to the anxiety. The clinical features of depression were often not present to any marked degree, that is, these men were not more depressed than the non-suicidal patients. They also did not show the commonly seen classical psychodynamic picture of depression characterized by dependent cravings, with rage toward someone who is felt to be frustrating these cravings — rage that becomes self-directed. These patients contrasted sharply with the Danish patients, for whom clinical depression was the outstanding symptom and was associated with the classical psychodynamic picture of depression. Together with this difference, the Danish patients exhibited degrees of passivity that were far greater than anything seen in the Swedish patients — even in those who would be labelled passive in Sweden. If depression in the Swedish suicidal patients was not severe, anxiety was; and it centered around getting ahead or, more commonly, around feelings of failure and lack of success. Performance and success-failure preoccupations can be seen in suicidal patients in the United States; so can concern over abandonment and loss. In the Danish men, the latter features are predominant; in the Swedish men the former.

.   .   .

Work served the Swedish man as an inordinate source of ego support. His self-image was of himself in his working role, and his self-esteem and feeling of worthwhileness rested heavily on his success at work. Failure here made him vulnerable to a good deal of self-hatred.

Work and performance also served as a major outlet for assertion and the discharge of aggression deriving from many sources. The aggression connected with work often gave a pleasureless, driven quality to the work or, more extremely, led to anxiety and difficulties in performance. Work failure struck very hard at both the man's self-evaluation and his usual outlet for the expression of aggression. The prohibition on the external expression of aggression, as will be seen, is very strong for the Swede and proved particularly so for the suicidal patient. Retroflexed aggression, in response to work failures and other failures, is a natural consequence. It is consistent with this that along with the high suicide rate, other ways of handling retroflexed aggression, such as alcoholism or hypochondriasis, are very common in Sweden. The Danish man is vulnerable to the termination of a relationship — a termination his own dependency may cause. The Swede is vulnerable to work or success difficulties that may be caused by his over-reliance on work as a source of self-esteem, by the aggression connected with his work and by his rigidly held expectations of himself for work success.

Emphasizing the performance success factors among the suicidal men does not mean that there is no problem in the relationship between the sexes, or that this does not play a significant role. The pattern of difficulties between men and women in Sweden has its own particular Swedish quality and is quite different from the patterns of difficulties between the sexes seen in either Denmark or the United States. For the man, although performance failure rather than immediate object loss is the more common precipitating factor with regard to suicide, his attitude toward women plays a crucial role, even in his attitude toward performance. For the woman, disappointment in the relationship between the sexes serves as one of the major precipitating motivations for suicide.

Even on the level of popular culture there is recognition of something of the nature of the trouble. There are standard jokes in Sweden that speak of the love and attention that the man bestows upon his car as compared with the lack of love and attention he shows his wife. There is the popular type of cartoon that depicts an attractive, well-built Swedish girl of 19 or 20 sitting in a restaurant while her boyfriend of about the same age ignores her and is busily engaged reading the sports pages in a newspaper. The stories for women, in the women's magazines, are particularly interesting in this regard. In these stories, there is one theme over and over: A woman, single or married, not too confident and only moderately attractive, loses her man — sometimes to a more sexually seductive woman, or sometimes the man just disappears after a misunderstanding. The story is designed to give a workout to the hurt and pain and, to a lesser degree, the anger that the woman feels. The stories generally have magical and unreal endings in which the man suddenly comes back, sometimes years later. If he left for another woman, he now realizes the more enduring virtues of the first one. If he disappeared, it was because he hadn't thought he was making enough money to marry the girl and had gone away to make his fortune — and, having done so, has now returned. The ending is unimportant, but the story seems to aim its appeal to great numbers of women who have experienced some such kind of loss.

However, from the patients, I got specific evidence as to the actual nature of the difficulties between the sexes.

The male suicidal patient showed a strong tendency to withdraw from a woman when he was in trouble over his work or performance. Typical was the attitude: She can't help me with it so why tell her about it? Nor were such men aware of any resentment toward the women in connection with this attitude. There was a tendency for the men to see their wives as women they came to for praise and admiration for successful performance. I saw non-suicidal men as well with histories of withdrawing from or giving up their relationship with women when experiencing anxiety as to their ability to cope with their work. I did see one suicidal patient who was able to go to his wife, and her reassurance had delayed his becoming acutely suicidal for many years. However, in general the men were far less able to utilize women as a source of comfort than are Danes or Americans. Seeing the woman chiefly as someone for whom to perform well is bound to make her something of a strain and probably contributes to the fact that in Sweden, far more than in Denmark or the United States, men like to relax and enjoy themselves in each other's company, without women. They often feel freer to be themselves and to enjoy themselves when only with other men.

If the man's tendency to withdraw from the woman when he is having trouble at work is great, his tendency to do so when there is trouble between the woman and himself is even greater. While the woman may want to have the difficulty aired and over with, the man is more likely to become silent and withdrawn, and stay angry longer. In this area, as well as in their work, the men gave evidence of difficulty in the handling and management of anger and aggression.

Men can seek an outlet for expressing anger in some activity away from home, ranging from intensified work to alcoholism and infidelity. However, it is noteworthy that infidelity was not characteristic of the suicidal men. This particular avenue for the discharge of aggression was generally one they did not take. Or, in reverse, those who took it were evidently not the group for whom retroflexed aggression is a cause of suicide.

Among the suicidal women patients, one sees the victims of infidelity rather than the perpetrators. Repeated infidelity on the part of a man was one of the major situations precipitating women's suicide attempts. These women occasionally had extramarital affairs but they were in the nature of retaliation for the male infidelity and neglect; and, for the woman, this did not serve as an adequate countermeasure.

.   .   .

One of the commonest marital complaints that one hears in Sweden concerns difficulty in reaching the marital partner emotionally, and it is usually the woman who is making this complaint about the man. There is an apt idiom in Swedish, *tiga ihjäl*, meaning, to kill somebody through silence. This tendency to control anger through detachment tends to result in a general dampening of affectivity and interference with the ability to sustain interest in a relationship, and it appears to be stronger in the man.

.   .   .

Strong feelings of detachment, repressed aggression and dampened affectivity are often perceived psychologically as a kind of emotional dying or death. Many of the suicidal patients were preoccupied with the feeling of being already dead — and not in a delusional sense, but in the sense of feeling emotionally dead. This deadness, associated with so much repressed rage, is experienced as extremely torturing. Individuals with such feelings in any culture (and this syndrome was characteristic for the Swedish patients) are more apt to take their lives than almost any other group of patients. They do so with the feeling that suicide is both a release from suffering and a carrying out of something that has already happened.

The relationship between lack of contact and underlying anger is beautifully expressed in the cartoons of the famous Swedish humorist and caricaturist Albert Engström. Over and over the lack of contact in the cartoons serves as a vehicle to permit the discharge of aggression. The judge asks the man in court why he beat up so many policemen. The man replies that if he had rained all those blows on one policeman he would have hurt him too badly.

However, probably the best examples and most graphic description of both aggressiveness and detachment and what they can mean in the

Swedish character come in the work of the Nobel-prize-winning writer Pär Lagerkvist. *Barabbas* is the epitomy of the man who goes through life more as the observer than the participant. His affectivity is stimulated a little by alcohol and his rage released by injustice — first by the murder of the hare-lipped girl and finally by his misunderstanding of the Christian cause. He contemplates a martyred religious view of life but never successfully or convincingly. For the most part, he is detached, but preoccupation with death never leaves him. With so much aggression within, death can be viewed as a frightening punishment and Barabbas sees it so. At the end: "Death! He always had that inside him, he had had that inside him as long as he had lived. It hunted him inside himself, in the dark mole's passages of his mind, and filled him with its terror."

The Dwarf is the personification of aggression, evil, avarice and destructiveness. At the end of the book, when he is shut up by the prince in a dungeon but knows the prince will call on him again it is made unmistakably clear that he is more than the prince's tool; he is the hidden part of the prince's personality. One could well take a slight license with the two books to say that behind the detachment of a Barabbas lies the need to control the aggression of the Dwarf.

In the *Eternal Smile, Guest of Reality, The Hangman* and his shorter stories and poems, Lagerkvist draws the equation of life with death, based on the inability to love or to feel. The "living dead" come to life when attacked — at least this permits them to release their rage. In this sense, the vicious or antisocial are more alive than others, and those who see society as the enemy are at least protected from such feelings of deadness. Without an enemy, there is only death in life, and psychologically this is due to strangulated rage and strangulated affectivity. Nor is Lagerkvist in any way alone in Swedish literature in this preoccupation with death. Lagerkvist, together with Sjöberg, Hallström, Dagelman and a host of other Swedish authors, has perhaps produced the world's most prolific and sensitive death literature.

For Americans who, to their own loss, are not familiar enough with Lagerkvist's work, this combination of detachment and destructiveness is seen in the films of Ingmar Bergman. The destructiveness is the more obviously familiar, but the knight in *The Seventh Seal* and the professor in *Wild Strawberries* are excellent examples of the kind of detachment referred to.

In a more minor key, the Swedish literary journals are filled with discussions of whether or not life is boring in Sweden. Foreigners who make this complaint of Stockholm could only have in mind that the city is not a playground, which is perhaps more of a compliment to it than an insult. However, the complaint, when made by Swedes themselves, has to be taken more seriously. The writer's suspicion is that the usual diagnoses made concerning *tråkighet* (boredom) that seek for its sources in external conditions are incorrect, and that it is merely a sign of internal affective difficulties with consequent diminished capacity to enjoy life on the part of the person who suffers most from it. Part of the Swedes' liking for the Danes and for the people of southern Europe stems from their perception of the greater emotional freedom these people have, at least in initial contacts.

The roots of the difficulty between the sexes, of the problem in affectivity and the control of anger and of the attitudes to work performance and competition have definite and striking origin in the Swedish pattern of bringing up children.

In Denmark, the writer had been struck by the Danish way of encouraging the child's dependency on its mother and delaying the separation between mother and child. In neighboring Sweden, exactly the reverse is true. The tendency in Sweden is to encourage a very early separation of the child from the mother and for the mother to be pleased with behavior that indicates that the child is self-sufficient and independent.

This does not simply refer to the problem of the working mother as seen in the United States and Denmark. This exists, and the tendency of Swedish mothers to go back to work three months after delivery is very evident. Some mothers admit honestly that they just cannot stay home and care for a young child, even though they know it would be better for the child; their own need not to do so is too strong for them. Very often their working is rationalized as being due to economic need; and, just as often, this is simply not true. The woman just doesn't enjoy caring for the child, and simply wants to get back to work. Or both the woman and her husband are more concerned with things they can buy with their combined earnings than they are with the effects on the child of separation from the mother. Day care centers care for children of from three months to six years of age whose mothers are working. "Key children" is the name given in Sweden to the young school children who are let out of school before their parents get out from work and who must let themselves in the house. The child is too young to be trusted not to lose his key, so it is tied around his neck.

However, even more important because it is so widespread, is the tendency on the part of those mothers who do stay home with their children to push the children into an extremely early independence. Often the mothers have some guilt over this, and they need to cover it up. But the emotional need to do it is marked. As one Swedish child psychiatrist put it — the mothers just don't seem to enjoy their children that much. They don't get the same pleasure from their children — whether caring for them or playing with them — that you see in Danish and American mothers.

This early separation is the source of a great deal of anxiety and resentment. However, since there is usually no physical neglect, and the child knows no other pattern, he finds no justification for being angry with his mother, and there is a tendency for the injury to be covered over, so that the average Swedish male patient tends to simply say that he had the nicest mother in the world — and he tries to change the subject. He has long since learned to consider his dependency needs unacceptable, to deny their existence and to mask them behind an apparent self-reliance.

Childhood phobias, particularly fears of darkness and thunder, were very frequent in the histories of both the Swedish patients and non-patients. Also common were fears of losing the mother through her dying. Such fears, which were a mixture of separation anxiety and anger, were often the first clue to disturbance in the mother-child relationship. Sleeping difficulties of the young child, which point to a similar type of anxiety, are one of the major problems that Swedish mothers with young children seek help about.

One patient described his mother with pride as having been a leading lady of the town when he was a boy. He spoke of her activities out of the home as far back as he could remember and felt that he had not suffered at all on account of them. However, he recalled severe fears of ghosts and darkness as a child, as well as fright over the possibility of his mother's dying. He described her as having been very ambitious for her children as well as rather perfectionistic. In his current situation, he had no conscious complaints about his wife, but his dreams and fantasies soon revealed a picture of all women and most importantly his wife and mother as demanding, expecting and potentially critical. He drove himself frantically at work, and tended to take his wife's not giving him all the praise and admiration he wanted as an indication of her expecting too much and of being at least potentially dissatisfied. His suicide attempt was tied up with his furious efforts at success at work and the difficulties he was having with it. All such difficulties he tried to keep from his wife; and, at the same time, he gave indications of resentment toward her for the position he found himself in. He ended up, without awareness on his part, by using his work to try to establish his worth-whileness in his own and his wife's eyes and was angry with her over his need to do so; thus he punished his wife for things that had initially happened with his mother. This combination was rather usual for the Swedish male patient.

The tendency for the young child's early separation from the mother is true for both sexes. At the later ages of five to 10, however, the boy is away from the home and out on his own more than the girl. He can play as he will and is free from any household chores and responsibilities. The little girl, on the other hand, has a fair number of household duties and grows to be competent in them. Both the girl and her mother will tend to cater more to the boy in the family, if there is one; and in this process the girls envy the boys their freedom although they may reap some advantage from the greater contact with their mothers that their role inevitably entails. The girl's self-confidence as well as the boy's is apt to be impaired by the early separation, though her experience between five and 10 can give her the feeling of being more competent than the boy.

.   .   .

With the suicidal women patients, the disturbance in the child mother relationship was easier to pick up since it was not covered over and buried in the same way as it was with the men. These women were able to express at least some bitterness over what they felt was maternal rejection in childhood.

One particular sexual problem in Sweden may throw further light on the disturbance in the mother-child relationship. Several of the Swedish psychiatrists and psychoanalysts spoke of the frequency with which they saw women withdraw sexually from their husbands after the birth of a child. This occurred in marriages that had been going well up to that point and was not a case of the women using the men merely to have the child and then no longer needing or wanting them afterward. Nor was the withdrawal initiated by the men. If this is so, the explanation probably lies in resentment on the part of the woman toward the man, because of the child. One is more used to the idea of a man resenting the birth of a child and the writer noted in his work on Denmark the frequency with which Danish analysts see impotence in the man following the birth of the child — stemming from the feeling that the man has been displaced. That the Swedish woman could be angry at the man because of the birth of a child would be an explanation consistent with many other facts in the situation. One of the woman's common complaints about her husband, in addition to the lack of emotionality mentioned earlier, is what she calls his "irresponsibility." By this, she means his freedom to come and go as he pleases while she is expected, even if she works, to care for the household and children in the evening. The wife's envy of the man in this regard is not unlike the young girl's envy of the boy's freedom to play as he pleases that was spoken of earlier. Her feeling of greater competence and responsibility is also similar to the young girl's feeling about the boy. A child could well aggravate this envy and resentment of the man's freedom and could force a reluctant woman into an unwilling acceptance of the female role. In addition, this reaction would be consistent with the encouragement of the child's independence and separation from the mother that has been described. Nor is it likely that women who have themselves experienced this early separation are going to be able emotionally to treat their children very differently from the way they themselves were treated, however much they may want to do so.

.   .   .

The differences in the expression of male and female affectivity also have a clear-cut origin in childhood. The Swedish child is actually taught not to show too much feeling, and this is more so for the boy than the girl. Great stress is put on the child's ability to be reasonable and unemotional even in disturbing situations. To be *"tyst och lugn,"* that is, quiet and calm, is something of a Swedish ideal, and more so for the boy and the man than for the girl and the woman.

Girls can cry, boys should not. Neither boys nor girls are allowed the degree of direct expression of anger toward parents and siblings that United States children have. However, the little girl is freer to have a somewhat undirected tantrum within the house. This may be tolerated as "hysterical" or "feminine." A boy's tantrum will be considered uncontrolled and unmanly. The situation is somewhat the reverse of what we see in the United States, where temper on the part of the boy may be considered masculine aggressiveness and that on the part of the girl may be regarded as rather unladylike.

While the boy, even more than the girl, should not directly express his anger, his freedom gives him at least one advantage over the Danish boy in this regard. He is in a better position to slam the door, to go out and play, and to express his anger in some form of disobedience. He thus learns to take his anger outside the family and to act it out; and, if as a husband, he continues this pattern, it is at least consistent.

All this results in a tendency on the part of the Swedish young man to regard all emotion as feminine. The affectivity difficulties that are to play such an important role in the relation between the sexes have already shown up by adolescence. While Swedish teenagers are somewhat freer sexually than is true for most teenage groups in the United States, the boy's coolness will force the girl into taking a little more initiative

with him than the American girl has to. The late teenager is not forced
to cover up what he or she does sexually as much as the American teenager is, and the parents make great efforts to be "reasonable."[1] However,
a fair amount of the sexual contact between teenagers is not simply a
matter of lesser restriction or prohibition, but rather takes place between
boys and girls who have difficulties with their affectivity and use sex in
the effort to try to make some kind of contact.

The teenagers in a Swedish movie audience take in stride scenes of
sexual intimacy on the screen that would cause American teenagers to
giggle and whistle. However, the Swedish teenager may evidence such
signs of anxiety or discomfort at scenes of a very romantic or tender nature, and will react this way far more readily than an American teenager.

By adulthood the Swedish man is likely to feel that strong emotion
in his wife and her expectation of a response from him is something of
a threat or even an attack. One Swedish psychoanalyst put it rather well
in saying that the Swedish woman is happiest who can make the transition from wanting emotional evidence from the man to settling for
loyalty and consideration as signs of his affection.

The man is also likely to be remote from any close emotional contact
with his children, and this certainly affects the image they have of him.
While the Swedish father is often popularly considered to rule the
family, his remoteness modifies the actual situation. For example, the
children will often see the mother catering to the father and acceding
to him in any open conflict yet at the same time managing some of the
most important family affairs by herself without the necessity of paternal
participation. In any case, half of the patients and nonpatients in the
present study considered the mothers to have been the stronger and more
effective force in their families.

What about the origin of the competitiveness and performance concern that has been spoken of? From the child's earliest age, Swedish
parents are more interested in his performance and how he compares
with other children than are Danish parents. The child learns to use his
performance to bolster his self-esteem, and to use it in the hope of being
more lovable in the eyes of his parents.

---

[1] The Swedish parents' attitude toward sexual activity on the part of their
young children is to prohibit it and to deny its existence at the same time, much
in the manner of American and Danish parents. If there is a difference with
young children, it is that the child is not educated to feel the same degree of
shame as children in the United States are with regard to bodily exposure. Children of five and six can be seen swimming undressed at the public beaches, while
in the United States this is generally stopped several years earlier. Thus the
adult, too, is not so apt to experience quite the pain or panic that we see here
if he or she is observed undressed.

At the age of about 10, a shift takes place in what is expected of Swedish boys and girls. The boy, who has been playing as he pleases, experiences a new and intense interest on the part of his family in his performance, particularly at school. He can win parental approval and admiration with success, and is expected to do so; and he can cause consternation with failure. The school competition for the boys who want to, or whose parents want them to, go on with their education is a fierce and intense one, for the number of places available for higher education is limited, and the system is based on merit. Many educated Swedes speak with great feeling of the toil between the age of 10 until the completion of the "student examen" necessary for their advanced education. Work and performance become a natural way of repairing whatever damage to self-esteem has been caused by early separation, and they can certainly win maternal admiration and attention. The boy whose self-esteem has not been too severely damaged by early separation, whose aggression is not too strongly curbed, and who can make this transition successfully, can become an extremely effective and productive person; but it is no easy task that is required of him.

The girls, on the other hand, at about the same age of 10, may experience the disappointment of seeing that their performance is no longer particularly appreciated. A girl's school failures are not the catastrophe that her brother's are, and her good marks receive less admiration. Her household chores may be taken for granted, although she may continue to try to build self-esteem and to control aggression by the obedient performance of these duties. If she does this, she may go on to become a meticulous housewife — often too meticulous for her husband's taste.[2] Both for the girls who follow this course and those who rebel against it, the idea of cleanliness and orderliness being psychologically equated with goodness and obedience remains strongly ingrained.

In her teens the girl's interest is expected to, and generally does, center around her popularity with boys. Here her self-confidence, if already impaired, is not helped by the boy's coolness. It is ironic that in a country famous for the beauty of its women, these same women are rather insecure about their attractiveness. Some of the girls take achievement and

[2] The woman puts more effort and concern into the neatness, cleanliness and dress of her child than is usual in the United States or in the rest of Scandinavia.

The writer's impression is that the child is also toilet trained earlier in Sweden and in a shorter period than are our children. This may be correlated as much with the mother's interest in an independently functioning child as with her interest in cleanliness and orderliness. There is a great deal of Swedish humor centering around bowel and bladder functions and the passing of flatus. These jokes generally serve to deflate or to humiliate someone through humorously calling attention to his natural functions.

success in work and career as their goals. However, too much achievement and success may be considered unfeminine. There is, for the adult
woman, a high prevalence of inhibition about success and doing one's
best that centers around the feeling that, in so doing, the woman will
give up her femininity and her chances of being happy with a man.
Women striving hard for success in career or work usually do not have
as rigid standards for themselves and their performance as do the men.
These are generally not the Swedish suicidal women and when I saw
them, they were patients with other problems or were the nurses or the
wives of the suicidal men.

Just who were the female suicidal patients and what were their motivations for suicide? One major group has been mentioned as being women
whose suicide attempts were reactions to infidelity or abandonment on
the part of a man. . . . The childhood histories of these women were
remarkably similar. They saw their mothers as demanding chores of
them, always critical and unloving. Their self-confidence had been impaired, their self-assertion and initiative crushed at an early age. They
went on to form relationships with men and managed to end up receiving abuse from their husbands, similar to that they had gotten from
their mothers. Criticism, neglect and infidelity were their lot in marriage; and suicide for them was the only way they could envisage striking
back.

As has been indicated, this pattern is not qualitatively unique to
Sweden. However, the Swedish girl goes into her relationship with a
man, on which her self-esteem is supposed to rest, hampered by the
prior injury to this self-esteem caused by early maternal separation. In
addition, her capacities for self-assertion and aggression have also been
impaired by parental attitudes toward such behavior. The woman's im-
pairments in self-assertion, aggression and self-esteem are also no help
in holding the man. And the man's attitudes toward women, based on
his own childhood experiences, are further not in her favor. If infidelity
or abandonment occurs, the woman is deprived of the very adaptative
tools she would need to cope with the situation. The whole combination
makes for more such disappointed women, more impotent rage and
self-hatred and more female suicides than one sees in the United States.

In the other major group of female suicidal patients, the relationship
with the mother was even more paramount. These women remained
rooted in their relationship with their mothers, and even if they formed
relationships with men, these were of secondary importance. They often
had histories of maternal separation or abandonment, followed by
later periods of what they felt was too much maternal control. Their
hatred of their mothers was focused on the period of control and inter-

ference, but the original and more important trauma was the separation or abandonment. These women were markedly paranoid and their hatred spilled over toward everyone. Those who were able to repress this rage developed more classical paranoid symptomatology often later in life — with delusions centering around their guilt over their rage toward the mother.

The male equivalent of this was best illustrated earlier by the patient whose suicide attempt represented psychodynamically a murderous attack on his mother. Such a man would become paranoid toward the world in a controlled way, while repressing his anger toward his mother and remaining rooted in his relationship with her. However, among the female paranoid patients the rage was more commonly overt; and, whatever they started talking about, they ended up returning to the unfairness and injustice of maternal treatment. Their suicide attempts were very much acts of destruction aimed at their mothers as well as themselves.

Most of the patterns stressed, that is, the early separation of the child, the relationship between the sexes, the control of aggression and its effect on affectivity and the attitudes toward competition and performance, are those patterns that seemed to be of the most widespread significance for Swedish life and character. Stockholmers come, or their parents do, from all parts of Sweden, and one can't work with patients there for long without getting a feeling for some of the variations and differences seen in different parts of the country. For example, competitiveness among the men is certainly greater in Stockholm than in the rural areas, and in many of the rural areas the control of affectivity is far greater than that seen in Stockholm. However, this study aims at defining the characteristics that distinguish Sweden, particularly in comparison with the United States and Denmark, rather than at defining those things that divide the Swedes. A comprehensive study of the variations in character and family patterns within the country would have to be a separate project, but one that the writer thinks would be extremely valuable for Swedish psychiatry and would also throw further light on the patterns that have been described.

. . .

How do the patterns that have been discussed fit together to produce the Swedish suicide rate?

The early separation of child from mother both stimulates anger and deflates self-esteem. The control that is required of anger and all strong affect results in the handling of anger with a good deal of detachment. Few combinations will provide such fertile soil for suicide as affective deadening, combined with, and based on, the need to control aggression. Competitive performance for the man is an acceptable salve for his self-esteem and an outlet for his aggression if he can so channel it. However, the rigid expectations he has of himself make him most vulnerable to self-hatred and suicide if he fails in this area.

For the woman, though her affectivity is somewhat better, the same factors operate, except that it is her relationship with the man that generally must restore her damaged self-esteem, and this very damage is no help in arousing and sustaining the man's interest in her. The man's attitude toward women only further aggravates the situation. The same difficulties in dealing with aggression can prove the woman's undoing if the relationship with the man turns out very badly for her.

In both male and female cases, where the injury in the maternal relationship is more severe or the reaction to it greater, the patient may become paranoid. Though with the paranoid man the anger toward the mother is more apt to be repressed than it is with the paranoid woman, both their suicides can then represent psychodynamically a murder of the mother. . . .

REFERENCES

Hendin, H. Attempted suicide: a psychiatric and statistical study. *Psychiat. Quart.*, 24:39-46, January 1950.
———. Psychodynamic motivational factors in suicide. *Psychiat. Quart.*, 25:672-678, October 1951.
———. Suicide. *Psychiat. Quart.*, 30:2, 267-282, April 1956.
———. Suicide in Denmark. *Psychiat. Quart.*, 34:3, 443-460, July 1960.
———. Suicide: Psychoanalytic point of view. In: The Cry for Help. Pp. 181-192. Farberow and Shneidman, editors. McGraw-Hill, 1961.
Ettlinger, Ruth. Ten-year follow-up study of attempted suicide in Stockholm. (Not yet published.)
Swedish Statistical Yearbooks (up to 1960). Swedish Central Bureau of Statistics. Stockholm.
Causes of Death in Sweden (up to 1959). Swedish Central Bureau of Statistics. Stockholm.

IV

Behavior Injurious to Others

Personal Violence

If one finds that female-based families in the American society produce more aggressive adolescent sons, the question may be raised whether this occurs because the female-based family deviates from the culturally expected American pattern, or whether such families generally, wherever they are found, produce more aggressive males. Does pathology result from maladjustment to an essentially arbitrary standard, or is a type of family structure inherently, by virtue of what it does to persons living under it everywhere, more effective in reducing male violence? If the first alternative is right, male violence in the United States could be reduced by making the female-based family type culturally acceptable. If the second alternative is valid, cultural legitimization of the female-based family type is likely to increase the amount of male violence (since presumably with cultural acceptance such families would become more prevalent). In the following article Beatrice Whiting shows how research in societies in which the female-based family is culturally acceptable helps to resolve the policy issue of how to deal with such families in any society.

7   BEATRICE B. WHITING

Sex Identity Conflict and Physical Violence:
A Comparative Study

This paper will attempt to compare the frequencies of assault and homicide[1] in six societies and to consider the differences in the light of the concept of "protest masculinity" and the status-envy hypothesis of identification. The ethnographic material used in the comparison is reported in *Six Cultures: Studies of Child Rearing* (B. Whiting, ed., 1963).[2]

Researchers in the field of delinquency and crime have, for the last 30 years, discussed the nature of the homes from which offenders have come. They have considered family composition and household structure as relevant antecedents of criminal behavior. Early on they discovered that a large number of the adults convicted of criminal offences had a history of delinquencies dating back to their childhood or adolescence (for a recent study see Robins and O'Neal 1958). Beginning around 1910, statistics were published indicating that "broken homes" might be an important predictor of delinquency (for summary of these studies see Monahan 1962). Of the early researchers, Healy and Bronner (1936) and Sheldon and Eleanor Glueck (1950) paid particular attention to family life and a boy's relationship to his father. In general, however, the description of "broken homes" was not specific and often did not indicate which parent was absent, why, at what stage in the child's life, and for how long. It would appear, however, that most often the home was "broken" by the absence of the father.

The interpretation of such findings centered on the importance of the intact nuclear family and the early stable, emotionally warm, but firm

Reproduced by permission of the author and the American Anthropological Association from the *American Anthropologist*, Vol. 67, No. 6, Part II (December 1965), pp. 123-140.

[1] Homicide is defined as killing another regardless of intent or circumstances.

[2] The interpretation of the data collected for the six culture project presented in this paper is that of the author. The field teams do not necessarily agree with it. Robert LeVine and Leigh Minturn have both been helpful in commenting on the manuscript.

rearing of the child. The emphasis was on the pathology of the home life and any family that did not fit the middle-class monogamous nuclear pattern was considered defective.

Paralleling the family studies, demographic studies reported consistently that certain areas in the United States and in other parts of the world have a higher crime rate than others. Slum areas in the United States which are overcrowded, have poor housing, poor job opportunity, and a higher percentage of Negro residents, have a consistently higher proportion of convictions for criminal offenses than do other areas. Negroes from these areas are arrested more frequently than whites.

Recent studies combining the demographic with the psychological approach suggest there is a type of culture with a well-established social structure that produces an adolescent and adult personality predisposed to behave at times in a violent and aggressive fashion. Two of the most articulate proponents of this theory are anthropologists who have studied lower-class populations. Unlike their predecessors, they have treated informants who do not maintain monogamous nuclear households as members of a functioning cultural subgroup rather than as deviants.

Walter Miller (1958:268-269) states this thesis clearly:

> There is a substantial segment of present-day American society whose way of life, values, and characteristic patterns of behavior are the product of a distinctive cultural system which may be termed "lower class." . . . The lower class way of life in common with that of distinctive cultural groups is characterized by a set of focal concerns.

The list of concerns includes the alternatives of being law-abiding vs. being law-violating; of having physical prowess, skill, and toughness as opposed to being weak, effeminate, and cowardly; of being smart and shrewd as opposed to being gullible; of seeking thrill, danger, and excitement as opposed to being bored, safe, and passive; of being lucky vs. being unlucky; of being independent vs. being cared for.

Miller characterizes lower-class social structure as having the female-based household rather than the two-parent family unit, and as having a prevalence of the one-sex peer group.

> Lower class society may be pictured as comprising a set of age-graded one-sex groups which constitute the major psychic focus and reference group for those over twelve or thirteen. . . . What has been called the "delinquent gang" is one subtype of this form, defined on the basis of frequency of participation in law-violating activity . . . (ibid. 273).

It is a subtype of the adolescent street-corner group.

> Members of the street-corner gangs are well aware of the law-violating nature of these acts; they are not psychopaths. . . . [The delinquent

> acts are] motivated primarily by the attempt to achieve ends, states,
> or conditions which are valued and to avoid those that are disvalued
> . . . (ibid. 275).

The delinquent acts, then, if one accepts Miller's findings, are attempts to prove that one has the valued characteristics of toughness,
smartness, and masculinity and to establish one's right to be a member
of the peer group.

The problem thus becomes one of the genesis of the values described
by Miller. He hypothesizes that the lower-class concern with "toughness"

> is probably related to the fact that a significant proportion of lower
> class males are reared in a predominantly female household and lack
> a consistently present male figure with whom to identify and from
> whom to learn essential components of a "male" role. Since women
> serve as a primary object of identification during pre-adolescent years,
> the almost obsessive lower class concern with "masculinity" probably
> resembles a type of compulsive reaction-formation (ibid. 270).

Rohrer and Edmonson (1960) come to a similar conclusion on the
basis of intensive work with New Orleans Negro subjects originally
studied by Davis and Dollard and reported upon in *Children of Bondage*
in 1940. Rohrer and Edmonson stress the function of the gang as a so-
cializing group one of whose functions is to replace the shadowy or
completely absent father in the lower-class "matriarchal" families. They
describe the gang as a highly structured organization characterized by a
code of secrecy, by remarkable displays of verbal aggression, and by a
clear pecking order that differentiates between the role of the bully and
the role of the sissy. "The pressures for conformity to gang standards
are severe; enforcement is physical and violent" (Rohrer and Edmonson
1960:162).

The authors continue to discuss the genesis of this social structural
form. They summarize:

> Thus an organizational form that springs from the little boy's search
> for masculinity he cannot find at home becomes at first a protest
> against femininity and then an assertion of hyper-virility. On the way
> it acquires a structuring in which the aspirations and goals of the
> matriarchy or the middle class are seen as soft, effeminate, and despic-
> able. The gang ideology of masculine independence is formed from
> these perceptions and the gang then sees its common enemy not as
> a class, nor even as a sex, but as the "feminine principle" in society
> (ibid. 162-163).

Despite the claim both of Miller and of Rohrer and Edmonson that
they are studying members of a legitimate culture, they have been
criticized by sociologists who claim that the groups they describe are in

fact deviant and hence not legitimate subcultures. Thus the critics argue that crime and delinquency can be attributed to the fact that the groups are economically depressed, are rejected caste groups, or are minority groups whose values conflict with the culture of the dominant group.

A cross-cultural study of the correlates of crime, published by Bacon, Child, and Barry (1963) includes some findings that should be considered in evaluating these criticisms of Miller's and Rohrer and Edmonson's work. Their study reports on 48 societies that are independent and self-contained in comparison with subcultures in Boston and New Orleans. In this study, the frequency of theft and personal crime (defined to include assault, rape, suicide, sorcery intended to make another ill, murder, making false accusation, and the like) was separately correlated with a number of variables

> which are suspected to be causal factors in the development of crime. Lack of or limitation of opportunity for the young boy to form an identification with his father was associated with both types of crime. A high degree of socialization anxiety in childhood and a high degree of status differentiation in adulthood were significantly associated with theft only; a general attitude of suspicion and distrust was more decidedly associated with personal crime (Bacon, Child, and Barry 1963:291).

Specifically, the "masculine protest" hypothesis was used to interpret the finding that crimes, including both theft and crimes defined as personal, are found more frequently in societies having polygynous mother-child households than in societies having monogamous and nuclear households. The assumption was made that since in at least a third of the first type of households a woman shares a house with her children and is visited by her husband in her turn, the child will not see his father so frequently as he will in the latter, nuclear-type, households.

Personal crimes were found to be associated with mother-child sleeping arrangements, which Bacon, Child, and Barry interpret as an index of strong dependence between mother and child, but which I, for reasons I will present later, prefer to consider an index of infrequent contact between an infant and his father and hence an index of low salience of the father in the child's infancy.

It should be noted that Miller's and Rohrer and Edmonson's studies do not discuss in detail the nature of the protest behavior of the street-corner gangs but, in both studies, physical violence is one of the types of deviance mentioned. For the purpose of this paper I would like to concentrate primarily on physical assault and homicide. The Bacon, Child, and Barry study, as well as studies by criminologists in our society, suggest that the personality profile of thieves is different from that of individuals involved in crimes of physical violence. Unfortunately, in the Bacon, Child, and Barry study, it is not possible to separate the assault and homicide cases from the rape, infanticide, suicide, and witchcraft and sorcery cases. This is particularly unfortunate as, for the purposes of this paper, I wish to confine myself to offenses committed by men. In the comparative material that I will present, all the cases of physical assault and homicide, as far as I can check, were committed by men. The other types of behavior, especially witchcraft and accusations of witchcraft, are more likely to be committed by women. That types of offenses may be differentiated according to the sex of the offender will not be surprising to those who have studied the differences between crimes committed by men and those committed by women in the United States and Europe (see Pollak 1950 and Tappan 1947). I would suspect that many of the differences will be found to be universal.

It should also be noted that in the studies cited above violent, aggressive behavior and concern over masculinity is interpreted as a *defense mechanism*. Although the antecedents are absence of, or infrequent contact with, the father, the theory does not explain the behavior as due to lack of discipline, lack of an adequate masculine role model, or faulty identification and low super-ego resulting from lack of a warm nurturant relationship with a man (McCord, McCord, and Zola 1959). Nor is this theory content to state simply that a boy commits violent, aggressive acts because he is a member of a sub-culture having gangs that approve and require such behavior; although the authors would agree to this statement they would go on to say that these societies or subcultures hold these values and have gangs because of psychological needs.

These studies do not present in any detail the theories of the genesis of the "masculine protest" defense syndrome. In this paper I follow the "status-envy" theory, which was developed at the Laboratory of Human Development at Harvard University and stated most explicitly but briefly by Whiting (1960a). In simplest terms, the theory states that an individual identifies with that person who seems most important to him, the person who is perceived as controlling those resources that he wants. If during the first two or three years of life a child is constantly with his mother and infrequently sees, and is handled by, his father, he will identify strongly with his mother and not with his father; in short, if he is a boy he will have a cross-sex identification. If, later in life, he is involved in a world that is obviously dominated by men, a world in which men are perceived to be more prestigeful and powerful than women, he will be thrown into conflict. He will develop a strong need to reject his underlying female identity. This may lead to an overdetermined attempt to prove his masculinity, manifested by a preoccupation with physical strength and athletic prowess, or attempts to demonstrate daring and valor, or behavior that is violent and aggressive. These types of behavior will be referred to as "protest masculinity."

It should be noted here that although this theory as presented is concerned with the fate of the male child, the theory also predicts sex conflict for the girl child. The important variable in her life is her perception of the status of women in the world she enters as a child. Although no extensive studies have been made, it would appear from the fragmentary evidence that women reared in mother-child households are more dominant and aggressive than women reared in nuclear households (see D'Andrade 1962 and Ridington 1964). This may be explained by secondary male identification engendered by the perception that in the "lower-class" world men have more power than women. It could also be the result of a primary identification with a masculine-type mother who has to fend for herself without a man and hence is more aggressive. The higher percentage of criminal offenses committed by Negro women in comparison with whites in the United States may be explained in part by the fact that a higher percentage of Negro women are reared in mother-child households.

In addition to the works mentioned above, studies which have discussed the consequences of father absence or low father salience during infancy have been conducted by: Whiting, Kluckhohn, and Anthony (1958); Burton and Whiting (1961); D'Andrade (1962); Longabaugh (1962); Carlsmith [Kuckenberg] (1963); R. Munroe (1964). These studies underline the fact that the consequences of father absence or low salience in infancy, with associated female identification, vary with the relative dominance of males and females in the adult world and the personal attributes valued by a society. Thus, Whiting *et al.* report that in societies having low father salience in infancy and an adult world in which men are more important and powerful than women the adolescent boy will undergo certain rituals that symbolically break the mother-son bond and prove the boy's masculine identity or manhood (Whiting, Kluckhohn, and Anthony 1958; Burton and Whiting 1961). Initiation is thus interpreted as a ritual solution to problems of cross-sex identity.

Contrariwise, where the dominance of males is less clear, the conflict for boys who have made an initial feminine identification may not be great. Karolyn Kuckenberg Carlsmith comments that the U.S. college boys she tested and interviewed who spent the first two years of their lives with their mothers while their fathers were overseas in World War II had feminine attributes but did not seem anxious or defensive about them. She summarizes her interpretation, "Although it is probable that men and women are about equally powerful in our middle and upper-middle class society, the evidence suggests that certain typically feminine attributes, such as sensitivity, aesthetic interests and verbal ability, are highly valued in academic or intellectual environments (Carlsmith [Kuckenberg] 1963:72)." Hence there is no serious problem of adjustment and no need for defensive protest.

Let us turn now to an examination of the comparative frequency of violence in the six societies reported in the Six Culture Study (Beatrice B. Whiting, ed., 1963) in the light of this theory of sex-identity conflict and "protest masculinity." It should be stressed that this paper is not proposing *any single explanation* for the existence of more violence in some societies than in others. It is merely exploring the status-envy/ protest-masculinity hypothesis to see if it can plausibly account *in part* for differences in the six societies.

The primary intent of the Six Culture Project was to maximize the comparability of data by trying to standardize as far as possible both the questions to be asked and the methods of data collection. The focus of the project was the relation of child-training practices to personality. Rather than relying on projective tests as a measure of personality, the senior investigators and their consultants decided to rely heavily upon the systematic observation of behavior. This led to the decision to study a relatively small number of subjects intensively and to make a small face-to-face community (Primary Social Unit) the social unit of investigation. Twelve girls and twelve boys between the ages of 3 and 10 were selected from such a community in each of the six societies. The behavior of these subjects was systematically observed and both they and their mothers were interviewed.

In addition to gathering standard ethnographic materials on the community, the field teams were asked to pay particular attention to two areas of behavior — leisure activities and incidents of conflict between individuals and groups of individuals. Each field team was asked to write a chapter in its ethnography on social control.

In Taira, Okinawa, Thomas and Hatsumi Maretzki studied 60 families who lived in the central part of town; the population of this section was approximately 300. The population of the entire group who considered themselves residents of Taira was 700; this included residents of hamlets scattered among the rice paddies several miles from the center of town. John and Ann Fischer studied 24 families in Orchard Town, New England. Most of the families were members of a Baptist Church in North Village (pop. 1,600), a subdivision of a town of 5,000. A. Kimball Romney and Romaine Romney worked in a Mixtecan barrio (pop. 600) of Juxtlahuaca, Oaxaca, Mexico. The Nydeggers studied families in three sitios ranging in size from three to 17 households in the 2-mile-square barrio of Tarong (pop. approximately 309) in Luzon, Philippines. Leigh Minturn and John Hitchcock studied families who were members of the Rājpūt caste in a subdivision of the town of

Khalapur (pop. 5,000), Uttar Pradesh, India. The subdivision included 602 members of the Rājpūt caste. Robert and Barbara LeVine studied 18 contiguous homesteads in the Gusii highlands of Kenya, Africa. The families belonged to a cooperative work group which the LeVines called Nyansongo (pop. 235).

In comparing these six societies it seems clear that more cases of assault and homicide occurred in Nyansongo and Khalapur than in any of the other four societies. This conclusion is based on total reported cases of assault and homicide that involved people known by name to members of the primary social unit (P.S.U.). Only one murder occurred during the period of field work: in a brawl in Khalapur one man was killed, one was injured, and several others were badly beaten (Minturn and Hitchcock 1963:252-262). During the field period one or two cases of physical violence were reported for each of the communities with the exception of Orchard Town. No comparative statement can be made on the basis of such a small sample for such a short period of time. The ethnographies and field notes, however, contain reference to past cases of assault or homicide that occurred to known people. On the basis of these remembered cases, the contrast between the Rājpūts of Khalapur and the Nyansongo and the other four societies becomes clear. Informants in the other four societies were not able to remember more than one case of murder involving relatives or friends; this one case is reported for Tarong (see Nydegger and Nydegger 1963:760). The members of all four of these societies had been involved in few, if any, court cases.

In contrast, in Khalapur, when John Hitchcock interviewed the 39 men between the ages of 25 and 65 in the sample they reported having been involved in 59 court cases; 17 of these concerned incidents that had taken a violent turn, and in three, men had been killed (Minturn and Hitchcock 1963:260). The ethnography and field notes contain examples of physical violence, such as the woman who lost an eye as a result of being beaten by her brother-in-law because her son, age 9, had allowed the cattle to stray into his uncle's crops. A similar case is reported in the Nyansongo field notes; a child who allowed the cattle to stray was beaten so severely that he had to be hospitalized.

The LeVines' chapter on social control deals with the court cases for the Gusii tribe as a whole.[3] In those trouble cases concerning individuals known to the P.S.U. there are at least seven instances of violence between named individuals, and numerous other accounts of knife and panga fights and accusations of assault. The LeVines state, "Almost

[3] The LeVines were able to collect a type of data which is not reported in the other monographs and hence cannot be used for comparative data except perhaps with Orchard Town, if it is typical of the figures given for urban United States. The following two charts taken from the monograph on Nyansongo

every Gusii adult male has been involved in a court case; many have had 10 or more" (LeVine and LeVine 1963:91).

The six societies also differ in their preoccupation with and attitude toward violence and strife. In Taira fights between husbands and wives over money were the only type of conflict that was reported to occur with any frequency. Such fights occur most often late at night after the participants have been drinking and sometimes end in physical violence. However, no specific cases were cited and the Maretzkis could summarize, "The absence of crime and the low incidence of quarrels, disputes and brawls would seem to make policing unnecessary" (Maretzki and Maretzki 1963:411).

Within the Mixtecan barrio, fights over women and the beating of adulterous wives were the only type of conflict that informants mentioned as occurring frequently. However, there were no such fights during the field work. A. Kimball Romney was with an informant when the latter discovered his wife in bed with another man. The aggrieved husband shrugged his shoulders and walked around the block and there was no subsequent beating or violence (Romney and Romney 1963:610).

The Mixtecans seem to fear aggression. Children are told they will die if they get angry and then eat. Parents like to keep their children at home in the courtyard lest they fight with other children. Unlike Nyansongo, Khalapur, and Taira, where alcohol seems to increase the probability of fights and arguments, in the Mixtecan barrio after intensive drinking at fiestas there was no violence.

(LeVine and LeVine 1963:98, 105) give comparative figures on homicide and rape for the United States and Nyansongo:

Average Annual Homicide Rates per 100,000 Population. Three Kenya Tribal Groups and the Urban United States, 1955 and 1956

Gusii	5.5
Kipsigis	4.8
South Nyanza Luo	4.5
United States, urban	4.85[a]

[a] Statistical Abstract of the United States, U.S. Department of Commerce, 78th Annual Edition, 1957, p. 139.

Average Annual Rate of Rape Indictments per 100,000 Population, Gusii and United States, 1955 and 1956

Gusii[a]	47.2
United States, urban[b]	13.85
United States, rural[b]	13.1

[a] This is an extremely conservative estimate; the procedures by which it was arrived at are described in LeVine (1959).

[b] Statistical Abstract of the United States, U.S. Department of Commerce, 78th Annual Edition, 1957, p. 139.

In Tarong verbal aggression seems to be more frequent than in Taira and Juxtlahuaca and appears to be condoned and even vicariously enjoyed. The Nydeggers summarize:

> In any small community where members so constantly interact, there are tensions, annoyances, fancied or real reasons to take offense. And a Tarongan has no hesitation about making his feelings loudly apparent to anyone within shouting distance. Stereotypically, women quarrel often but men are more silent, fighting with their bolos when angered. Nevertheless, bolos are used most often for threatening, not chopping, and men roaring imprecations and curses are heard not infrequently throughout the sitio.
>
> Since it is shameful to fight with neighbors and relatives, such arguments occasion no family support and are quickly smoothed over. Although heated, they leave little bitterness: instead they seem to clear the air and are openly enjoyed and kibitzed by noninvolved sitio members (Nydegger and Nydegger 1963:749-750).

Both the Rājpūt of Khalapur and the Nyansongo, in contrast, have a warrior and cattle-thieving tradition. The Rājpūt still cherish a martial self image. They are proud to claim a connection with the Rājpūt heroes of the medieval period (Hitchcock 1958:216-223). They believe that they have an "innate capacity for ruling and a right to do so." Angered by lower-caste disobedience, a Rājpūt will often slap an offender or strike him with his staff. He considers it his duty to keep his inferiors in line.

Within the caste group itself there are quarrels which have often led to violence and bloodshed. Hitchcock (1958:218) states,

> The Rājpūt is brave, mettlesome, and very quick to perceive and resent an insult. It is part of his code that a slight to his prestige should be avenged. The preferred method of taking revenge is to wait and plan until the just moment has come. As one Rājpūt said, "We like to wait until we get our enemy to the edge of the pond and then push him in."

Hitchcock describes a feud between two Rājpūt families involving a severe beating followed six months later by a revenge murder; no action was taken by the police as they had been bribed. Hitchcock continues (219):

> One of the most characteristic qualities of the martial Rājpūt is his tendency to carry his warrior and regal virtues to extremes. His ambition tends to become overweening; his concern for his reputation tends to become immoderate pride; and his bravery often borders on the rash. One Khalapur Rājpūt of the more martial type when he had been drinking, sometimes used to come alone from his side of the village to a side where several large families of his enemies

lived. He would walk up and down before the platform of their
men's houses and challenge any or all of them to come and fight him.

Family retaliation is still an important factor in social control and family
power is reckoned in part on how many able-bodied men can be mustered
for staff fights.

The Khalapur Rājpūt also have a tradition of marauding outside the
village:

> Throughout the nineteenth century . . . [they] and their kinsmen in
> nearby villages were a problem to the British because of their cattle
> thieving, their marauding for grain (especially when crops were poor),
> and their unremitting resistance to revenue collectors. The police and
> some government officials still speak of Khalapur as a criminal village,
> and some of the village Rājpūt still do augment their incomes
> through cattle theft" (Minturn and Hitchcock 1963:220-221; see
> also Hitchcock 1959:396).

It will be argued by some that the Rājpūt are not so aggressive as the
description above would suggest. They are Hindus and subscribe to the
doctrine of pacifism and passive resistance which has been reinforced by
recent religious and political leaders. The Rājpūt themselves commented
that they found their present lot as agriculturists at odds with their
martial tradition. One Rājpūt who, in good Hindu tradition, joined a
religious order as a wandering holy man, soon returned, stating that he
was too proud to beg for a living (Hitchcock 1959). It would seem to
me that the Rājpūt, like many other people, have conflicting values. If
our theory is correct they will find it easier to give up their martial ideal
when they also give up purdah and the seclusion of their women.

In Nyansongo, until 1912 when the British abolished the age-grade
cattle villages, skirmishes against other clans involving not only the
theft of cattle but also physical violence and homicide were part of a
young man's experience. It would appear that violence within the community was forbidden but violence between clans was permitted and
expected. The seemingly high percentage of fights between fathers and
sons and between half-brothers reported by R. LeVine may have been
lower when cattle villages still existed.

The initiation rites that every adolescent boy in Nyansongo experiences stress the values of manliness—especially toughness and bravery.
In the old days, after initiation, a boy joined other warriors in the cattle
villages and spent his time defending the herds and raiding other groups,
stealing their cattle and sexually assaulting their women. Nowadays
sexual exploits are still possible but often end in arrest and litigation.

It should be noted that there is a court system and delegated authority
available in all of the six societies. At the time of the field work the legal

way to settle personal crimes in Khalapur was through the Indian National Government Courts and in Nyansongo through the courts introduced by the British. In both societies, however, the families studied preferred not to use the system. The families in Khalapur still preferred to settle disputes through the local panchayat. Before they turned to colonial courts, the Nyansongo, even though the homestead elders were no longer capable of settling some disputes as they did in precolonial times, sought out the chief who had been appointed by the British government. In Juxtlahuaca, Taira, and Tarong there is probably even more resistance to using the available courts because of the fear of being discriminated against by the more "civilized" people of the town. This is probably true of the Mixtecans who are derogated by the ladinos of El Centro, Juxtlahuaca.

In sum, although there is no adequate statistical material for comparing the six societies, I would feel reasonably safe in stating that there were more cases of physical violence reported for Khalapur and Nyansongo than for the other four societies. Accusations of sorcery and witchcraft are highest by far in Nyansongo, next highest in Tarong. As stated earlier, I prefer to separate assault and homicide from sorcery and witchcraft as I do not think the antecedents are identical. Sexual assault is more frequent in Nyansongo. It is not mentioned in the Khalapur ethnography. If one accepts the Bacon, Child, and Barry definition of personal crimes, Nyansongo would probably score very high. It is less clear where they would have placed the Rājpūts on a ten-point scale.

I would now like to consider how the role of the father in relation to his son in Khalapur and Nyansongo differs from his role in the other societies. It will be remembered that the nature of this relationship before the child is three and the importance of men in later life are crucial variables in the "status envy" hypothesis for the development of cross-sex identity and masculine-protest behavior.

If one assumes that the infant's perception of the importance of the father will in large part be determined by how often he sees his father then it is necessary to assess the amount of this contact. Since infants spend most of their time with their mothers in all the societies, a crude estimate can be made by determining how much time the father or father surrogate spends in the company of the mother. Does he sleep with her at night, eat with her, work with her, and spend his leisure time with her? How often is any man around?

One of the major differences between the Rājpūt and Nyansongo samples and the other groups is the relation between men and women. In the first two groups husband and wife may neither sleep nor eat together and seldom work or play together.

The Nyansongo man shares a hut with his wife if he is a monogamist.

However, the hut is divided into two sections, one of which belongs to the husband exclusively. Here he entertains his guests, keeps his possessions, and sleeps when he wishes. He has a private entrance (LeVine and LeVine 1963:25-26). A polygynist builds a similar house for each wife and either rotates among them or sleeps in a special house which he may share with his unmarried sons who are over 12 and have been initiated. He may spend most time with his youngest, most recent wife, but he must be careful to spend some time with each lest they bring suit against him for sexual neglect or, out of jealousy, make the life of the youngest wife intolerable (ibid. 38-39). He seldom if ever visits a wife who has a nursing baby. The LeVines state that:

> As children grow older, they are excluded from sleeping with the parents and it is usually the father who takes the initiative on this score because of his sexual embarrassment. He excludes girls at an earlier age, mostly 5 to 6, then boys who are told to sleep outside at 7 or 8. The girl goes to sleep with the mother's co-wife or, even more frequently, a grandmother (ibid. 179; see also LeVine 1959).

The LeVines estimate that at least two-thirds of the children grow up in polygynous households. For these children, as well as for the children of monogamists who are working away from home, the father is a visitor in the house rather than a permanent resident. Twenty-four of the 28 adult males in the Nyansongo sample had been employed at some time in their lives outside South Nyanza district.

The pattern at mealtime also varies with the type of household and again the polygynist's children may eat alone with their mother for part, if not all, of the year. A polygynist receives a basket of food from each wife at every meal and takes at least one mouthful from each. At this signal the wife may bring the rest of it back to be eaten by herself and the children in her own hut.

Nyansongo men and women seldom work together. Men do the heavy preparation of the gardens, mend fences, build houses, and tend to the coffee plantings. Women do the planting and harvesting, often working in cooperative groups with other women of their own and neighboring homesteads. Women milk the cattle and children tend them. If the husband works as an agricultural laborer or artisan or as a servant or policeman in Nairobe, he is seldom home and his wife must do all the work in the gardens. The Nyansongo man is the manager of his wives and their gardens. If he does not have a wage-earner's job, the work he does is seasonal. Most of the time he is an executive. He spends many hours at the chief's camp attending court sessions and he spends time visiting, keeping up with the political developments of the day. He spends many hours with other men of his lineage, drinking beer and gossiping.

Women are excluded from most of these beer parties (LeVine & LeVine 1963:79). In general the social life of a married woman is with other women.

The life of a Rājpūt woman, though very different from that of a Nyansongo woman, has certain characteristics in common with it. She too lives a life which is to a great degree separate from men. Women are in purdah and spend most of their young married life behind the mud walls of the courtyard which they usually share with their mother-in-law and sister-in-law. They are not allowed to wander in town or to work in the fields until their children have married. They may visit over the rooftops and attend religious festivals and occasionally go home to their own villages for prolonged visits, but most time is spent with other women and with the children of the courtyard.

With few exceptions a wife never sleeps or eats with her husband. The men sleep in a separate structure, a sleeping platform, which may be adjacent to the women's courtyard or several blocks away. When a husband visits his wife at night, they repair surreptitiously to a deserted part of the courtyard or to one of the unused rooms. Ideally a man does not visit his wife at night for two or three years after the birth of her child. Boys, when they are considered old enough, anywhere from 6 to 14 years of age, are sent to sleep with the men.

Eating is a private affair and there are no family meals. "When a man has entered the house for his meal, he will quickly retire into a room or behind the wall of his hearth. . . . His meal will usually be served to him by his mother, if she is living, or by an adult sister. Only if some woman of his own family is not present or does not wish to assert her prerogatives will his wife be allowed to serve his meal" (Minturn and Hitchcock 1963:240). A man may request that his food be carried out to him at the sleeping platform or in the fields. Women also eat alone. "Each woman takes her food into her room or into a corner of the courtyard where she can turn her back toward the other women. Children are fed when they demand food and may eat together or separately depending on whether they get hungry at the same time" (ibid. 244).

Almost all leisure activities are spent in the company of one's own sex. Men visit men, sitting and smoking and discussing politics. Women visit each other and occasionally go in groups to religious functions and fairs. Although a married woman has an institutionalized joking relationship with her husband's younger brothers, her most relaxed contact with men is when she returns to her own village and may visit and talk with her brothers and cousins.

Thus, in both the Rājpūt and Nyansongo household, the infant sees his father infrequently. When the father is present he does not interact with the mother or infant as frequently as in the other societies. In contrast to this is the intimacy of the Taira household in Okinawa and the Philippine household in Tarong, where members of a family lie down together in the evening. All ages and both sexes stretch out side by side on their mats closing their doors or shutters to the outside world. Father and mother discuss the events of the day. It would be unbelievable to the members of these societies that a child could grow up without ever hearing his mother and father talk to each other, as has been reported by a Rājpūt who grew up in a village not too different from Khalapur (R. Singh, personal communication). Although the case of this Rājpūt is probably extreme, it indicates the nature of interaction between parents. In Taira and Tarong in families where there are several children, one is sure to share the same mat with his father; often this is the newly weaned and displaced two-year-old. Although the father is more frequently away from home in Juxtlahuaca than in Taira or Tarong, there is a shared intimacy at night when he is home. Although the Orchard Town infant sleeps in his own crib in his own or his parent's room, his parents sleep together in the same room or house and he may visit them in their bed.

In contrast to Nyansongo and Khalapur, in Taira, Tarong, Juxtlahuaca, and Orchard Town there are family meals. Although the women serve the men and older boys first in the Mixtecan households, the father is home and the wife and children may talk to him as he eats.

During leisure time in Tarong, Taira, Juxtlahuaca, and Orchard Town, men and women are together, drinking, chatting, and sharing jokes and pleasantries. Although men and women eat and drink separately at the Mixtecan fiestas, women are present and participate in the festivities.

In these four societies men and women also work together more frequently than in Khalapur and Nyansongo. The Taira husband and wife are a cooperative team in lumbering, and in both Taira and Tarong men and women work together in the rice paddies. The Mixtecan husband and wife may work together less but certainly do so more frequently than Rājpūt or Nyansongo married couples. The Orchard Town sample mothers did not work with their husbands but they sometimes helped them with bookkeeping and typing, and the men joined their wives in cooperative projects in the house and yard.

All the mothers in the six societies were asked the extent to which the father helped care for their children in infancy.[4] The Nyansongo mothers reported the least help from their husbands. Most Nyansongo babies have child nurses who are 5 to 6 years old. Fathers occasionally supervise these nurses when the mother is not home, but they seldom touch the infants. The Rājpūt fathers handle their infant children

[4] See Minturn and Lambert 1964:93-116 for discussion of caretakers.

slightly more. A few of the mothers reported that the father might hold the child while they cooked. Occasionally fathers, uncles, or grandfathers carry a very young child out to the men's sleeping platform and keep it there for a short time.

It is difficult to rank the other four societies by the degree to which the father helps in infant care, but it is clear that in each one he is more involved than in the Nyansongo and Khalapur households. About half the Okinawan mothers reported that their husbands helped. In Orchard Town and Juxtlahuaca the fathers helped in the evening and at night. The fathers in Tarong seem to have helped their wives when they needed help and they were proud of the fact that they could run the household completely during the postpartum period when their wives were confined to bed.

One could argue that a father is not essential as an object of identification and that grandfathers, uncles, and other male figures can take his place. This seems to be substantiated by the recent work of Robert Munroe in British Honduras. In a study of the couvade and cross-sex identity among the Black Carib (Munroe 1964) he found that the important variable seemed to be the presence of a man in the household. The only households in our sample that included adult males other than the father were in Taira, Okinawa, and Khalapur. In Taira, grandparents live with one of their sons, preferably the oldest. In Khalapur there are large patrilocal extended households which share a courtyard and may include as many as eight adult males — if for example two brothers and all their married sons remain together. However, the grandfathers and uncles, like the fathers, do not sleep or spend much time in the courtyard. When the child is older, however, and can leave the courtyard and visit the sleeping platform on his own, the influence of these male relatives may be great.

It is during these later years, when the child can walk securely and can move out into the larger world of the courtyard and the immediate neighborhood of his house, that, according to our theory, conflict in sex identity may occur. The conflict will develop in those male children who move from a world dominated by women and children into a world dominated by men. It will be a problem for those boys who have formed a strong identification with women only if the people in the world make it clear that being a man is very different from being a woman and that men are more important and more powerful. For these boys there is a dramatic change in their evaluation of who controls resources.

In his cross-cultural work on identity conflict J. Whiting (1960b) has found that patrilineage and patrilocal residence are good predictors of sex-identity conflict. This suggests that from a young child's point of view the number of male relatives who live within the area that he can explore in early childhood is important. For both the Rājpūt and the Nyansongo boy these male relatives are numerous. On his father's sleeping platform, the young Rājpūt boy can sit with his father, his paternal uncles, and his paternal grandfather. His older brothers already sleep and work with these men. He can hear them discuss family matters. It is probably here that he learns about the lineage to which he belongs. Any of these men may reprimand or teach him. He must now be aware that he can escape from the courtyard and his mother into the men's world.

The Nyansongo homestead is also patrilocal. A young boy's uncles and grandparents live in separate houses within the area in which he may wander when he is under seven.

On a deeper level the behavior of a mother in a patrilocal environment may differ from that of a mother who has her own relatives near at hand. Rājpūt men marry wives from villages to the north and a woman may not see her own family unless arrangements are made to take her to her home. Nyansongo men traditionally took their wives from clans with whom they engaged in warfare. It would seem that a mother may well have less self-confidence and self-esteem if she is separated from the backing and support of members of her own family (see Minturn and Lambert 1964). In addition, it may well be that a woman's behavior to her children alters when her husband is present and helping her.

It is in Nyansongo and Khalapur, then, that our theory would predict "protest masculinity." For the little boys brought up in the other four societies, the problem of male control in the world of the three-to-six-year-olds is not theoretically relevant, as they have already had a chance to identify with males. They have seen men and women interact in intimate settings since birth. Moreover, even if they have made a strong feminine identification, there will be less conflict later in life since the importance of men and women will be more nearly equal and the contrast between the behavior and personal profiles of the sexes will be less. In Orchard Town, Taira, and Tarong the equality of the sexes seems greatest. In Juxtlahuaca the discrepancy is greater and it may be that the perceived importance of the father in infancy is greater than in the other societies since he always eats before the women and children. The Mixtecan boy may make an earlier and stronger identification with his father. This is also suggested by the analysis of the behavior of three-to-ten-year-old Mixtecan children. There are more significant sex differences between young boys and girls than in any of the other societies (J. Whiting et al. n.d.).

In both Nyansongo and Khalapur there are other cultural factors besides residence rules that must underline the inferiority of women and the importance of men. The Rājpūt three-year-old must notice that the women get down on the floor and cover their heads every time a male enters the courtyard. The hungry young three-year-old in Nyansongo must have looked with longing at the basket of food prepared for his father. He must have learned that his father has a private world in his special room or house. He knows that when he is older he will sleep with his brothers and his father, and will be initiated with other boys in a ceremony from which all women are excluded. He will then join the society of adult men.

It would seem as if there were a never-ending circle. The separation of the sexes leads to a conflict of identity in the boy children, to unconscious fear of being feminine, which leads to "protest masculinity," exaggeration of the difference between men and women, antagonism against and fear of women, male solidarity, and hence to isolation of women and very young children.

In sum, this analysis of the six societies seems to support the sex-identity conflict theory. If one interprets violence as "protest masculinity" then its higher frequency among the Nyansongo and Khalapur is, as the theory would predict, in those societies where the father has lower salience in infancy and where he and other men have higher prestige and salience from childhood on. Nyansongo undoubtedly fits the Bacon, Child, and Barry findings reported earlier; the Khalapur Rājpūt may fit these findings.

One might well ask what relevance this paper has to a conference on primitive law. I would like to suggest four hypotheses derived from the analysis above that may be relevant. (1) I would predict that in those societies whose social structure engenders sex-identity conflict and "protest masculinity" there will be more forms of violence that are considered lawful by the society than in societies that do not engender such conflict. (2) There will be more conflict in the resolution of trouble cases in these societies because it will be considered unmanly to admit guilt and, hence,[5] (3) there will be more formalized legal codes and procedures and more litigation than in societies of equal size and integration that do not engender such conflict; and finally (4) punishment for what the society considers deviant behavior will be more severe in these societies and will be characterized by desire for revenge.

References

Bacon, Margaret K., Irvin L. Child, and Herbert Barry, III. A cross-cultural study of correlates of crime. Journal of Abnormal and Social Psychology 66:291-300, 1963.

[5] See Freda Rebelsky's findings (1963) showing confession to be more prevalent in females than males.

Burton, Roger V. and John W. M. Whiting. The absent father and cross-sex identity. Merrill-Palmer Quarterly 7:85-95, 1961.

Carlsmith, Karolyn Kuckenberg. Effect of early father absence on scholastic aptitude. Ph.D. dissertation, Harvard University, 1963.

———. Effect of early father absence on scholastic aptitude. Harvard Educational Review, 1964.

Cutter, W. Bowman. Household structure, behavior, and personality in Barbados. Senior honors thesis, Harvard College, 1964.

D'Andrade, Roy C. Father-absence and cross-sex identification. Ph.D. dissertation, Harvard University, 1962.

Davis, Allison and John Dollard. Children of bondage. Washington, American Council of Education, 1940.

Fischer, John L. and Ann Fischer. The New Englanders of Orchard Town, U.S.A. In Six Cultures: studies in child rearing, Beatrice B. Whiting, ed., New York, John Wiley and Sons, Inc., 1963.

Glueck, Sheldon and Eleanor Glueck. Unraveling juvenile delinquency. New York, the Commonwealth Fund, 1950.

Healy, William and Augusta F. Bronner. New light on juvenile delinquency and its treatment. New Haven, Yale University Press, 1936.

Hitchcock, John T. The idea of the martial Rājpūt. American Journal of Folklore 71, 281:216-223, 1958.

———. Leadership in a North Indian village: two case studies. In Leadership and political institutions in India, R. I. Park and I. Tinker, eds., Princeton, Princeton University Press, 1959.

LeVine, Robert A. Gusii sex offenses: a study in social control. American Anthropologist 61:965-990, 1959.

———. Witchcraft and co-wife proximity in southwestern Kenya. Ethnology 1:39-45, 1962.

———. Witchcraft and sorcery in a Gusii community. In Witchcraft and sorcery in East Africa, John Middleton and Edward Winter, eds., New York, Frederick A. Praeger, 1963.

LeVine, Robert A. and Barbara B. LeVine. Nyansongo: a Gusii community in Kenya. In Six cultures: studies in child rearing, Beatrice B. Whiting, ed., New York, John Wiley and Sons, Inc., 1963.

Longabaugh, Richard H. W. The description of mother-child interaction. Ph.D. dissertation, Harvard University, 1962.

Maretzki, Thomas W. and Hatsumi Maretzki. Taira: an Okinawa village. In Six cultures: studies in child rearing, Beatrice B. Whiting, ed., New York, John Wiley and Sons, Inc., 1963.

McCord, William, Joan McCord, and Irving K. Zola. Origins of crime. New York, Columbia University Press, 1959.

Miller, Walter D. Lower class culture as a generating milieu of gang delinquency. In The sociology of crime and delinquency, Marvin E. Wolfgang, Leonard Savitz and Norman Johnston, eds., New York, John Wiley and Sons, Inc., 1958.

Minturn, Leigh and John T. Hitchcock. The Rājpūts of Khalapur, India. In Six cultures: studies in child rearing, Beatrice B. Whiting, ed., New York, John Wiley and Sons, Inc., 1963.

Minturn, Leigh and William Lambert. Mothers of six cultures. New York, John Wiley and Sons, Inc., 1964.

Monahan, Thomas P. Family status and delinquency. *In* The sociology of crime and delinquency, Marvin E. Wolfgang, Leonard Savitz and Norman Johnston, eds., New York, John Wiley and Sons, Inc., 1962.

Munroe, Robert L. Couvade practices of the Black Carib: a psychological study. Ph.D. dissertation, Harvard University, 1964.

Nydegger, William F. and Corinne Nydegger. Tarong: an Ilocos barrio in the Philippines. *In* Six cultures: Studies in child rearing, Beatrice B. Whiting, ed., New York, John Wiley and Sons, Inc., 1963.

Pollak, Otto. The criminality of women. Philadelphia, University of Pennsylvania Press, 1950.

Rebelsky, Freda. An inquiry into the meaning of confession. Merrill-Palmer Quarterly 9:287, 1963.

Ridington, Antonia Kern. The relation of household structure to child-rearing practices in St. Christopher, Barbados. Senior honors thesis, Radcliffe College, 1964.

Robins, L. N. and Patricia O'Neal. Mortality, mobility and crime: problem children 30 years later. American Sociological Review 23:162-171, 1958.

Rohrer, John H. and Munro S. Edmonson. The eighth generation. New York, Harper and Brothers, 1960.

Romney, Kimball and Romaine Romney. The Mixtecans of Juxtlahuaca, Mexico. *In* Six cultures, studies in child rearing, Beatrice B. Whiting, ed., New York, John Wiley and Sons, Inc., 1963.

Tappan, Paul W. Delinquent girls in court. New York, Columbia University Press, 1947.

Whiting, Beatrice B., ed. Six cultures: studies in child rearing. New York, John Wiley and Sons, Inc., 1963.

Whiting, John W. M. Resource mediation and learning by identification. *In* Personality development in children, Ira Iscoe and Harold Stevenson, eds., Austin, University of Texas Press, 1960a.

———. Social structure and identification. Paper read at the Mona Bronfen Sheckman Lectures, Tulane University, New Orleans, 1960b.

———. The effects of climate upon certain cultural practices. *In* Cultural anthropology, W. Goodenough, ed., New York, McGraw-Hill, 1964.

Whiting, John W. M., Richard Kluckhohn, and Albert Anthony. The function of male initiation ceremonies at puberty. *In* Readings in social psychology, Eleanor E. Maccoby, Theodore M. Newcomb and Eugene L. Hartley, eds., New York, Henry Holt and Company, Inc. (3rd Edition), 1958.

Whiting, John W. M., *et al.* The learning of values. *In* The Peoples of Rimrock, E. Z. Vogt, ed. Harvard University Press. In press.

Whiting, John W. M., *et al.* Field guide for the study of socialization in five societies. Mimeographed m.s., 1954. To be published by John Wiley and Sons, Inc., New York.

Whiting, John W. M., William Lambert, Richard Longabaugh, Beatrice Whiting, *et al.* The behavior of children: six culture study. In preparation.

Prejudice

More clearly than any other reading in this volume, Pettigrew's analysis of the social sources of racial prejudice proves the distinctness and independent variability of causal factors operating from within the personality, the organization of the society, and its cultural tradition. The relative importance of each type of factor may well vary with respect to different pathologies (cultural tradition is clearly less important in determining the amount of mental illness than in determining the amount of prejudice) and among different societies. The relative importance of the psychological, social, and cultural levels of causation may also vary over time. Policies intended to contain pathologies and reduce their prevalence have to be directed to all three types of pathogenic variables simultaneously. However, if one type of causation is more important than another in respect to a specific pathology in a particular society, social control would be most effective if directed chiefly toward that type. Comparative study of social problems should increase our currently minimal ability to generalize along these lines.

8   THOMAS F. PETTIGREW

*Personality and Sociocultural
Factors in Intergroup Attitudes:
A Cross-National Comparison*

I. INTRODUCTION

Along the continuum of prejudice theories, two extreme positions have been popular. One strongly emphasizes the personality of the bigot and neglects his cultural milieu; the other views intolerance as a mere reflection of cultural norms and neglects individual differences. Recent evidence lends little support to either pole. As further data are gathered

Reprinted by permission of the author and publisher from the *Journal of Conflict Resolution*, Vol. 2 (March 1958), pp. 29-42.

with more refined research tools, it becomes increasingly apparent that the psychological and sociological correlates of prejudice are elaborately intertwined and that both are essential to provide an adequate theoretical framework for this complex phenomenon.

Carrying this viewpoint further, Smith, Bruner, and White (38, pp. 41-44) have delineated three functions that attitudes may serve for an individual. First, there is the *object-appraisal* function; attitudes aid in the process of understanding "reality" as it is defined by the culture. Second, attitudes can play a *social-adjustment* role by contributing to the individual's identification with, or differentiation from, various reference groups. It should be noted that both these functions — object appraisal and social adjustment — are important reflections on the personality level of sociocultural conditions. But the most studied function of attitudes, *externalization*, is somewhat unique. "Externalization occurs when an individual, often responding unconsciously, senses an analogy between a perceived environmental event and some unresolved inner problem . . . [and] adopts an attitude . . . which is a transformed version of his way of dealing with his inner difficulty." Such a process may serve to reduce anxiety. The principal psychological theories of prejudice — frustration-aggression (9), psychoanalytic (20), and authoritarianism (1) — all deal chiefly with this third process.

External expression of inner conflict is relatively more independent of sociocultural factors than are the other functions of attitudes. Indeed, a heuristic distinction between externalized personality variables and sociological variables contributes to our understanding of much that is known about intergroup conflict.

Minard's observations of race relations in the coal-mining county of McDowell, West Virginia, serve as a direct illustration of the point (26). The general pattern in this region consists of white and Negro miners being integrated below the ground and almost completely segregated above the ground. Minard estimates that roughly 60 per cent of the white miners manage to reverse roles almost completely; they can accept Negroes as equals in the mines but cannot accept them as equals elsewhere. Furthermore, he feels that, at one extreme, about 20 per cent accept the black miners as equals in both situations, while, at the other extreme, about 20 per cent never accept them in either situation. In our terms, the behavior of the majority of these whites studied by Minard can be predicted largely by sociocultural expectations, and the behavior of the consistent minorities can be accounted for largely by externalized personality variables.

The research literature abounds with further examples in which a separation of psychological and sociological factors is helpful. The many papers on interracial contact in housing (7, 40), at work (11), and in the army (39) show the marked effects that can be brought about by certain changes in the social situation between races. But personality factors are still operating. Usually these studies report that some individuals hold favorable attitudes toward minorities even before the contact and that other individuals still hold unfavorable attitudes after the contact. Many of these studies also find that the changes brought about by the contact are quite specific and delimited in nature. That is, the intergroup changes occur only under a narrow range of conditions, since the basic personality orientations of the participants have not changed fundamentally. Thus white department-store employees become more accepting of Negroes in the work situation after equal status contact but not in other situations (11). And the attitudes of white army personnel toward the Negro as a fighting man improve after equal status in combat, but their attitudes toward the Negro as a social companion do not change (39).

Desegregation findings furnish further illustrations where the distinction is useful. Social demands for racial desegregation and the irresistible trend of the times are counteracting personality predispositions in many communities. Thus a 1954 public opinion survey in Oklahoma found an overwhelming majority of the residents sternly against desegregation, and yet today mixed schools have become accepted throughout most of the state without incident (17). And in Wilmington, Delaware, two years after successful school integration without apparent public opposition, a poll indicated that only a minority approved of the school desegregation decision of the Supreme Court (17). Indeed, this discrepancy between opinions and demands is a general phenomenon throughout the border states. Hyman and Sheatsley (16) report that only 31 per cent of the white population in those border areas that have already integrated their school systems indorse desegregation.

This conflict between authority-supported cultural changes and personal preferences is underscored by another finding that public opinion polls have uncovered in the South. Several investigators have independently shown that respondents themselves make a distinction between what they individually favor and what they expect to happen in their community. Thus the huge majority of southern whites favor racial segregation, but most of them also feel that desegregation is inevitable (16, 28).

Finally, the work originally done by La Piere (19) in 1934 and more recently replicated in different contexts by Saenger and Gilbert (34) and by Kutner, Wilkins, and Yarrow (18) furnishes further justification for a theoretical separation of social and externalization aspects of intergroup conflict. These investigations illustrate the results of conflicting personality predispositions and actual social situations with minority-group members; frequently the face-to-face conditions override previous practices.

Such work has led several authorities in the field to make the sociocultural and personality differentiation. Psychologist G. W. Allport discusses the two classes of factors separately in his definitive volume, *The Nature of Prejudice* (2), and sociologist Arnold Rose makes a similar distinction in a recent theoretical article on intergroup relations (33).

The present paper is a summary report on research conducted chiefly to gain cross-national perspective on these two sets of prejudice factors. The studies were made in two parts of the world where racial conflict today is highlighted and cultural sanctions of intolerance are intense and explicit: the Union of South Africa and the southern United States. First, a more detailed report of previously unpublished data will be presented on the South African study. Following this, a comparison will be made with the southern United States based on a summary of data presented in detail elsewhere (29).

II. RACIAL PREJUDICE IN THE
UNION OF SOUTH AFRICA

The limited evidence available supports the general belief that white South Africans are unusually prejudiced against Africans (14, 21, 24). This raises the intriguing question as to whether this increased hostility represents (*a*) more externalizing personality potential for prejudice among South Africans, (*b*) the effects of different cultural norms and pressures, or (*c*) both of these.

To provide a tentative answer, a questionnaire study was undertaken of the racial attitudes of students at the English-speaking University of Natal in the Union of South Africa. A non-random sample of 627 undergraduates — approximately one-third of the entire university — completed an anonymous instrument containing three scales and a number of background items.[1] The three scales are a thirteen-item measure of authoritarianism (F scale) whose statements are shown in Table 2, a sixteen-item measure of social conformity (C scale) whose statements are shown in Table 3, and an eighteen-item measure of anti-African attitudes (A scale) whose statements are shown in Table 8.[2] Background

[1] Comparisons between this one-third sample and the total student body of the University of Natal reveal that, in terms of sex, age, and field of concentration, the sample's distributions are quite similar to the student body at large.

[2] All thirteen of the F-scale items are from the original California study on authoritarianism (1, pp. 255-57); the C scale is a new scale composed of both new items and adaptations from the conformity measures of Hoffman (15) and MacCrone (22); and fourteen of the A-scale items are new, while four are adaptations from the E scale (1, items 8, 31, and 34 on p. 105 and item 29 on p. 117).

information includes place of birth, political party preference, father's occupation, and ethnic-group membership.

Taken as a group, these students evidence considerable hostility toward Africans, accepting in large degree the white-supremacy ideology so adamantly propounded by the present government of their country. Thus 72 per cent of the sample agree that "there is something inherently primitive and uncivilized in the native, as shown in his music and extreme aggressiveness"; and 69 per cent agree that "manual labor seems to fit the native mentality better than more skilled and responsible work." And yet their F-scale responses are roughly comparable to those of American student populations.[3] Thus these South Africans are sharply prejudiced against blacks without possessing any greater externalizing personality potential for intolerance than peoples in more tolerant areas.

In addition, authoritarianism correlates with anti-African attitudes at a level comparable to relationships between authoritarianism and prejudice in other parts of the world. Table 1 shows that the A and F scales correlate +0.56 among the Afrikaans-speaking members of the sample and +0.46 among the English-speaking members. Similar scales typically correlate in the fifties in American college samples.[4] The C-scale measure of social conformity — employed for the first time in this investigation — relates to the A-scale scores significantly, too, in both ethnic groups (Table 1).

More detailed analyses of the F and C scales' relationships with anti-African attitudes are provided in Tables 2 and 3. Each of the thirteen authoritarian statements separates the less and more prejudiced halves of the sample in the predicted direction, seven of the differences proving to be significant at better than the 0.001 level of confidence. The sixteen C-scale items predict almost as well; the more anti-African students in every case agree more often than the less prejudiced. Perhaps the con-

────────────

[3] Comparisons across diverse groups with varying forms of the F scale are difficult and tenuous at best. American college samples generally average slightly below the neutral point on F-scale statements, while the present South African sample averages slightly above the neutral point. This small difference can probably be accounted for by (a) the use of a disproportionate number of high-agreement items in the thirteen-item F scale employed with the South African sample and (b) the inclusion in the South African group of fields of concentration not usually included in tested American college groups (e.g., agriculture) whose members tend to score high on the F scale (due probably to social class factors).

[4] Again, comparisons are difficult. Correlations between long-form F scales and ethnocentrism scales (measuring prejudice against a variety of out-groups) have sometimes reached the sixties and even occasionally the seventies in American college samples (1, 2, 5). But correlations of the magnitude found in this study have been consistently reported when — as in this study — a short-form F scale and a prejudice scale against a single out-group are related.

TABLE 1. CORRELATIONS BETWEEN ANTI-AFRICAN SCALE (A) AND
AUTHORITARIANISM (F) AND CONFORMITY (C) SCALES[a]

| Variables | Ethnic Group[b] | |
	Afrikaners	English
N	50	513
A and F	+0.56	+0.46
A and C	+0.42	+0.46

[a] All four of these product-moment correlations are significantly different from zero at better than the 1 per cent level of confidence. The scale scores that were correlated vary between 0 and 10. They were calculated on the basis of +4 for agree strongly, +3 for agree, +2 for omitted response, +1 for disagree and 0 for disagree strongly for each item, and then the total scores were collapsed into the 0-10 categories for machine analysis.

[b] Separate analyses by ethnic group are made necessary by the sharply divergent A-scale means of the two groups (see Table 7).

forming attitude of the bigots is capsuled in the first item of Table 3. While only a third of the tolerant members of the group agree with the statement, over half the prejudiced students feel that "it's better to go along with the crowd than to be a martyr."

These personality relationships suggest (*a*) that personality factors are as important correlates of prejudice in this sample as they are in other, non-South African samples; (*b*) that social conformity (as measured by the C scale) is a particularly crucial personality variable in this sample's attitudes toward Africans; and (*c*) that personality components do not in themselves account for the heightened intolerance of this sample.

We must turn to sociocultural factors to explain the extreme prejudice of these respondents, and the unusual importance of these variables is made clear by the data. For instance, the 560 students who were born on the African continent are significantly more intolerant of Africans than the remaining 65, but they are *not* more authoritarian. Table 4 shows that those not born in Africa are much less likely to fall into the most prejudiced third of the distribution than other sample members. And yet the two groups do not differ significantly in their F-scale scores. More thoroughly influenced throughout their lives by the culture's definition of the white man's situation in Africa, students born on the Dark Continent are more anti-African without the usual personality concomitants of ethnocentrism.

Another such relationship involves students who support the Nationalist party — the pro-*Apartheid* political faction that is presently in power. Table 5 indicates that these respondents score significantly higher on the A scale than their fellow undergraduates, but these two groups do

TABLE 2. Anti-African Prejudice and F-Scale Items

F-Scale Item	Less Preju-diced Half	More Preju-diced Half	$2 \times 2 \chi^2$	p
a) Nowadays when so many different kinds of people move around and mix together so much, a person has to be especially careful not to catch an infection or disease from them	13.6	33.2	33.5	0.001
b) There is hardly anything lower than a person who does not feel a great love and respect for his parents	52.6	70.5	21.2	.001
c) People can be put into two distinct classes: the weak and the strong	23.5	37.8	15.1	.001
d) Most of our social problems would be solved if we could somehow get rid of the immoral, crooked, and feebleminded people	45.4	60.6	14.8	.001
e) The most important thing a child should learn is obedience to his parents	79.8	90.2	13.2	.001
f) Every person should have faith in some supernatural power whose decisions he obeys without question	46.7	60.9	13.0	.001
g) When a person has a problem or worry, it is best for him not to think about it, but to keep busy with more cheerful things	39.4	53.2	11.8	.001
h) Nowadays more and more people are prying into matters that should remain private and personal	63.5	74.5	8.6	.01
i) If people would talk less and work more, everybody would be better off	67.8	78.2	8.3	.01
j) An insult to our honor should always be punished	31.8	40.3	4.7	.05
k) No sane, normal person would ever think of hurting a close friend or relative	67.9	76.6	4.3	.05
l) Science has its place, but there are many important things that can never possibly be understood by the human mind	80.7	85.8	2.9	0.10
m) Some day it will probably be shown that astrology can explain a lot of things	44.4	48.0	0.9	n.s.

Percentage Agreement[a]

[a] The respondent was given four categories: agree strongly, agree, disagree, and disagree strongly. Percentage agreement is calculated by combining the first two of these replies.

TABLE 3. ANTI-AFRICAN PREJUDICE AND C-SCALE ITEMS

C-Scale Item	Less Preju- diced Half	More Preju- diced Half	$2 \times 2 \chi^2$	p
a) It's better to go along with the crowd than to be a martyr	34.8	53.2	21.8	0.001
b) When almost everyone agrees on something, there is little reason to oppose it	16.6	31.1	18.5	.001
c) Adherence to convention produces the best kind of citizen	31.8	46.8	14.9	.001
d) To be successful, a group's members must act and think alike	45.7	60.0	12.5	.001
e) It is important for friends to have similar opinions	28.5	42.2	12.1	.001
f) It is more important to be loyal and conform to our own group than to try to co-operate with other groups	25.6	38.5	11.7	.001
g) We should alter our needs to fit society's demands rather than change society to fit our needs	42.4	55.1	11.4	.001
h) A good group member should agree with the other members	21.2	33.2	11.1	.001
i) It is best not to express your views when in the company of friends who disagree with you	23.8	32.9	6.1	.02
j) Before a person does something, he should try to consider how his friends will react to it	54.6	63.1	4.4	.05
k) To become a success these days, a person has to act in the way that others expect him to act	33.2	41.5	4.2	.05
l) A group cannot expect to maintain its identity unless its members all think and feel in very much the same way	59.3	66.8	3.9	.05
m) It is one's duty to conform to the passing demands of the world and to suppress those personal desires that do not fit these demands	43.7	51.1	3.4	.10
n) A person should adapt his ideas and his behavior to the group that happens to be with him at the time	45.7	52.6	3.1	.10
o) It is extremely uncomfortable to go accidentally to a formal party in street clothes	78.5	83.1	2.0	.20
p) To get along well in a group, you have to follow the lead of others	27.2	31.1	1.1	0.30

[a] Percentage agreement calculated as in Table 2.

TABLE 4. Place of Birth and Anti-African Prejudice[a]

| Anti-African Attitudes[b] | N | Place of Birth | |
		On African Continent	Not on African Continent
		560	65
Least prejudiced	176	28%	29%
Medium prejudiced	246	38%	54%
Most prejudiced	203	34%	17%

[a] 2×3 chi-square $= 9.33$; $p < 0.01$.

[b] The least prejudiced are the students who rated A-scale scores from 0 through 4 by disagreeing with a heavy majority of the items; the medium prejudiced received scores of either 5 or 6 by agreeing with roughly half of the 18 A-scale items; and the most prejudiced obtained scores of 7 through 10 by agreeing with a majority of the statements.

TABLE 5. Political Party Preference and Anti-African Prejudice[a]

| Anti-African Attitudes | N | Political Party Preference[b] | |
		Nationalist Party	Other Parties
		72	483
Least prejudiced	157	8%	35%
Medium prejudiced	210	26%	36%
Most prejudiced	188	66%	29%

[a] 2×3 chi-square $= 38.60$; $p < 0.001$.

[b] Seventy-two of the 627 students did not indicate any political preference.

TABLE 6. Father's Occupational Status and Anti-African Prejudice[a]

| Anti-African Attitudes | N | Father's Occupational Status[b] | |
		Manual	Non-Manual
		146	417
Less prejudiced half	280	34%	55%
More prejudiced half	283	66%	45%

[a] 2×2 chi-square $= 18.90$; $p < 0.001$.

[b] Sixty-four of the 627 students did not indicate their fathers' occupations.

not differ on the F scale. Again a prejudice difference is not accompanied by a personality potential difference. These relationships with political party preference and prejudice hold for each of the major ethnic groups — Afrikaners and English — considered separately.

Two other comparisons yield statistically significant differences in both authoritarianism and anti-African prejudice. Table 6 indicates that those sample members whose fathers are manually employed are significantly more intolerant of the African than those whose fathers are non-manually employed. The two groups differ in the same manner in their F-scale scores. But when authoritarianism is controlled for, the groups still differ significantly in their attitudes toward blacks.[5] In other words, the children of manual fathers are more prejudiced and more authoritarian than other students, and they remain more prejudiced even after the difference in authoritarianism is partialed out of the relationship. These upwardly mobile students must be carefully in step with the mores to establish firmly their rise in the social structure, and the mores of South Africa lead to intolerance.

Table 7 shows the sharp difference between the Afrikaner and English subjects in the sample. Afrikaners are both more anti-African and more authoritarian, and, when the F-scale differences are corrected for, they remain significantly more hostile to the African.[6] These 50 students are directly subject to the national ethos and have no conflicting national reference, as many English-speaking South Africans have in Great Britain. Like the upwardly mobile, they are in roles that demand unusual conformity.

TABLE 7. ETHNIC GROUP AND ANTI-AFRICAN PREJUDICE[a]

| Anti-African Attitudes | N | Ethnic Group[b] | |
		Afrikaners	English
		50	513
Less prejudiced half	264	14%	50%
More prejudiced half	299	86%	50%

[a] 2×2 chi-square $= 23.7$; $p < 0.001$.
[b] Ethnic group is determined by both the student's own ethnic identification and the principal language spoken in his home. Sixty-four of the students identified with other groups (e.g., Jewish, French, German) and are not included in this analysis.

[5] Authoritarianism can be controlled out in two ways. First, separate chi-square analyses of father's employment and anti-African attitudes were made for low and high F-scale halves. Second, the A- and F-scale scores were employed in an analysis of covariance that partialed out F scores. Both analyses indicate that father's employment is a significant correlate of anti-African attitudes even after authoritarianism is controlled out of the relationship.

[6] Authoritarianism was controlled out by both of the analyses described in the previous footnote. With their F-scale differences corrected for, Afrikaners in the sample are still significantly more hostile to the African than the English students. The cultural determination of this ethnic-group difference is made apparent when we survey the attitudes of the English students toward the Indians of South Africa. In sharp contrast to their African attitudes, the English members of the sample are considerably more anti-Indian — one-fifth of them "wish someone would kill all of them."

Table 8 clarifies further the ethnic differences in attitudes toward the African. Sixteen of the A scale's eighteen statements significantly separate the Afrikaners from the English, the former scoring higher in all cases. And, moreover, there is a definite trend in these differences. The five items which discriminate poorest between the ethnic groups (items *n* through *r*) are all stereotyped-belief statements; they refer to the standard traits frequently associated with Africans — lazy, primitive, happy-go-lucky, and bad-smelling. Conversely, five of the six best discriminators (items *b* through *f*) are all exclusion-discrimination statements; they deny equal rights to Africans in employment, housing, and voting. Africans-speaking and English-speaking students, then, do not differ sharply in the degree to which they harbor the traditional stereotype of the African, but they do possess markedly divergent views on discrimination against the African. A key to these differences may be provided in the lone exception to this trend, item *a*. Seven out of every ten Afrikaners, as compared with only a third of the English, believe that the "natives will always have a greater tendency toward crimes of violence than Europeans." Strong projection may be operating for those agreeing with this statement, but, in any event, it suggests that physical fear of the black man is especially prevalent among our Afrikaans-speaking respondents and that this may be the fundamental motivation for their emphasis on excluding and discriminating against the African.

All these findings point to the crucial role of the cultural milieu in shaping the attitudes of the white South African toward the blacks in his midst. While externalizing personality factors do not account for the students' unusually prejudiced attitudes concerning Africans, variables which reflect the dominant norms of the white society prove to be important. Students who are especially responsive to these norms — those who were born in Africa, those who identify with the Nationalist party, those who are upwardly mobile, and those who have been molded by the conservative traditions of the Afrikaans-speaking people — tend to be intolerant of Africans to some degree, regardless of their basic personality structure.

III. RACIAL PREJUDICE IN THE SOUTHERN UNITED STATES

Similar considerations led to an earlier comparative study of anti-Negro prejudice in the southern and northern United States. While considerable evidence indicates that white southerners are typically more intolerant of the Negro than white northerners (16, 27, 30, 35, 36, 39), little work has been focused on the factors underlying this difference. But, like the South African data, the scant data available suggest that sociocultural

TABLE 8. ETHNIC-GROUP DIFFERENCES ON A-SCALE ITEMS

| A-Scale Items | Percentage Agreement[a] | | | |
	Afri-kaners	Eng-lish	$2 \times 2 \ \chi^2$	p
a) Because of their primitive background, natives will always have a greater tendency toward crimes of violence than Europeans	70.0	34.9	33.6	0.001
b) Native musicians are sometimes as good as Europeans at swing music and jazz, but it is a mistake to have mixed native-European bands	86.0	54.2	18.8	.001
c) Most of the natives would become officious, overbearing, and disagreeable if not kept in their place	80.0	48.3	18.2	.001
d) Laws which would force equal employment opportunities for both the natives and Europeans would not be fair to European employers	74.0	44.2	16.2	.001
e) The natives have their rights, but it is best to keep them in their own districts and schools and to prevent too much contact with Europeans	86.0	63.7	9.9	.01
f) The natives do not deserve the right to vote	64.0	41.3	9.5	.01
g) The natives will never have the intelligence and organizing ability to run a modern industrial society	42.0	23.2	8.7	.01
h) As the native will never properly absorb our civilization, the only solution is to let him develop along his own lines	68.0	46.3	8.6	.01
i) Manual labor seems to fit the native mentality better than more skilled and responsible work	88.0	68.9	8.0	.01
j) Seldom, if ever, is a native superior to most Europeans intellectually	72.0	52.2	7.1	.01
k) The natives tend to be overly emotional	66.0	46.5	7.1	.01
l) Because of his immaturity, the South African native is likely to be led into all sorts of mischief and should therefore be strictly controlled in his own best interests	92.0	75.6	6.9	.01
m) The granting of wide educational opportunities to natives is a dangerous thing	36.0	19.9	6.9	.01
n) Most natives are lazy and lack ambition	60.0	44.1	4.6	.05
o) There is something inherently primitive and uncivilized in the native, as shown in his music and extreme aggressiveness	86.0	72.1	4.4	.05
p) Due to the differences in innate endowment, the Bantu race will always be inferior to the white race	54.0	39.6	4.0	.05
q) Most of the natives are happy-go-lucky and irresponsible	70.0	60.0	1.9	0.20
r) In spite of what some claim, the natives do have a different and more pronounced body odor than Europeans	84.0	81.5	0.2	n.s.

[a] Percentage agreement calculated as in Table 2.

and not externalization factors may be the crucial determinants of the contrasting regional attitudes toward the Negro.

Thus, if the South did have more externalizing personality potential for prejudice than other American areas, it should also be more anti-Semitic.[7] But Roper (31, 32) has twice found in his national polls that the South is one of the most tolerant regions toward Jews, and Prothro (30) has noted that 40 per cent of his adult white Louisiana sample is at the same time favorable in its attitudes toward Jews and highly anti-Negro. Furthermore, there is no evidence that the stern family pattern associated with "prejudiced personalities" (1, 12) is more prevalent in the South than in the North (6, 8). And, finally, the few white southern populations that have been given the F scale have obtained means that fall easily within the range of means reported for non-southern populations (1, 25, 37).

Rose categorically concludes: "There is no evidence that 'authoritarian personality' or frustration-aggression or scapegoating, or any known source of 'prejudice' in the psychological sense, is any more prevalent in the South than in the North" (33). And Prothro adds: "Situational, historical and cultural factors appear to be of considerable, perhaps major, import in addition to personality dynamics" in determining anti-Negro attitudes in the South (30).

In testing these ideas in the two regions, different methods were employed than those used in South Africa. Public opinion polling techniques were utilized with 366 randomly selected white adults in eight roughly matched communities in the North and South. The four small southern towns, located in Georgia and North Carolina, were chosen to have Negro population percentages ranging from 10 to 45 per cent, while the small northern towns, all located in New England, have less than 1 per cent Negroes each.

The interview schedule contained a ten-item measure of authoritarianism (F scale), an eight-item measure of anti-Semitism (A-S scale), and a twelve-item measure of anti-Negro prejudice (N scale), together with numerous background questions.[8] The poll purported to be concerned

---

[7] This is true because the prejudiced personality is predisposed to disliking all socially recognized out-groups — Negroes, Jews, Catholics, etc. — and not just one. Being functionally necessary, prejudice generalizes to out-groups of all varieties (1, 2, 13).

[8] There is considerable overlap in items used in the two investigations. Again, all ten of the F items are taken from the work of Adorno *et al.* (1); seven were used in South Africa (Table 2, items *a, b, c, f, h, i,* and *k*); and the others are items 1, 13, and 21 of p. 255 in *The Authoritarian Personality* (1). The A-S items are all from the California investigations, too (1, items 3, 4, 13, 15, 22, and 24 on pp. 68-69 and items 4 and 15 on p. 70). Save for the word substitu-

with the effects of the mass media upon public opinion, and it seems largely due to this guise that the blatantly phrased prejudice statements caused no interview breakoffs.

Of greatest immediate interest is the striking similarity in these results with those of the South African investigation. First, the southern sample is considerably more anti-Negro than the northern sample but is *not* more authoritarian. Similar to the Afrikaner-English differences (Table 8), the southerners respond in the more prejudiced direction on each of the N-scale statements but are most unique in their extreme attitudes concerning excluding and discriminating against the Negro. That is, southerners and Northerners in the samples both share in large degree the lazy, primitive, happy-go-lucky, and bad-smelling stereotype of the Negro, but southerners far more than northerners wish to deny equal rights to the Negro in employment, housing, and voting. And yet there is no difference in the externalization potential for intolerance; the F-scale means of the two samples are almost identical.

Further similarities to the South African data support the contention that personality dynamics, such as authoritarianism, are not responsible for the sharp North-South divergence in attitudes toward the Negro. When age and education are partialed out,[9] the N and F scales correlate to a comparable degree in the two populations. Moreover, with age and education partialed out again, the N and A-S scales relate at equivalent levels in the two regional samples. In other words, the externalizing prejudiced personality as tapped by the F and A-S scales does not account for any more of the anti-Negro variance in the southern sample than it does in the northern sample. This finding, combined with the previously mentioned fact that the two groups do not differ in their F-scale responses, indicates that externalization factors do not explain the heightened bigotry of the southerners. As with the South African results, we must turn to social variables in an effort to account for the regional discrepancy in attitudes toward the Negro.

All six of the sociocultural dimensions tested yield meaningful relationships with Negro prejudice in the southern sample: sex, church attend-

---

tions of "white" for "European" and "Negro" for "native," all twelve N-scale items were used in the South African A scale (Table 8, items *b, c, d, e, f, j, k, m, n, o, q,* and *r*). That virtually the same prejudice and authoritarian statements can be successfully used in the Union of South Africa and in the northern and southern United States suggests that racial prejudice and its personality concomitants take extremely similar forms in many parts of the Western world.

[9] This was not necessary in the South African data because the college sample is relatively homogeneous in terms of age and education. In heterogeneous, randomly drawn adult samples, however, age and education must be controlled, since both authoritarianism and prejudice are positively related to age and negatively related to education (2, 5, 16, 23).

ance, social mobility, political party identification, armed service, and education. These variables reflect southern culture in a manner similar to the social variables tested in the South African study. And as in South Africa, those southerners, who by their roles in the social structure can be anticipated to be conforming to the dictates of the culture, prove to be more prejudiced against Negroes than their counterparts. For example, females, the "carriers of culture," are significantly more anti-Negro than men in the southern sample but *not* in the northern sample.

Two other groups of southerners who manifest conforming behavior in other areas are also more intolerant of Negroes.[10] Respondents who have been to church within the week are significantly more anti-Negro than those who have not been within the month, and there is a tendency (though not statistically significant) for the upwardly mobile to be more anti-Negro than others in the non-manual occupational class. The latter result recalls the finding in the South African study that students whose fathers are manual workers tend to be more anti-African (Table 6). In the northern sample, no such trends appear. Protestant church-goers in the North tend to be more tolerant of the Negro than Protestant non-attenders, and no relationship between upward mobility and attitudes toward Negroes is discernible. Conformity to northern norms — unlike conformity to southern or South African norms — is not associated with hostility for the black man.

In contrast to the conformers, southerners who evidence deviance from the mores in some area of social life tend to be *less* anti-Negro. Non-attenders of church furnish one example. Another example are respondents who explicitly identify themselves as political independents, which also represents a degree of deviance: they tend to be considerably more tolerant of the Negro than are southerners who consider themselves either Democrats or Republicans.[11] Again, no such discrepancy occurs in the northern population.

Downward mobility has been noted by other investigators to be positively related to intolerance in the North (3, 10), and this finding is replicated in the present northern data. But in the southern data a striking reversal occurs. The downwardly mobile in the South are much less anti-

[10] The church attendance, social mobility, political party identification, and armed service findings reported here were all established with matched-pair analyses. This design made it possible to control the age, education, and sex variables out of these relationships. The detailed results are published elsewhere (29).

[11] It might be thought that Republican party membership in the South constitutes deviance, too. Actually, the "solid South" is not that politically solid; three of the four southern communities polled have favored some Republican candidates in recent elections.

Negro than other manually employed respondents, though the two groups do not differ in authoritarianism. Perhaps in a culture that emphasizes status and family background, that makes a sharp distinction between "poor whites" and "respectable whites," and that cherishes its aristocratic traditions (4, 6, 8), the downwardly mobile southerner learns to reject much of his culture. And rejecting the culture's stress on tradition and status makes it easier to reject also the culture's dicta concerning the Negro.

Two groups of southerners — armed service veterans and the highly educated — are potential deviants from southern culture simply because their experience and study have brought them into contact with other ways of life. And, as we might expect, we find that both veterans and college-educated southerners are considerably more tolerant of the Negro than non-veterans and the poorly educated. Veterans in both regions prove to be more authoritarian than non-veterans,[12] and, consistent with this, northern veterans are less tolerant of Negroes than northerners who had not served. Education is negatively related to N-scale scores in the northern sample, too, but significantly less than in the southern sample. Exposure to non-southern culture leads to deviance from the strict southern norms concerning the Negro; little wonder that southerners who have been out of the region for any considerable length of time are generally viewed as suspect by their neighbors upon return.

These consistent relationships with social factors in the southern data have been interpreted in terms of conformity and deviance from the narrowly prescribed mores of small-town southern life. Evidence for such an analysis comes from a final intra-southern difference. Southern communities with high Negro population ratios (38 and 45 per cent) have significantly higher N-scale means than the other communities sampled in the South with low Negro ratios (10 and 18 per cent), though they are *not* different in authoritarianism or anti-Semitism. In southern areas with the most intensely anti-Negro norms, prejudice against the black southerner is greater, even though there is not a greater amount of externalizing personality potential for prejudice.

Though limited by the restricted samples employed, this evidence indicates that socio-cultural factors — as in the South African sample — are indeed the key to the regional difference in attitudes toward the Negro. In spite of the marked contrast in samples and method between the two investigations, both the South African and the southern results underline

---

[12] Presumably this increased authoritarianism of veterans is related to their service experience in authoritarian environments, though Christie (5) failed to note an increase in F scores of army recruits after six weeks of infantry basic training.

the unique importance of social variables in prejudice that is sanctioned by the cultural norms.

IV. SUMMARY AND CONCLUSIONS

Finely interwoven personality and sociocultural variables together form the foundation upon which a broad and satisfactory theory of racial prejudice must be built. Neither set of factors can be neglected, but a heuristic separation between the relatively culture-free externalization factors and social factors aids analysis. The present paper uses this distinction to interpret prejudice data from two parts of the world with tense racial conflict — the Union of South Africa and the southern United States.

Externalization factors such as authoritarianism are associated with prejudice in both the South African and the southern samples at levels roughly comparable with other areas. Data from the South African students hint, however, that susceptibility to conform may be an unusually important psychological component of prejudice in regions where the cultural norms positively sanction intolerance. In addition, there is no indication in either of these samples that there is any more externalizing personality potential for prejudice in these areas than in more tolerant parts of the globe.

The extensive racial prejudice of the South African and southern groups seems directly linked with the antiblack dictates of the two cultures. Sociocultural factors which reflect the mores consistently relate to prejudice — place of birth, political party preference, upward mobility, and ethnic-group membership in the South African data and sex, church attendance, social mobility, political party identification, armed service, and education in the southern data. The pattern is clear: conformity to South African or southern mores is associated with racial intolerance, while deviance from these mores is associated with racial tolerance.

Taken together with other published work, these limited results suggest a broad, cross-national hypothesis:

In areas with historically imbedded traditions of racial intolerance, externalizing personality factors underlying prejudice remain important, but sociocultural factors are unusually crucial and account for the heightened racial hostility.

Should future, more extensive, research support such a hypothesis, its implications for prejudice theory would be considerable. Regions or peoples with heightened prejudice against a particular outgroup would not necessarily be thought of as harboring more authoritarianism; the special conflict may reflect the operation of particular historical, cultural, and social factors. Such a prospect may be encouraging to many action programs — efforts which typically are more successful at changing a person's relation to his culture than they are at changing basic personality structure. Desegregation is a case in point. The success of the movement in the South does not depend — this hypothesis would contend — on changing the deeply ingrained orientations of prejudice-prone personalities; rather, it rests on the effectiveness with which racial integration now going on in the South can restructure the mores to which so many culturally intolerant southerners conform.

A second implication of the hypothesis is that personality factors such as authoritarianism and susceptibility to conform cannot be overlooked in understanding bigotry even in parts of the world like the Union of South Africa and the southern United States. Most psychological approaches to prejudice, it has been noted, are concerned chiefly with the externalization function of attitudes. Perhaps, as the object-appraisal and social-adjustment functions of attitudes are studied in more detail, the direct personality concomitants of cultural pressures will be isolated and better understood.

REFERENCES

1. Adorno, T. W., Frenkel-Brunswik, Else, Levinson, D. J., and Sanford, R. N. *The Authoritarian Personality*. New York: Harper & Bros., 1950.
2. Allport, G. W. *The Nature of Prejudice*. Cambridge, Mass.: Addison-Wesley Press, 1954.
3. Bettelheim, B., and Janowitz, M. *Dynamics of Prejudice*. New York: Harper & Bros., 1950.
4. Cash, W. *The Mind of the South*. New York: Knopf, 1941.
5. Christie, R. "Authoritarianism Re-examined." In R. Christie and M. Jahoda (eds.), *Studies in the Scope and Method of "The Authoritarian Personality,"* pp. 123-96. Glencoe, Ill.: Free Press, 1954.
6. Davis, A., Gardner, B., and Gardner, Mary. *Deep South*. Chicago: University of Chicago Press, 1941.
7. Deutsch, M., and Collins, M. *Interracial Housing*. Minneapolis: University of Minnesota Press, 1951.
8. Dollard, J. *Caste and Class in a Southern Town*. New Haven, Conn.: Yale University Press, 1937.
9. Dollard, J., Doob, L., Miller, N., Mowrer, O., and Sears, R. *Frustration and Aggression*. New Haven, Conn.: Yale University Press, 1939.
10. Greenblum, J., and Pearlin, L. "Vertical Mobility and Prejudice: A Sociopsychological Analysis." In R. Bendix and S. Lipset (eds.), *Class, Status, and Power*, pp. 480-91. Glencoe, Ill.: Free Press, 1953.
11. Harding, J., and Hogrefe, R. "Attitudes of White Department Store Employees toward Negro Co-workers," *Journal of Social Issues*, VIII, No. 1 (1952), 18-28.

12. Harris, D. B., Gough, H. G., and Martin, W. E. "Children's Ethnic Attitudes. II. Relationship to Parental Beliefs concerning Child Training," *Child Development*, XXI (1950), 169-81.

13. Hartley, E. L. *Problems in Prejudice*. New York: Kings Crown Press, 1946.

14. Hellmann, Ellen (ed.), *Handbook on Race Relations in South Africa*. Cape Town, South Africa: Oxford University Press, 1949.

15. Hoffman, M. L. "Some Psychodynamic Factors in Compulsive Conformity," *Journal of Abnormal and Social Psychology*, XLVIII (1953), 383-93.

16. Hyman, H. H., and Sheatsley, P. B. "Attitudes toward Desegregation," *Scientific American*, CXCV (1956), 35-39.

17. Jones, E. "City Limits." In D. Shoemaker (ed.), *With All Deliberate Speed*, pp. 71-87. New York: Harper & Bros., 1957.

18. Kutner, B., Wilkins, Carol, and Yarrow, Penny. "Verbal Attitudes and Overt Behavior Involving Racial Prejudice," *Journal of Abnormal and Social Psychology*, XLVII (1952), 649-52.

19. La Piere, R. T. "Attitudes versus Actions," *Social Forces*, XIII (1934), 230-37.

20. McLean, Helen V. "Psychodynamic Factors in Racial Relations," *Annals of the American Academy of Political and Social Science*, CCXLIV (1946), 159-66.

21. MacCrone, I. D. *Race Attitudes in South Africa*. London: Oxford University Press, 1937.

22. ————. "Ethnocentric Ideology and Ethnocentrism," *Proceedings of the South African Psychological Association*, IV (1953), 21-24.

23. MacKinnon, W. J., and Centers, R. "Authoritarianism and Urban Stratification," *American Journal of Sociology*, XLI (1956), 610-20.

24. Malherbe, E. G. *Race Attitudes and Education*. Johannesburg, South Africa: Institute of Race Relations, 1946.

25. Milton, O. "Presidential Choice and Performance on a Scale of Authoritarianism," *American Psychologist*, VII (1952), 597-98.

26. Minard, R. D. "Race Relations in the Pocahontas Coal Field," *Journal of Social Issues*, VIII, No. 1 (1952), 29-44.

27. Myrdal, G. *An American Dilemma*. New York: Harper & Bros., 1944.

28. Pettigrew, T. F. "Desegregation and Its Chances for Success: Northern and Southern Views," *Social Forces*, XXXV (1957), 339-44.

29. ————. "Regional Differences in Anti-Negro Prejudice" (manuscript presently submitted for publication).

30. Prothro, E. T. "Ethnocentrism and Anti-Negro Attitudes in the Deep South," *Journal of Abnormal and Social Psychology*, XLVII (1952), 105-8.

31. Roper, E. "United States Anti-Semites," *Fortune*, XXXIII (1946), 257-60.

32. ————. "United States Anti-Semites," *Fortune*, XXXVI (1947), 5-10.

33. Rose, A. M. "Intergroup Relations vs. Prejudice: Pertinent Theory for the Study of Social Change," *Social Problems*, IV (1956), 173-76.

34. Saenger, G., and Gilbert, Emily. "Customer Reactions to the Integration of Negro Sales Personnel," *International Journal of Opinion and Attitude Research*, IV (1950), 57-76.

35. Samelson, Babette. "The Patterning of Attitudes and Beliefs Regarding the American Negro: An Analysis of Public Opinion." Unpublished doctoral dissertation, Radcliffe College, 1945.
36. Sims, V. M., and Patrick, J. R. "Attitude towards the Negro of Northern and Southern College Students," *Journal of Social Psychology*, VII (1936), 192-204.
37. Smith, C. U., and Prothro, J. W. "Ethnic Differences in Authoritarian Personality," *Social Forces*, XXXV (1957), 334-38.
38. Smith, M. B., Bruner, J. S., and White, R. W. *Opinions and Personality*. New York: John Wiley & Sons, 1956.
39. Stouffer, S. A., Suchman, E. A., DeVinney, L. C., Star, Shirley A., and Williams, R. M., Jr. *The American Soldier: Adjustment during Army Life*. ("Studies in Social Psychology in World War II," Vol. I.) Princeton: Princeton University Press, 1949.
40. Wilner, D. M., Walkley, R. P., and Cook, S. W. "Residential Proximity and Intergroup Relations in Public Housing Projects," *Journal of Social Issues*, VIII, No. 1 (1952), 45-69.

V

Pathological Institutions

Oppression

*Few social institutions can be regarded as pathological by their
very nature, that is, organized for destruction or the promotion
of self-destructive behavior. Slavery and concentration camps
come as close to being pathological institutions as it seems possible to imagine. In his analysis of the effects of these two types
of pathological institutions on the personality of their victims,
Elkins argues that an extremely oppressive social setting has
essentially the same effect on those who are exposed to it, regardless of differences in their cultural tradition or their personality organization. However, some inmates of concentration
camps — both Nazi and Soviet — were able to resist the de-
humanizing effect of extreme oppression. Both personality and
ideological factors seem to have played a part in maintaining
their capacity for resistance. And there have been revolts of
Negro slaves, even in Virginia. But neither the camps (at least
in Nazi Germany) nor slavery (at least in the American South),
in spite of their predominantly pathological nature, crumbled
from an accumulation of internal strains. Both had to be destroyed by the "secondary pathology" of violence from without.*

The Psychological Effects of Slavery and Concentration Camps

PERSONALITY TYPES AND STEREOTYPES

An examination of American slavery, checked at certain critical points against a very different slave system, that of Latin America, reveals that a major key to many of the contrasts between them was an institutional key: The presence or absence of other powerful institutions in society made an immense difference in the character of slavery itself. In Latin America, the very tension and balance among three kinds of organizational concerns — church, crown, and plantation agriculture — prevented slavery from being carried by the planting class to its ultimate logic. For the slave, in terms of the space thus allowed for the development of men and women as moral beings, the result was an "open system": a system of contacts with free society through which ultimate absorption into that society could and did occur with great frequency. The rights of personality implicit in the ancient traditions of slavery and in the church's most venerable assumptions on the nature of the human soul were thus in a vital sense conserved, whereas to a staggering extent the very opposite was true in North American slavery. The latter system had developed virtually unchecked by institutions having anything like the power of their Latin counterparts; the legal structure which supported it, shaped only by the demands of a staple-raising capitalism, had defined with such nicety the slave's character as chattel that his character as a moral individual was left in the vaguest of legal obscurity. In this sense American slavery operated as a "closed" system — one in which, for the generality of slaves in their nature as men and women, *sub specie aeternitatis*, contacts with free society could occur only on the most narrowly circumscribed of terms. The next question is whether living within such a "closed system" might not have produced noticeable effects upon the slave's very personality.

The name "Sambo" has come to be synonymous with "race stereo-

Reprinted from *Slavery* by Stanley M. Elkins by permission of The University of Chicago Press. © 1959 by The University of Chicago. Abridgment and omission of most documentary footnotes approved by the author and publisher.

177

type." Here is an automatic danger signal, warning that the analytical difficulties of asking questions about slave personality may not be nearly so great as the moral difficulties. The one inhibits the other; the morality of the matter has had a clogging effect on its theoretical development that may not be to the best interests of either. And yet theory on group personality is still in a stage rudimentary enough that this particular body of material — potentially illuminating — ought not to remain morally impounded any longer.

Is it possible to deal with "Sambo" as a type? The characteristics that have been claimed for the type come principally from Southern lore. Sambo, the typical plantation slave, was docile but irresponsible, loyal but lazy, humble but chronically given to lying and stealing; his behavior was full of infantile silliness and his talk inflated with childish exaggeration. His relationship with his master was one of utter dependence and child-like attachment: it was indeed this childlike quality that was the very key to his being. Although the merest hint of Sambo's "manhood" might fill the Southern breast with scorn, the child, "in his place," could be both exasperating and lovable.

Was he real or unreal? What order of existence, what rank of legitimacy, should be accorded him? Is there a "scientific" way to talk about this problem? For most Southerners in 1860 it went without saying not only that Sambo was real — that he was a dominant plantation type — but also that his characteristics were the clear product of racial inheritance. That was one way to deal with Sambo, a way that persisted a good many years after 1860. But in recent times, the discrediting, as unscientific, of racial explanations for any feature of plantation slavery has tended in the case of Sambo to discredit not simply the explanation itself but also the thing it was supposed to explain. Sambo is a mere stereotype — "stereotype" is itself a bad word, insinuating racial inferiority and invidious discrimination. This modern approach to Sambo had a strong counterpart in the way Northern reformers thought about slavery in ante-bellum times: they thought that nothing could actually be said about the Negro's "true" nature because that nature was veiled by the institution of slavery. It could only be revealed by tearing away the veil. In short, no order of reality could be given to assertions about slave character, because those assertions were illegitimately grounded on race, whereas their only basis was a corrupt and "unreal" institution. "To be sure," a recent writer concedes, "there were plenty of opportunists among the Negroes who played the role assigned to them, acted the clown, and curried the favor of their masters in order to win the maximum rewards within the system. . . ."[1] To impeach Sambo's legitimacy in this way is the next thing to talking him out of existence.

[1] Kenneth Stampp, "The Historian and Southern Negro Slavery," *American Historical Review*, LVII (April, 1952), 617.

There ought, however, to be still a third way of dealing with the Sambo picture, some formula for taking it seriously. The picture has far too many circumstantial details, its hues have been stroked in by too many different brushes, for it to be denounced as counterfeit. Too much folk-knowledge, too much plantation literature, too much of the Negro's own lore, have gone into its making to entitle one in good conscience to condemn it as "conspiracy." One searches in vain through the literature of the Latin-American slave systems for the "Sambo" of our tradition — the perpetual child incapable of maturity. How is this to be explained? If Sambo is not a product of race (that "explanation" can be consigned to oblivion) and not simply a product of "slavery" in the abstract (other societies have had slavery), then he must be related to our own peculiar variety of it. And if Sambo is uniquely an American product, then his existence, and the reasons for his character, must be recognized in order to appreciate the very scope of our slave problem and its aftermath. The absoluteness with which such a personality ("real" or "unreal") had been stamped upon the plantation slave does much to make plausible the ante-bellum Southerner's difficulty in imagining that blacks anywhere could be anything but a degraded race — and it goes far to explain his failure to see any sense at all in abolitionism. It even casts light on the peculiar quality of abolitionism itself; it was so all-enveloping a problem in human personality that our abolitionists could literally not afford to recognize it. Virtually without exception, they met this dilemma either by sidetracking it altogether (they explicitly refused to advance plans for solving it, arguing that this would rob their message of its moral force) or by countering it with theories of infinite human perfectibility. The question of personality, therefore, becomes a crucial phase of the entire problem of slavery in the United States, having conceivably something to do with the difference — already alluded to — between an "open" and a "closed" system of slavery.

If it were taken for granted that a special type existed in significant numbers on American plantations, closer connections might be made with a growing literature on personality and character types, the investigation of which has become a wide-spread, respectable, and productive enterprise among our psychologists and social scientists. Realizing that, it might then seem not quite so dangerous to add that the type corresponded in its major outlines to "Sambo."

Let the above, then, be a preface to the argument of the present essay. It will be assumed that there were elements in the very structure of the plantation system — its "closed" character — that could sustain infantilism as a normal feature of behavior. These elements, having less to do with "cruelty" per se than simply with the sanctions of authority, were effective and pervasive enough to require that such infantilism be characterized as something much more basic than mere "accommodation." It will be assumed that the sanctions of the system were in themselves sufficient to produce a recognizable personality type.

It should be understood that to identify a social type in this sense is still to generalize on a fairly crude level — and to insist for a limited purpose on the legitimacy of such generalizing is by no means to deny that, on more refined levels, a great profusion of individual types might have been observed in slave society. Nor need it be claimed that the "Sambo" type, even in the relatively crude sense employed here, was a universal type. It was, however, a plantation type, and a plantation existence embraced well over half the slave population. Two kinds of material will be used in the effort to picture the mechanisms whereby this adjustment to absolute power — an adjustment whose end product included infantile features of behavior — may have been effected. One is drawn from the theoretical knowledge presently available in social psychology, and the other, in the form of an analogy, is derived from some of the data that have come out of the German concentration camps. It is recognized in most theory that social behavior is regulated in some general way by adjustment to symbols of authority — however diversely "authority" may be defined either in theory or in culture itself — and that such adjustment is closely related to the very formation of personality. A corollary would be, of course, that the more diverse those symbols of authority may be, the greater is the permissible variety of adjustment to them — and the wider the margin of individuality, consequently, in the development of the self. The question here has to do with the wideness or narrowness of that margin on the ante-bellum plantation.

The other body of material, involving an experience undergone by several million men and women in the concentration camps of our own time, contains certain items of relevance to the problem here being considered. The experience was analogous to that of slavery and was one in which wide-scale instances of infantilization were observed. The material is sufficiently detailed, and sufficiently documented by men who not only took part in the experience itself but who were versed in the use of psychological theory for analyzing it, that the advantages of drawing upon such data for purposes of analogy seem to outweigh the possible risks.

The introduction of this second body of material must to a certain extent govern the theoretical strategy itself. It has been recognized both implicitly and explicitly that the psychic impact and effects of the concentration-camp experience were not anticipated in existing theory and that consequently such theory would require some major supplementation. It might be added, parenthetically, that almost any published discussion of this modern Inferno, no matter how learned, demonstrates how "theory," operating at such a level of shared human experience, tends to shed much of its technical trappings and to take on an almost literary quality. The experience showed, in any event, that infantile personality features could be induced in a relatively short time among large numbers of adult human beings coming from very diverse backgrounds. The particular strain which was thus placed upon prior theory consisted in the need to make room not only for the cultural and environmental sanctions that sustain personality (which in a sense Freudian theory already had) but also for a virtually unanticipated problem: actual change in the personality of masses of adults. It forced a reappraisal and new appreciation of how completely and effectively prior cultural sanctions for behavior and personality could be detached to make way for new and different sanctions, and of how adjustments could be made by individuals to a species of authority vastly different from any previously known. The revelation for theory was the process of detachment.

These cues, accordingly, will guide the argument on Negro slavery. Several million people were detached with a peculiar effectiveness from a great variety of cultural backgrounds in Africa — a detachment operating with infinitely more effectiveness upon those brought to North America than upon those who came to Latin America. It was achieved partly by the shock experience inherent in the very mode of procurement but more specifically by the type of authority-system to which they were introduced and to which they had to adjust for physical and psychic survival. The new adjustment, to absolute power in a closed system, involved infantilization, and the detachment was so complete that little trace of prior (and thus alternative) cultural sanctions for behavior and personality remained for the descendants of the first generation. For them, adjustment to clear and omnipresent authority could be more or less automatic — as much so, or as little, as it is for anyone whose adjustment to a social system begins at birth and to whom that system represents normality. We do not know how generally a full adjustment was made by the first generation of fresh slaves from Africa. But we do know — from a modern experience — that such an adjustment is possible, not only within the same generation but within two or three years. This proved possible for people in a full state of complex civilization, for men and women who were not black and not savages.

.   .   .

SHOCK AND DETACHMENT

We may suppose that every African who became a slave underwent an experience whose crude psychic impact must have been staggering and whose consequences superseded anything that had ever previously hap-

pened to him. Some effort should therefore be made to picture the series
of shocks which must have accompanied the principal events of that enslavement.

The majority of slaves appear to have been taken in native wars, which
meant that no one — neither persons of high rank nor warriors of
prowess — was guaranteed against capture and enslavement. Great numbers were caught in surprise attacks upon their villages, and since the
tribes acting as middlemen for the trade had come to depend on regular
supplies of captives in order to maintain that function, the distinction
between wars and raiding expeditions tended to be very dim. The first
shock, in an experience destined to endure many months and to leave its
survivors irrevocably changed, was thus the shock of capture. It is an
effort to remember that while enslavement occurred in Africa every day,
to the individual it occurred just once.

The second shock — the long march to the sea — drew out the night-
mare for many weeks. Under the glaring sun, through the steaming
jungle, they were driven along like beasts tied together by their necks; day
after day, eight or more hours at a time, they would stagger barefoot
over thorny underbrush, dried reeds, and stones. Hardship, thirst, brutalities, and near starvation penetrated the experience of each exhausted man
and woman who reached the coast. One traveler tells of seeing hundreds
of bleaching skeletons strewn along one of the slave caravan routes. But
then the man who must interest us is the man who survived — he who
underwent the entire experience, of which this was only the beginning.

The next shock, aside from the fresh physical torments which accompanied it, was the sale to the European slavers. After being crowded
into pens near the trading stations and kept there overnight, sometimes
for days, the slaves were brought out for examination. Those rejected
would be abandoned to starvation; the remaining ones — those who had
been bought — were branded, given numbers inscribed on leaden tags,
and herded on shipboard.

The episode that followed — almost too protracted and stupefying to
be called a mere "shock" — was the dread Middle Passage, brutalizing to
any man, black or white, ever to be involved with it. The holds, packed
with squirming and suffocating humanity, became stinking infernos of
filth and pestilence. Stories of disease, death, and cruelty on the terrible
two-month voyage abound in the testimony which did much toward
ending the British slave trade forever.

The final shock in the process of enslavement came with the Negro's
introduction to the West Indies. Bryan Edwards, describing the arrival of
a slave ship, writes of how in times of labor scarcity crowds of people
would come scrambling aboard, manhandling the slaves and throwing

them into panic. The Jamaica legislature eventually "corrected the enormity" by enacting that the sales be held on shore. Edwards felt a certain mortification at seeing the Negroes exposed naked in public, similar to that felt by the trader Degrandpré at seeing them examined back at the African factories. Yet here they did not seem to care. "They display . . . very few signs of lamentation for their past or of apprehension for their future condition; but . . . commonly express great eagerness to be sold." The "seasoning" process which followed completed the series of steps whereby the African Negro became a slave.

The mortality had been very high. One-third of the numbers first taken, out of a total of perhaps fifteen million, had died on the march and at the trading stations; another third died during the Middle Passage and the seasoning. Since a majority of the African-born slaves who came to the North American plantations did not come directly but were imported through the British West Indies, one may assume that the typical slave underwent an experience something like that just outlined. This was the man — one in three — who had come through it all and lived and was about to enter our "closed system." What would he be like if he survived and adjusted to that?

Actually, a great deal had happened to him already. Much of his past had been annihilated; nearly every prior connection had been severed. Not that he had really "forgotten" all these things — his family and kinship arrangements, his language, the tribal religion, the taboos, the name he had once borne, and so on — but none of it any longer carried much meaning. The old values, the sanctions, the standards, already unreal, could no longer furnish him guides for conduct, for adjusting to the expectations of a complete new life. Where then was he to look for new standards, new cues — who would furnish them now? He could now look to none but his master, the one man to whom the system had committed his entire being: the man upon whose will depended his food, his shelter, his sexual connections, whatever moral instruction he might be offered, whatever "success" was possible within the system, his very security — in short, everything.

The thoroughness with which African Negroes coming to America were detached from prior cultural sanctions should thus be partly explainable by the very shock sequence inherent in the technique of procurement. But it took something more than this to produce "Sambo," and it is possible to overrate — or at least to overgeneralize — this shock sequence in the effort to explain what followed. A comparable experience was also undergone by slaves coming into Latin America, where very little that resembled our "Sambo" tradition would ever develop. We should also remember that, in either case, it was only the first generation that actually experienced these shocks. It could even be argued that the shock sequence is not an absolute necessity for explaining "Sambo" at all.

So whereas the Middle Passage and all that went with it must have been psychologically numbing, and should probably be regarded as a long thrust, at least, toward the end product, it has little meaning considered apart from what came later. It may be assumed that the process of detachment was completed — and, as it were, guaranteed — by the kind of "closed" authority-system into which the slave was introduced and to which he would have to adjust. At any rate, a test of this detachment and its thoroughness is virtually ready-made. Everyone who has looked into the problem of African cultural features surviving among New World Negroes agrees that the contrast between North America and Latin America is immense. In Brazil, survivals from African religion are not only to be encountered everywhere, but such carry-overs are so distinct that they may even be identified with particular tribal groups. "The Negro religions and cults," Arthur Ramos adds, "were not the only form of cultural expression which survived in Brazil. The number of folk-lore survivals is extremely large, the prolongation of social institutions, habits, practices and events from Africa."[2] Fernando Ortiz, writing of Cuba in 1905, saw the African witchcraft cults flourishing on the island as a formidable social problem.[3] One of our own anthropologists, on the other hand, despite much dedicated field work, has been put to great effort to prove that in North American Negro society any African cultural vestiges have survived at all.[4]

ADJUSTMENT TO ABSOLUTE POWER IN THE CONCENTRATION CAMP

A certain amount of the mellowness in Ulrich Phillips' picture of ante-bellum plantation life has of necessity been discredited by recent efforts not only to refocus attention upon the brutalities of the slave system but also to dispose once and for all of Phillips' assumptions about the slave as a racially inferior being. And yet it is important — particularly in view of the analogy about to be presented — to keep in mind that for all the

[2] Arthur Ramos, *The Negro in Brazil* (Washington: Associated Publishers, 1939), p. 94. Ramos devotes two full chapters to "The Cultural Heritage of the Brazilian Negro." Donald Pierson, in his *Negroes in Brazil* (Chicago: University of Chicago Press, 1942), likewise devotes two chapters to African influences in the customs of the Negroes of Bahia.

[3] Fernando Ortiz, *Los Negros Brujos* (Madrid: Libería de F. Fé, 1906). This entire book is devoted to occult African practices in Cuba, including a chapter called "The Future of Witchcraft."

[4] Melville Herskovits, *The Myth of the Negro Past* (New York: Harper, 1941).

system's cruelties there were still clear standards of patriarchal benevolence inherent in its human side, and that such standards were recognized as those of the best Southern families. This aspect, despite the most drastic changes of emphasis, should continue to guarantee for Phillips' view more than just a modicum of legitimacy; the patriarchal quality, whatever measure of benevolence or lack of it one wants to impute to the regime, still holds a major key to its nature as a social system.

Introducing, therefore, certain elements of the German concentration-camp experience involves the risky business of trying to balance two necessities — emphasizing both the vast dissimilarities of the two regimes and the essentially limited purpose for which they are being brought together, and at the same time justifying the use of the analogy in the first place. The point is perhaps best made by insisting on an order of classification. The American plantation was not even in the metaphorical sense a "concentration camp"; nor was it even "like" a concentration camp, to the extent that any standards comparable to those governing the camps might be imputed to any sector of American society, at any time; but it should at least be permissible to turn the thing around — to speak of the concentration camp as a special and highly perverted instance of human slavery. Doing so, moreover, should actually be of some assistance in the strategy, now universally sanctioned, of demonstrating how little the products and consequences of slavery ever had to do with race. The only mass experience that Western people have had within recorded history comparable in any way with Negro slavery was undergone in the nether world of Nazism. The concentration camp was not only a perverted slave system; it was also — what is less obvious but even more to the point — a perverted patriarchy.

The system of the concentration camps was expressly devised in the 1930's by high officials of the German government to function as an instrument of terror. The first groups detained in the camps consisted of prominent enemies of the Nazi regime; later, when these had mostly been eliminated, it was still felt necessary that the system be institutionalized and made into a standing weapon of intimidation — which required a continuing flow of incoming prisoners. The categories of eligible persons were greatly widened to include all real, fancied, or "potential" opposition to the state. They were often selected on capricious and random grounds, and together they formed a cross-section of society which was virtually complete: criminals, workers, businessmen, professional people, middle-class Jews, even members of the aristocracy. The teeming camps thus held all kinds — not only the scum of the underworld but also countless men and women of culture and refinement. During the war a specialized objective was added, that of exterminating the Jewish populations of subject countries, which required special mass-production methods of which the gas chambers and crematories of Auschwitz-Birkenau were outstanding examples. Yet the basic technique was everywhere and at all times the same: the deliberate infliction of various forms of torture upon the incoming prisoners in such a way as to break their resistance and make way for their degradation as individuals. These brutalities were not merely "permitted" or "encouraged"; they were prescribed. Duty in the camps was a mandatory phase in the training of SS guards, and it was here that particular efforts were made to overcome their scruples and to develop in them a capacity for relishing spectacles of pain and anguish.

The concentration camps and everything that took place in them were veiled in the utmost isolation and secrecy. Of course complete secrecy was impossible, and a continuing stream of rumors circulated among the population. At the same time so repellent was the nature of these stories that in their enormity they transcended the experience of nearly everyone who heard them; in self-protection it was somehow necessary to persuade oneself that they could not really be true. The results, therefore, contained elements of the diabolical. The undenied existence of the camps cast a shadow of nameless dread over the entire population; on the other hand the *individual* who actually became a prisoner in one of them was in most cases devastated with fright and utterly demoralized to discover that what was happening to *him* was not less, but rather far more terrible than anything he had imagined. The shock sequence of "procurement," therefore, together with the initial phases of the prisoner's introduction to camp life, is not without significance in assessing some of the psychic effects upon those who survived as long-term inmates.

The arrest was typically made at night, preferably late; this was standing Gestapo policy, designed to heighten the element of shock, terror, and unreality surrounding the arrest. After a day or so in the police jail came the next major shock, that of being transported to the camp itself. "This transportation into the camp, and the 'initiation' into it," writes Bruno Bettelheim (an ex-inmate of Dachau and Buchenwald), "is often the first torture which the prisoner has ever experienced and is, as a rule, physically and psychologically the worst torture to which he will ever be exposed."[5] It involved a planned series of brutalities inflicted by guards making repeated rounds through the train over a twelve- to thirty-six-hour period during which the prisoner was prevented from resting. If transported in cattle cars instead of passenger cars, the prisoners were sealed in, under conditions not dissimilar to those of the Middle Passage.

[5] Bruno Bettelheim, "Individual and Mass Behavior in Extreme Situations," *Journal of Abnormal Psychology*, XXXVIII (October, 1943), 424.

Upon their arrival — if the camp was one in which mass exterminations were carried out — there might be sham ceremonies designed to reassure temporarily the exhausted prisoners, which meant that the fresh terrors in the offing would then strike them with redoubled impact. An SS officer might deliver an address, or a band might be playing popular tunes, and it would be in such a setting that the initial "selection" was made. The newcomers would file past an SS doctor who indicated, with a motion of the forefinger, whether they were to go to the left or to the right. To one side went those considered capable of heavy labor; to the other would go wide categories of "undesirables"; those in the latter group were being condemned to the gas chambers. Those who remained would undergo the formalities of "registration," full of indignities, which culminated in the marking of each prisoner with a number.[6]

There were certain physical and psychological strains of camp life, especially debilitating in the early stages, which should be classed with the introductory shock sequence. There was a state of chronic hunger whose pressures were unusually effective in detaching prior scruples of all kinds; even the sexual instincts no longer functioned in the face of the drive for food. The man who at his pleasure could bestow or withhold food thus wielded, for that reason alone, abnormal power. Another strain at first was the demand for absolute obedience, the slightest deviation from which brought savage punishments. The prisoner had to ask permission — by no means granted as a matter of course — even to defecate. The power of the SS guard, as the prisoner was hourly reminded, was that of life and death over his body. A more exquisite form of pressure lay in the fact that the prisoner had never a moment of solitude: he no longer had a private existence; it was no longer possible, in any imaginable sense, for him to be an "individual."

[6] One aspect of this registration ceremony involved a sham "inspection" of the body, whose effect on the women prisoners in particular was apparently very profound. See Olga Lengyel, *Five Chimneys: The Story of Auschwitz* (Chicago, 1947), p. 19; Ella Lingens-Reiner, *Prisoners of Fear* (London: Victor Gollancz, 1948), p. 26. This may be compared with Degrandpré's description of a similar "inspection" on the African slave coast in the 1780's; see his *Voyage à la côte occidentale d'Afrique, fait dans les années 1786 et 1787* (Paris, 1801), II, 55-56. "Apart from the fact that for every newcomer his transformation into a 'prisoner' meant a degradation," writes an ex-prisoner of Auschwitz and Mauthausen, "there was also the *loss of his name*. That this was no trifling circumstance should be apparent from the great importance which, according to Freud, a man attaches to his name. This is, in Freud's view, sufficiently proven by 'the fact that savages regard a name as an essential part of a man's personality. . . .' Anyhow, whether one agrees with Freud or not, the loss of one's name is not without significance, for the name is a personal attribute. Because he no longer had a name, but had become a number, the prisoner belonged to the huge army of the nameless who peopled the concentration camp." Elie Cohen, *Human Behavior in the Concentration Camp* (New York: Norton, 1953), pp. 145-46.

Another factor having deep disintegrative effects upon the prisoner was the prospect of a limitless future in the camp. In the immediate sense this meant that he could no longer make plans for the future. But there would eventually be a subtler meaning: it made the break with the outside world a *real* break; in time the "real" life would become the life of the camp, the outside world an abstraction. Had it been a limited detention, whose end could be calculated, one's outside relationships — one's roles, one's very "personality" — might temporarily have been laid aside, to be reclaimed more or less intact at the end of the term. Here, however, the prisoner was faced with the apparent impossibility of his old roles or even his old personality ever having any future at all; it became more and more difficult to imagine himself resuming them. It was this that underlay the "egalitarianism" of the camps; old statuses had lost their meaning. A final strain, which must have been particularly acute for the newcomer, was the omnipresent threat of death and the very unpredictable suddenness with which death might strike. Quite aside from the periodic gas-chamber selections, the guards in their sports and caprices were at liberty to kill any prisoner any time.

In the face of all this, one might suppose that the very notion of an "adjustment" would be grotesque. The majority of those who entered the camps never came out again, but our concern here has to be with those who survived — an estimated 700,000 out of nearly eight million. For them, the regime must be considered not as a system of death but as a way of life. These survivors did make an adjustment of some sort to the system; it is they themselves who report it. After the initial shocks, what was the nature of the "normality" that emerged?

A dramatic species of psychic displacement seems to have occurred at the very outset. This experience, described as a kind of "splitting of personality," has been noted by most of the inmates who later wrote of their imprisonment. The very extremity of the initial tortures produced in the prisoner what actually amounted to a sense of detachment; these brutalities went so beyond his own experience that they became somehow incredible — they seemed to be happening no longer to him but almost to someone else. "[The author] has no doubt," writes Bruno Bettelheim, "that he was able to endure the transportation, and all that followed, because right from the beginning he became convinced that these horrible and degrading experiences somehow did not happen to 'him' as a subject, but only to 'him' as an object."[7] This subject-object "split" appears to have served a double function: not only was it an immediate psychic defense mechanism against shock, but it also acted as the first thrust toward a new adjustment. This splitting off of a special "self" — a self

---

[7] Bettelheim, "Individual and Mass Behavior," p. 431. See also Cohen, *Human Behavior*, pp. 116-17, 172.

which endured the tortures but which was not the "real" self — also provided the first glimpse of a new personality which, being not "real," would not need to feel bound by the values which guided the individual in his former life. "The prisoners' feelings," according to Mr. Bettelheim, "could be summed up by the following sentence: 'What I am doing here, or what is happening to me, does not count at all; here everything is permissible as long and insofar as it contributes to helping me survive in the camp.' "[8]

One part of the prisoner's being was thus, under sharp stress, brought to the crude realization that he must thenceforth be governed by an entire new set of standards in order to live. Mrs. Lingens-Reiner puts it bluntly: "Will you survive, or shall I? As soon as one sensed that this was at stake everyone turned egotist."[9] ". . . I think it of primary importance," writes Dr. Cohen, "to take into account that the superego acquired new values in a concentration camp, so much at variance with those which the prisoner bore with him into camp that the latter faded."[10] But then this acquisition of "new values" did not all take place immediately; it was not until some time after the most acute period of stress was over that the new, "unreal" self would become at last the "real" one.

"If you survive the first three months you will survive the next three years." Such was the formula transmitted from the old prisoners to the new ones,[11] and its meaning lay in the fact that the first three months would generally determine a prisoner's capacity for survival and adaptation. "Be inconspicuous": this was the golden rule. The prisoner who called attention to himself, even in such trivial matters as the wearing of glasses, risked doom. Any show of bravado, any heroics, any kind of resistance condemned a man instantly. There were no rewards for martyrdom: not only did the martyr himself suffer, but mass punishments were wreaked upon his fellow inmates. To "be inconspicuous" required a special ·kind of alertness — almost an animal instinct — against the apathy which tended to follow the initial shocks. To give up the struggle for survival was to commit "passive suicide"; a careless mistake meant death. There were those, however, who did come through this phase and who managed an adjustment to the life of the camp. It was the striking contrasts between this group of two- and three-year veterans and the

[8] Bettelheim, "Individual and Mass Behavior," p. 432. "We camp prisoners," writes Mrs. Lingens-Reiner, "had only one yardstick: whatever helped our survival was good, and whatever threatened our survival was bad, and to be avoided." *Prisoners of Fear*, p. 142.

[9] Lingens-Reiner, *Prisoners of Fear*, p. 23.

[10] *Human Behavior*, p. 136.

[11] Bettelheim, "Individual and Mass Behavior," p. 438.

perpetual stream of newcomers which made it possible for men like
Bettelheim and Cohen to speak of the "old prisoner" as a specific type.

The most immediate aspect of the old inmates' behavior which struck
these observers was its *childlike* quality. "The prisoners developed types
of behavior which are characteristic of infancy or early youth. Some of
these behaviors developed slowly, others were immediately imposed on
the prisoners and developed only in intensity as time went on."[12] Such
infantile behavior took innumerable forms. The inmates' sexual impotence brought about a disappearance of sexuality in their talk; instead,
excretory functions occupied them endlessly. They lost many of the
customary inhibitions as to soiling their beds and their persons. Their
humor was shot with silliness and they giggled like children when one of
them would expel wind. Their relationships were highly unstable.
"Prisoners would, like early adolescents, fight one another tooth and nail
. . . only to become close friends within a few minutes."[13] Dishonesty
became chronic. "Now they suddenly appeared to be pathological liars,
to be unable to restrain themselves, to be unable to make objective evaluation, etc."[14] "In hundreds of ways," writes Colaço Belmonte, "the
soldier, and to an even greater extent the prisoner of war, is given to
understand that he is a child. . . . Then dishonesty, mendacity, egotis-
tic actions in order to obtain more food or to get out of scrapes reach
full development, and theft becomes a veritable affliction of camp life."[15]
This was all true, according to Elie Cohen, in the concentration camp
as well.[16] Benedikt Kautsky observed such things in his own behavior:
"I myself can declare that often I saw myself as I used to be in my
school days, when by sly dodges and clever pretexts we avoided being
found out, or could 'organize' something."[17] Bruno Bettelheim remarks
on the extravagance of the stories told by the prisoners to one another.
"They were boastful, telling tales about what they had accomplished in
their former lives, or how they succeeded in cheating foremen or guards,
and how they sabotaged the work. Like children they felt not at all set
back or ashamed when it became known that they had lied about their
prowess."[18]

This development of childlike behavior in the old inmates was the

[12] Bettelheim, "Individual and Mass Behavior," p. 141.
[13] Bettelheim, "Individual and Mass Behavior," p. 445.
[14] *Ibid.*, p. 421.
[15] Quoted in Cohen, *Human Behavior*, p. 176.
[16] *Ibid.*
[17] *Ibid.*, p. 174.
[18] Bettelheim, "Individual and Mass Behavior," pp. 445-46. This same phenomenon is noted by Curt Bondy: "They tell great stories about what they have
been before and what they have performed." "Problems of Internment Camps,"
Journal of Abnormal and Social Psychology, XXXVIII (October, 1943), 453-75.

counterpart of something even more striking that was happening to them: "*Only very few of the prisoners escaped a more or less intensive identification with the SS.*"[19] As Mr. Bettelheim puts it: "A prisoner had reached the final stage of adjustment to the camp situation when he had changed his personality so as to accept as his own the values of the Gestapo."[20] The Bettelheim study furnishes a catalogue of examples. The old prisoners came to share the attitude of the SS toward the "unfit" prisoners; newcomers who behaved badly in the labor groups or who could not withstand the strain became a liability for the others, who were often instrumental in getting rid of them. Many old prisoners actually imitated the SS; they would sew and mend their uniforms in such a way as to make them look more like those of the SS — even though they risked punishment for it. "When asked why they did it, they admitted that they loved to look like . . . the guards." Some took great enjoyment in the fact that during roll call "they really had stood well at attention." There were cases of nonsensical rules, made by the guards, which the older prisoners would continue to observe and try to force on the others long after the SS had forgotten them. Even the most abstract ideals of the SS, such as their intense German nationalism and anti-Semitism, were often absorbed by the old inmates — a phenomenon observed among the politically well-educated and even among the Jews themselves. The final quintessence of all this was seen in the "Kapo" — the prisoner who had been placed in a supervisory position over his fellow inmates. These creatures, many of them professional criminals, not only behaved with slavish servility to the SS, but the way in which they often outdid the SS in sheer brutality became one of the most durable features of the concentration-camp legend.

To all these men, reduced to complete and childish dependence upon their masters, the SS had actually become a father-symbol. "The SS man was all-powerful in the camp, he was the lord and master of the prisoner's life. As a cruel father he could, without fear of punishment, even kill the prisoner and as a gentle father he could scatter largesse and afford the prisoner his protection."[21] The result, admits Dr. Cohen, was that "for all of us the SS was a father image. . . ."[22] The closed system, in short, had become a kind of grotesque patriarchy.

The literature provides us with three remarkable tests of the profundity of the experience which these prisoners had undergone and the thoroughness of the changes which had been brought about in them.

---

[19] Cohen, *Human Behavior*, p. 177. Italics in original.
[20] Bettelheim, "Individual and Mass Behavior," p. 447.
[21] Cohen, *Human Behavior*, pp. 176-77.
[22] *Ibid.*, p. 179.

One is the fact that few cases of real resistance were ever recorded, even among prisoners going to their death.

> With a few altogether insignificant exceptions, the prisoners, no matter in what form they were led to execution, whether singly, in groups, or in masses, never fought back! . . . there were thousands who had by no means relapsed into fatal apathy. Nevertheless, in mass liquidations they went to their death with open eyes, without assaulting the enemy in a final paroxysm, without a sign of fight. Is this not in conflict with human nature, as we know it?[23]

Even upon liberation, when revenge against their tormentors at last became possible, mass uprisings very rarely occurred. "Even when the whole system was overthrown by the Allies," says David Rousset writing of Buchenwald, "nothing happened. . . . The American officer appointed to command of the camp was never called upon to cope with any inclination toward a popular movement. No such disposition existed."[24]

A second test of the system's effectiveness was the relative scarcity of suicides in the camps. Though there were suicides, they tended to occur during the first days of internment, and only one mass suicide is known; it took place among a group of Jews at Mauthausen who leaped into a rock pit three days after their arrival.[25] For the majority of prisoners the simplicity of the urge to survive made suicide, a complex matter of personal initiative and decision, out of the question. Yet they could, when commanded by their masters, go to their death without resistance.

The third test lies in the very absence, among the prisoners, of hatred toward the SS. This is probably the hardest of all to understand. Yet the burning spirit of rebellion which many of their liberators expected to find would have had to be supported by fierce and smoldering emotions; such emotions were not there. "It is remarkable," one observer notes, "how little hatred of their wardens is revealed in their stories."[26] . . .

[23] Eugene Kogon, *The Theory and Practice of Hell* (New York: Farrar, Straus, 1946), p. 284.

[24] David Rousset, *The Other Kingdom* (New York: Reynal and Hitchcock, 1947), p. 137.

[25] Kogon, *Theory and Practice*, pp. 166-67. This occurred during fearful tortures at the quarry, where the Jews knew they were about to be killed anyway.

[26] A. Hottinger, *Hungerkrankheit, Hungerödem, Hungertuberkulose*, p. 32, quoted in Cohen, *Human Behavior*, p. 197. "After the liberation many writers were struck by the callousness of the onetime prisoners, and particularly by their apathy when relating their experiences, even the most horrible." *Ibid.*, p. 144.

War

The apparent association of warfare with social evolution in preliterate societies suggests that, at least in these relatively simple societies, warfare has some "evolutionary value," possibly by activating energy and promoting political consolidations.[1] Warfare seems to lose this evolutionary value in more advanced societies, and in the nuclear age full-fledged wars may well be said to have become totally pathological. Cultural attitudes toward warfare have been affected in modern times by a technological change — increase in the destructive power of armaments. In the following selection Deutsch's analysis of ideological orientations toward warfare suggests that, while ideologies regarding an organized pathology may increase or reduce the chances of its occurrence, there is in complex societies a considerable degree of freedom of choice among such ideologies. Several ideological orientations (traditional as well as novel) co-exist, and relatively rational choices may be made among them by considering their "fit" with the current sociohistorical situation and the likely future effects of a current choice. How one thinks about a form of pathological behavior is itself a major influence on the prevalence and virulence of such behavior.

10 KARL W. DEUTSCH

Changing Images of International Conflict

Political thinkers and philosophers long have held several different images of international conflict. Some of these basic images or themes

Reprinted by permission of The Society for the Psychological Study of Social Issues from the *Journal of Social Issues*, Vol. 23, No. 1 (January 1967), pp. 91-107.

[1] Quincy Wright, *A Study of War* (Chicago: The University of Chicago Press, 1942), Vol. I, pp. 60-74; Raoul Naroll, "Does Military Deterrence Deter?" *Trans-Action*, 3 (January/February, 1966), pp. 19-20.

have persisted for thousands of years, with only surface variations. Others have developed during the last few centuries, and some are still more recent. Today all of them are confronted with the reality of world-spanning transport and communication and with the accelerating development of potentially world-devastating weapons. All of our major images of international conflict, therefore, are now undergoing reappraisal and reexamination.

SEVEN MAJOR IMAGES OF WAR

The Image of Necessity

One of the oldest images of war is the image of necessity. War, like famine, plague, hailstorm or earthquake, is seen as an inexorable act of God or nature, an event that comes and will come again, in response to the will of a deity or to some processes of nature too vast to be concerned with any acts, desires, hopes or fears of human beings.

This image pictures war as a catastrophe in which human attitudes and emotions are irrelevant. Just as no individuals or peoples can stop Shiva's dance of destruction once it has begun to run its course, so no such act could stop the ride of the Four Horsemen in the Book of Revelations. All that remains for human beings to do is to bow down and take what fate befalls them and to adjust their minds and souls to its acceptance. In a slightly varied version of the same image, war is still seen as a catastrophe, but now as one sent as divine punishment for some human transgression of divine law or ritual. If war seems to strike down the seemingly just with the unjust, it may still be a punishment for some hidden sin of the former, or else the justice of the deity may be beyond mere human comprehension. In either case, this image once again demands passive acceptance and adjustment.

Still another version of the same image depicts war as desirable and good, in which believers participate enthusiastically and emotionally, for war and all other catastrophes are gigantic testing devices through which a deity — or nature — selects the best of human beings. In some of its religious versions particularly the old Norse and the Moslem religions, the best are selected for salvation after death in some paradise of warriors. In its secularized version such as Social Darwinism, the selection is for survival on earth, if not for best young men — who are more frequently killed off in wars — then at least for their offspring, their relatives or their nations.

Such images of war as a perpetual necessity and a basically beneficial process have been held by theorists ranging from Heraclitus, to Machiavelli and finally to Adolf Hitler. It was Hitler who described nature as "the cruel queen of all wisdom" and saw the German people inescapably committed to an unending Malthusian chain of future world wars for survival.[1]

Finally, if it should turn out that whole nations might perish in war, an extreme version of this image still could picture war as a selection device to bring out the noblest attitudes; actions and emotions within each individual personality and each social group. Men cannot master fate, says Oswald Spengler (1950, and Hughes, 1952) but they can choose the attitude with which they bear it. In this philosophy, war becomes a selection device for styles of histrionics on the stage of history.

The Augustinian and Thomistic Images of Human Weakness and Limited Just Wars

A second group has an image of war in which war is not a result of the grandeur of God or of nature, but of the weakness of men. For Augustine, as for Thomas Aquinas and for Edmund Burke, man was a weak and limited creature, prone to error and conflict, and burdened with original sin (Augustine, 1948). Where the group, who held to the first image of war, exhorted man to bow down to the divine right of necessity, the second group of thinkers dared, at most, to hope for the limited right of justice. Justice they felt, in so far as men's erring minds could discern it, could turn the secular state from a city of robbers into an orderly city of man and into a fit secular shelter for the city of God on earth, the Church. The Church, Augustine taught, had to help and guide men, both subjects and rulers, to recognize justice and to strive for it, but the reason and conscience of individuals could help them in the same direction. St. Thomas strengthened this stress on reason and by implication stressed the conscience that accepted reason. His doctrine of the single truth asserted that right reason could never lead men astray from truth and from the faith. Even though some matters could not be understood by reason but by faith alone, reason could never contradict faith and, therefore, could be trusted.

[1] For Heraclitus' view of war as "the father of all things," cf. fragment 44, p. 91 in Milton C. Nahm, Ed., *Selections from Early Greek Philosophy*, 34th Edition, New York: Appleton-Century-Crofts, 1947; Werner Jaeger, *Paideia*, New York: Oxford University Press, 1943, Vol. I, p. 182; and Bertrand Russell, *History of Western Philosophy*, New York, Simon and Schuster, 1945, 41-42. For Machiavelli, cf. Leo Strauss, *Thoughts on Machiavelli*. Glencoe, Ill.: Free Press, 1958. See also Niccolo Machiavelli, *The Prince*, Ch. 14, "The Prince's Duty in Military Matters," tr. by Thomas G. Bergin, New York: F. S. Crofts, 1947, 41-43. See also Jacques Maritain, "The End of Machiavellianism," *Review of Politics*, 1942; and "The Concept of Sovereignty," *American Political Science Review*, Vol. 44 (2), June, 1950, 343-357. See also Adolph Hitler, *Mein Kampf*, German edition, Munich: F. Eher, 1939; English translation, edition sponsored by John Chamberlain, Sidney B. Fay *et al.*, New York: Reynal & Hitchcock, 1939, see especially 606-10, 888-91, 935-67.

St. Thomas' doctrine of the single truth logically leads to his doctrine of the just war. Each war had to be judged in reason and conscience, he suggested, by every Christian. If the war appeared just, it was one's duty to support it; but if the war was unjust, it was to be opposed. It was not consistent with Thomistic philosophy, therefore, for Christians to support patriotically and uncritically all wars fought by their governments.[2] "My country, right or wrong," would have sounded to Aquinas more like the battle cry of a pagan tribe or the slogan of a newly risen Antichrist than a fit sentiment for a prelate of the Church.[3]

To expect men to judge discerningly the justice or injustice of a war, or that of the cause of one or the other side in such a war, required precisely the "curiously darting confidence" of Thomas — as G. K. Chesterton has called it — in the limited but real powers of human reason and judgment. More timid or conservative thinkers, such as Edmund Burke, would prefer tò stress the "weak and giddy" nature of most men.[4] They would then suggest that, in their inability to discern truth or justice, the common people of each country should rest content to leave such judgment to their betters in society, to their ruling classes, such as the nobility, and to the secular governments — even if those governments, at war with each other, should summon their subjects to mutual killing. From this Burkean viewpoint, however, the traditional elites or governments would be expected to resort to war only in a limited fashion, with due regard to justice, or at least to prudence and moderation. In all cases, force and war were to be kept in bounds appropriate to the end sought, and that end always remained the continued living together of many imperfect rulers, governments and populations. Within these limits, recurrent wars might seem inevitable, and at least for one side in each war, they might seem legitimate.

[2] For the testimony of an eminent Catholic historian on this point, see Carlton J. H. Hayes, *Nationalism: A Religion*, New York: Macmillan, 1960, 181, 71-72.

[3] The philosophy implicit in these words, from a celebrated toast by Stephen Decatur, was explicitly rejected by John Quincy Adams, who commented: "I disclaim all patriotism incompatible with the principles of eternal justice." (Cited in W. E. Woodward, *A New American History*, New York: Garden City Publishing Co., 1939, 363.) The words themselves, it was reported in 1945, were found by troops of the United States inscribed in German above the main gate of the Nazi concentration camp at Buchenwald. In late 1965, Francis Cardinal Spellman was reported using the words, "right or wrong, my country" as expressing his attitude to the United States military effort in Viet Nam.

[4] G. K. Chesterton, *Orthodoxy*, New York: Dodd Mead, 1924, London-New York: J. Lane, 1918. Edmund Burke, *Reflections on the French Revolution*, London: J. M. Dent, New York: E. P. Dutton, 1955. Cf. also Ross J. S. Hoffmann and Paul Levack, Eds., *Burke's Politics*, New York: Knopf, 1949, see 285. For Burke's emphasis on prudence see xxxi-xxxiv.

The Rationalistic Image of War as Last Resort

Closely related to the image of recurrent wars as the result of human limitation and error is a third group of images in which war is pictured as a last resort, either of governments in their disputes with one another, or of men confronting their rulers. *Ultima ratio regum* — "the last argument of kings" — was engraved on the cannons of a European king. "As a last means, when nothing else will serve," wrote Friedrich Schiller about man's vindication of his inalienable rights "the sword is given him."[5]

These images show the intellectual style of naive rationalism, untroubled by any self-criticism of its own perceptions or judgments. The limited right of justice among fallible men is here replaced by their inalienable rights, or else by the divine right of kings or of nations. In any case, it is replaced by rights that in the last emergency can or must be asserted to their full extent by violence or war. The naive rationalist images focus our attention on the legitimacy or necessity of this assertion, leaving its limits to be defined at most by implication. They do imply, to be sure, that force and war are not legitimate where they are not an unavoidable last resort, and not necessary to vindicate some essential truth or right. But they pay little attention to the possibility that men could err, and that they could be mistaken about the substance of their asserted right or claim, or else about the supposed necessity to resort to force. The government or parties, who claim to have exhausted all peaceful means to press their cause, may be claiming for their side not only more justice but also more infallibility of judgment than may be warranted in fact.

The Optimistic Image of War as Obsolescent

If rationalism sees war as the last resort of reason or justice against otherwise invincible ignorance or the denial of justice, then a more optimistic version of the same outlook may expect that such unenlightened opposition to righteousness and reason will in time diminish and ultimately disappear. This optimism gives rise to a fourth group of images. These are the images of the obsolescence of war and of organized large-scale violent conflict, and of their eventual disappearance from the affairs of men. Here we find the great and familiar visions of Immanuel Kant (1957) and Alfred Lord Tennyson (1938) of a warless world, brought

---

[5] Cf. the poem by Stephen Spender, "Ultima ratio regum," in R. Eberhard & S. Rodman, Eds., *War and the Poet*, New York: Devin-Adair, 1945, 185-86. Spender's poem attacks the philosophy implied in its title. The citation from Friedrich Schiller is from *Wilhelm Tell*, New York: Macmillan, 1898.

about by the growth of human consciousness, education and enlightenment. Here we also find in our own century Sir Norman Angell's (1933)
hope that men will outgrow war as "the great illusion," Norman Cousin's
(1946) hope that nation-bound modern man will perceive himself and
his nation-state as "obsolete," and Stanley Hoffmann's (1965) more
understated but essentially not less optimistic notion of the possible
gradual "atrophy of war" in the last decades of our century.

The Image of Transitory Historical Necessity

A combination of the preceding elements gives rise to the classic Marxist
images of war, from Marx and Engels to Lenin and Mao Tse Tung. In
the thought of these theorists, war among feudal or capitalist regimes
is a historical necessity, due to the relative backwardness and error inherent in these social systems. With economic, social and intellectual
development socialism becomes technologically and politically possible.
It becomes a vital interest of a growing international working class. In
country after country a new kind of struggle, the struggle for the abolition of capitalism and for socialism, is expected to follow. In most countries, according to this classic Marxist theory, this struggle is expected to
be a violent revolution, or a revolutionary war waged in order to establish or spread the new order or to defend it against the expected attacks
of the counter-revolution of the ruling classes. During the same period,
according to some versions of the theory, vast wars will break out among
the capitalist countries, but these wars will offer added opportunities to
the proletariat and to the Marxist parties to transform these wars into
struggles to overthrow some of the capitalist regimes and put communist ones in their place. Such conflicts, civil wars and wars — particularly
those for the establishment of the new Socialist or Communist regimes
— are held to be inevitable at this stage of history, but this age of violence is then to lead to a new socialist era of history in which the main
economic, social and psychological motives for war will disappear. Out
of the age of wars and revolutions will come, according to this view, a
warless world and indeed a world free from all large-scale social conflict
and organized repression. In this image of the world, revolutionary violence now will lead to universal peace and harmony later.

This view may crucially underestimate the destructiveness of modern
weapons, particularly nuclear weapons. It may also underestimate the
complexities of international politics among a plurality of nationally
based Communist regimes. Such a plurality of Communist countries
has existed for nearly two decades, and no war has in fact occurred between any two such countries. It may even be conceded that the Marxist
system of beliefs would make a conflict among Socialist countries unexpected, illegitimate, and on the whole less probable. In recent years,

however, the evidence from the USSR and Communist China has by no means been conclusively against the possibility of a conflict occurring at some time in the future.[6] The divine right of historical necessity, as it can be glimpsed in some version of this Marxist view, seems more likely to encourage militant conflict behavior now than to guarantee a long-run peaceful future. Moreover, by involving such grand prospects of future peaceful rewards for present violence, the Marxist imagery has seriously contributed to the rise of totalitarian or quasi-totalitarian ideologies of "holy wars" and "last battles" in our century.

The Images of Armageddon and
the Manichean Heresy

The images in this sixth group are based on two themes which are combined in varying proportions. One theme is that of a holy war of good against evil. The other theme is that of a last battle of good against evil, in which evil finally and forever will be defeated.

The theme of a holy war is old. It is recurrent in the Old Testament whose views on the wars of the Israelites, fighting with the aid of the Almighty against unbelievers, are, as A. J. Toynbee once put it, "very clear and very savage." The same theme is made general and absolute in the Zoroastrian religion of ancient Persia, which saw a deity of goodness and light, Ahuramazda, locked in everlasting combat with a deity of evil and darkness, Ahriman. Men could only choose their side in this inexorable struggle; but those who believed themselves fighting for the good and for the side of light could then perceive their adversaries as the servants of the forces of darkness and smite them with pitiless enthusiasm.

Much of this imagery recurred in the Manichean heresy of the first centuries of the Christian era. The followers of the teachings of Mani believed that evil was just as substantial, strong and enduring as good and that the world was a perpetual battleground between God and the Devil, who appeared evenly matched. The Manicheans thus saw their adversaries as tools or incarnations of Satan, and so they could struggle against them in an exalted mood of mingled pessimism, self-glorification and

[6] For recent examples of Chinese Communist thinking along these lines, see *Jen-min jih pao* and *Hung-ch'i*, Editorial Department, "Two Different Lines on the Question of War and Peace — Comment on the Open Letter of the Central Committee of the CPSU (5)," translated in *Peking Review*, VI. No. 47 (November 27, 1963), 6-16, reprinted under the title "The Fantasy of a Warless World," Walter C. Clemens, Jr., *Toward a Strategy of Peace*, New York: Rand-McNally, 1965, 76-103. I am indebted to Mr. Clemens for help in completing this reference. Also cf. documents in Clemens, Ed., *op. cit.*, and *World Perspectives on International Politics*, Boston: Little, Brown, 1965. For a broader discussion, see also Marshall D. Shulman, *Beyond the Cold War*, New Haven: Yale Univ. Press, 1966.

self-righteousness. Manicheanism thus was a doctrine of eternal conflict in which men could deify their own side and themselves and at the same time Satanize their opponents. Seeing themselves as instruments of God and their adversaries as tools of Satan, they felt little need to see themselves and their enemies as men, imperfect, fallible, with good and bad traits intermingled and much in need of humility, self-doubt, kindness and compassion.

Just these aspects of man, which Manicheanism slighted, were implicit in the thought of St. Augustine who denied that evil had any substance of a kind comparable to good. A shadow, the Saint reasoned, is nothing more than the absence of light and not a beam of "black light" cast by any "source of darkness." Likewise, a hole is the absence of matter not the presence of any "negative matter." Similarly, as Augustine saw it, evil was nothing more than the absence of good. It was certainly real, as shadows or holes are real, but it had no substance or powers of its own comparable to those of good. In modern terms, Augustine might have compared evil to a deficiency disease, caused by the absence of some needed vitamin or other nutrient, and not by the presence of any poison or hostile organism. This view leads to the Augustinian and Thomist view set forth in an earlier section: of possible just wars within limits, of the likelihood of some evil being intermingled even on the side of goodness or justice, and of the ever-present need for moderation, self-criticism, realism and compassion.

Across the centuries, these alternative intellectual positions have persisted. Despite many and important intellectual differences something of the Augustinian and Thomist tradition lives on in the thought of Albert Camus, Winston Churchill and of such contemporary writers on international conflict as Reinhold Niebuhr, Jacques Maritain, Hans Morgenthau, George Kennan, Kenneth Thompson and Arnold J. Toynbee.[7]

[7] See Albert Camus, *Resistance, Rebellion and Death*, New York: Knopf, 1961, esp. "Pessimism and Courage," 57-60, and "The Unbeliever and Christians," 67-74. Reinhold Niebuhr, *Moral Man and Immoral Society*, New York: Scribner, 1955, and *The Structure of Nations and Empires*, New York: Scribner, 1959. Hans Morgenthau, *Politics Among Nations*, 3rd Edition, New York: Knopf, 1964. George Kennan, *American Diplomacy 1900-1950*, Ch. 6, "Diplomacy in the Modern World," Chicago: Univ. of Chicago Press, 1951, 91-103; Cf. also Kennan, *Totalitarianism in the Modern World* in Carl J. Friedrich, Ed., *Totalitarianism*, Cambridge: Harvard Univ. Press, 1954, New York: Grossett & Dunlop, Universal Library, 1964, 17-31. Kenneth Thompson, *Political Realism and the Crisis of World Politics*, Ch. 4, "The Limits of Principle in International Politics: Necessity and the New Balance of Power," Princeton: Princeton Univ. Press, 1960. Arnold J. Toynbee, *A Study of History*, 12 vols., New York: Oxford Univ. Press, 1935-1961, and especially the excerpts collected in A. J. Toynbee, *War and Civilization*, selected by A. V. Fowler from "A Study of History," Oxford University Press, 1950.

The Manichean view of conflict has flourished more strongly. Islam, it seems, brought to the world from the seventh century onward the concept of the *jehad*, the Holy War against the infidels. From the eleventh century, Western Christendom developed its own form of the *jehad* or Holy War in its Crusades. With the spread of mass armies and mass politics from the age of the French Revolution onward, there also spread the tendency to see one's own side, country or ideology as endowed with quasi-religious sanctity and to ascribe to one's adversaries unrelieved Satanic evil. By the time of the First World War, Satanism had become a standard technique of war propaganda for depicting enemies, and the collective self-worship of one's own side was not far behind (Lasswell, 1965 & Wright, 1965).

In the Second World War, these traits culminated in the quasi-paranoia of Nazism; however, similar though weaker psychological tendencies also appeared on the Allied side. How they contributed there to the gradual acceptance by public opinion of the previously abhorred practice of area bombing of cities and civilian populations, culminating in the dropping of the atom bomb on Hiroshima in 1945, is recounted in Robert Batchelder's book, *The Irreversible Decision* (1962).

During the nineteenth and twentieth centuries, the Manichean view of political conflict also became associated with political ideologies. Liberals and Abolitionists saw themselves as fighters for Light and Goodness against Darkness and Evil. So they were shown in Julia Ward Howe's *Battle Hymn of the Republic*, and in the liberal poems of Ferdinand Freiligrath in 1848. From the last third of the nineteenth century on, the Socialist and Labor movements took up the same themes, with the same unhesitating identification of themselves as the children of light and their opponents as the incarnations or servants of darkness.

In all these political movements a second theme was added, the theme of the "last battle." Julia Ward Howe's *Battle Hymn* took some of its chief symbols from the Book of Revelations.[8] Freiligrath's poem "The Battle at the Birth Tree" is a vision of the final battle of the forces of goodness and the liberal West, including liberal Germany, against the forces of darkness and the — then — conservative East, notably including Russia. The Armageddon symbol recurred in the liberal rhetoric of Theodore Roosevelt and, on a larger scale, of Woodrow Wilson, whose appeal for "a war to end war" combined the symbols of the last battle and of a crusade. From 1878 on, followers of Socialist — and later also Communist — parties in many countries would sing the "International" with its vision "C'est la lutte finale . . ." (". . . and the last fight let

---

[8] "Mine eyes have seen the glory of the coming of the Lord, He is trampling out the vintage where the grapes of wrath are stored. . . ." Cf. *Revelations*, 14: 19-20, 19:15, etc.

us face . . .") and its promise that ". . . et demain l'international sera le genre humain" ("tomorrow the international will be mankind").

The themes of the sacred war and the last fight were then echoed and reechoed in many other songs of the continental European labor movement, and they reached the peak of emotional commitment in the imagery and ideology of the various Communist movements and parties. At the same time they also reached there the peak of potential intolerant self-righteousness and of the rejection of any need for doubt or pity. Pitilessness against "traitors" — which might be no more than ideological or political dissenters or "deviationists" — became a specific theme in some of the leftist songs in the Spanish Civil War, just as it became a strident theme in the bloody purges of the Stalin era. Communist parties and regimes have retained much of this political Manicheanism to this day, and with it they have retained its dangerous link of self-glorification with the devil image of one's adversaries and, perhaps even, of all dissenters. Purges and splits within parties and countries and the tendency toward lasting ideological divisions among the Communist regimes of different countries have been the result, at least in the sense, of the built-in intolerance, fanaticism and self-righteousness of the Manichean imagery shared by many Communists. This has tended to aggravate any disagreements among them, in some cases possibly beyond repair.

Since the end of World War II and the coming of the Cold War, many anti-Communists in the West have adopted much of the Manichean imagery of the Communists, only with inverted value signs. Now it is anti-Communism that is held to represent *ipso facto* the cause of goodness, truth and light and that spreads an aura of sanctity to all its allies, however dictatorial — from Generalissimo Franco to Generalissimo Chiang Kai Shek — their governments may be. And it is Communism, of course, of whatever variety, that is now seen as unrelieved evil and the cause of Hell. Moreover, whoever lags, doubts, falters or dissents in this sacred struggle may well be tainted with evil. Extreme anti-Communists and Communists agree in suspecting treason in every instance of dissent. With this adoption of the Manichean imagery comes, of course, the adoption of its weaknesses: rigidity and self-righteousness of outlook, suspicion of diversity, the incapacity to keep many genuine allies and to maintain for long the unity of any broad coalition. It is worth bearing in mind that the most effective leaders of the West against the challenge of Communism have had little or no use for such Manichean images.

The divine right of ideology is no less dangerous and obsolete today than the divine right of kings. In the age of nuclear weapons, Manichean images of politics might well point the way to mutual suicide for any parties to a major international conflict. Different, more flexible and effective images of conflict are needed. Some images of this kind are now being developed from the viewpoint of communication and control.

The Image of War as Failure of Control

The writers and poets were the first to explore the image of war as a failure of control; however, only the philosophers could begin to sort out its implications and to pursue them to their consequences. G. K. Chesterton used words that could apply to many a dispute between the globe-girdling political ideologies of the 1960's when he spoke of the ideological conflict between certain interpretations of science and religion in his day as "the clash between two very impatient forms of ignorance" (1918). Matthew Arnold saw man in the world "as on a darkling plain . . . where ignorant armies clash by night" (1949).

The image of the blind collision is sometimes combined with a perception of some underlying unity of the clashing forces. Two armies fighting each other, wrote the French writer Henri Barbusse in World War I, "are one great army committing suicide" (Barbusse, 1928).

The conception implicit in such images is that of some interdependent system within which control has failed in regard to some crucial interactions, and violent conflict has arisen as a result of this failure.

The implications of this concept of an interdependent system in which control has failed can be stated more precisely. It requires, first of all, a high degree of interdependence between at least two actors, such that the actions of at least one of them makes a significant difference to the outcomes of some important actions of the other. And, it presupposes, in the second place, a time lag in the actual performance of control, or a lack of ability in one or the other actor, for the level of control required for the continued smooth functioning of the larger system (Deutsch, 1954, 1963).

This failure of control may occur at the level of the subsystem or the actor. A collision will occur if there is a failure of the steering mechanism of a car or of the navigation of a ship. The failure can even occur at the level of the larger system. This would produce an "irrational conflict system out of rational components" such as a frustrating jam made up of cars with purposeful drivers or the great economic depression of 1929. A mathematical and experimental example of classic simplicity for this phenomenon is found in the "Prisoners' Dilemma" game, in which the most rational individual decisions of the two players who make up the system result only in conflict and penalties for both of them. They can avoid this outcome only by coordinating their behavior at the level of the larger system which consists of both of them together. From this viewpoint, Anatol Rapoport's important theoretic and experimental studies of the "Prisoners' Dilemma" can be considered as evidence of the success or failure of the players in achieving joint control and coordination of their actions. Overt conflict between them is the result of their failure to achieve that coordination.

Failure to achieve or maintain adequate control in the larger system then means that at least one actor finds himself confronting at least one specific frustrating partner — now become an adversary — or a more general frustrating environment, now perceived as hostile. Power or force are then likely to be resorted to by the threatened or frustrated actor. Efforts to threaten, to compel or to use outright violence represent his attempts at escape from or damage control in, an intolerable situation in which the injured, frustrated or threatened actor cannot continue without what seems to him even more severe damage to his material or psychic self-system. Where control failed in forestalling the intolerable situation, force and violent conflict may yet serve to resolve it. They may modify the environment and overcome obstacles or opposing actors, until a more tolerable situation has been reached, or they may at least be expected by the actor to accomplish this result. Even if violence should fail to produce any significant change in the environment of the actor, it may reduce some disequilibrium within his own acting system and thus relieve his inner tensions. Psychiatrists are familiar with this function of violence in relieving the inner tensions of individuals in the behavior patterns sometimes called "*Abreaction*" or "cathexis."

The behavior of nation-states in international politics may show some limited similarities to these phenomena. A nation-state often finds itself driven by its own inner structure and processes to seek a certain relation with another state, or with its larger international environment — a relation in which some inner disequilibrium or tension would be lessened. This is called its *goal*. The inner tension or disequilibrium driving the nation-state and its government to seek to attain this goal in the international arena may arise from tension between different interest groups, between different economic reward mechanisms, between contradictory elements in its prevailing political imagery and ideology or from some combinations of all these. If the nation-state cannot control its own internal political processes sufficiently to stop this drive toward a goal situation in foreign policy which this nation-state is unlikely to attain or preserve without violence, and if this nation-state is at the same time unable to control its environment sufficiently to permit the nonviolent attainment of the national foreign policy goal to which it has become committed, then a situation of intense national frustration, mounting domestic political pressures and finally violent international conflict is likely to ensue.

What causes conflicts in such situations, according to this image, is a triple failure of control. First, there is a failure at the level of the international system to maintain a state of affairs in which nation-states can pursue without violent international conflict their probable goals — that is those goals which they are likely to choose and to pursue. Second, there is a failure on the part of at least one of the nation-states within the system to control its environment sufficiently so as to reach its goal without violent conflict. And third, there is a failure on the part of the same nation-state to control its own domestic-political processes and to modify its own foreign policy goals and strategies so that violent international conflict would be avoided.

In this image of war — and generally of prolonged large-scale violent conflict — such a failure of control would lead to several predictions. It predicts that, if other things are equal, the intensity or duration of violence in a conflict will increase the greater the interdependence between the contending parties. Conversely, other things being equal, the probability or intensity of violent conflict between two nations, groups or persons could be reduced by reducing their material or psychic interdependence, that is, the amount and/or importance of the matter-energy transactions, communication flows or memories that connect them.

Another prediction is that violence will become more likely as the tasks, burdens or difficulties of control increase. If other things remain equal, any substantial increase in the speed, complexity, or variability of transactions, or in any other loads upon the limited control capabilities of the participants will increase the chances of some failure of control, and hence the chances of violent conflict. Correspondingly, and again other things being equal, any decline in the steering and control facilities and capabilities of any relevant participant in the system will have the same effect of making war more likely.

According to this image, the crucial relation is that between the tasks or burdens of control, if violence is to be avoided, and the capabilities for such control at any relevant point in the system. If a critical gap between limited control capabilities and varying control tasks is to be avoided, it may seem rational to centralize control capabilities as much as possible at what seems to be the most important point, and to hope that the control burdens will not reach a critical level at any other point. This may be the basis of many of the proposals for political centralization, limited world government, a world police force and the like.[9] Such

[9] For an early example, see Emery Reves, *The Anatomy of Peace*, New York-London: Harper, 1945. For a far more careful and in many ways impressive scheme, see Grenville Clark & Louis Sohn, *World Peace through World Law*, Cambridge: Harvard Univ. Press, 1958.

schemes often beg a decisive question. They assume that controls will not break down at any other crucial point in the international system and particularly not in regard to the policies of any major national state or world region.

A related fallacy is the belief that the maintenance of peace requires a monopoly of force in the hands of a single government or central authority.[10] No such monopoly of force existed for several centuries in the Swiss Confederation, nor for the United States from 1790 to 1860, nor for Scandinavia since 1815. Only a plurality of cantonal forces existed for a long time in Switzerland; only several national forces exist in Scandinavia; and the state militia forces in the United States long remained much stronger than the Federal army. Yet peace was kept in each of these political systems for prolonged periods, and long enough to let the Swiss and the American community each become sufficiently consolidated to withstand later challenges. What counts is not whether control facilities are monopolized or centralized, but whether they are adequate to the burden of coping with the relevant transactions, and thus of avoiding or preventing war (Deutsch, 1957). The ecology of international conflict depends on this balance between burdens and controls, overall and at every critical point in the international system, and in each of the major national actors within it.

THE CHANGING ECOLOGY
OF INTERNATIONAL CONFLICT

During the 20th century, there has been a rising trend in the burden placed upon the control capabilities of national governments and of the international system. About 0.75 per cent of the population of many developing countries has been shifting each year from traditionalism, rural isolation and political apathy into the sector of the socially mobilized population and into its potentially politically relevant strata. By now the politically relevant strata usually includes well above the majority of the population in the highly developed countries, and the developing countries are moving over the next few decades toward similar levels of potential and actual political participation. Between 1900 and 1913, the attitudes and feelings of perhaps 200 million people had to be taken into account in international politics. This was perhaps five or ten times as many as had to be taken into account in 1815 or 1820, but it was only perhaps one-quarter of the politically relevant populations — about 1 billion scattered from Pakistan to Nigeria, Cyprus and China

---

[10] For a recent discussion of this view, and for the evidence of the relevant actual facts of United States history, see Ronald Spector, "Force and Nation-Building," unpublished draft, Yale University, 1966.

— whose mass attitudes and actions have at least a potential effect on world politics and international peace today. The order of magnitude of the tasks of political control may thus have risen by as much as a factor of five in the last half century, and it may still double or treble during the next.[11]

A consideration of the much smaller fractions of the politically active populations — those whom Ithiel Pool once called the "activists" and whom he put in the United States at about 3 per cent of the population — leads to a similar perspective. In 1815 the politically active fraction of the population was perhaps no more than 0.5 per cent of a world population of about 500 million, or a total of perhaps 2.5 million persons — even if distance had not separated many of them effectively from each other. In 1900, perhaps less than 2 per cent of a world population of 1,500 million were politically active, or a total of 30 million — far too many, it seems, to permit the national governments and the almost nonexistent international institutions of the time to prevent the outbreak of World War I. In the world of 1966, perhaps 3 per cent are politically active in some way, out of a world population of over 3,100 million. This is a total of over 90 million political activists, and it indicates a broadening and diversification of the basic political elites of the world. It quite possibly might mean a proportional expansion of the top elites of the world, and this might turn out to be far beyond what our national and international instruments of effective political communication and control can manage.

At the same time, improvement in transport and weaponry have increased the strategic interdependence of the world far beyond its economic, cultural and social interdependence, and still farther beyond the capacities of national states to respond adequately and peaceably to the urgent messages, demands and needs of their neighbors.

Interdependence has been outstripping responsiveness among nations and populations, at least temporarily; and narrowly power-oriented psychological interdependence has outstripped the broader and varied forms of interdependence in economics, society and culture.

At the same time, the rising levels of social mobilization and political participation in many countries have led to steadily rising costs of foreign intervention. Countries are getting harder to govern, even from within, and very much harder to occupy and govern from abroad.

All this produces an increasing sense of a loss or lack of control among

[11] For partial data on relevant rates of change, see K. W. Deutsch, "Social Mobilization and Political Development," *American Political Science Review*, Vol. 55 (3), September 1961, 493-514; and Bruce M. Russett, *et al.*, *World Handbook of Political and Social Indicators*, New Haven: Yale Univ. Press, 1964.

many elite members particularly in the old and formerly well-established elites, and even more so perhaps among some of the new entrants into such elites who now are finding their new positions so much less powerful and secure than they had imagined. Some militant neoconservatives among the first and second generation industrialists and financiers in the South and West of the United States may be examples of this trend; and so may be, in a very different context, some militant members of the new elites of Communist China.

Anxiety, disappointment and frustration often breed resentment and an aggressive mood and cast of mind. It is with such a cast of mind that many elite members — and indeed large sections of the population in some countries — are turning to the old images of conflict, so as to find there some reassuring picture of their own situation and some simple directives upon which to act. Some of them will select images that lead to war. Others are retaining or adopting images that may lead to actions that may promote peace. What contrasts and alignments, what coalitions and what strategies of peace can be expected to develop in such a situation?

IMAGES OF CONFLICT AND
POSSIBLE STRATEGIES OF PEACE

Our age of mass mobilization and mass anxiety has produced attempts at escapism and denial of the threat of war on the part of many individuals in all strata, but it has also produced among several significant and influential minorities an increased acceptance of war-promoting images of international — and sometimes interracial — conflict.

The virtual coalition of war-promoting images has several components. It includes the traditional images of war as necessity, either as an inevitable pseudo-Darwinian or Malthusian process of selection, or else in somewhat rarer versions a fundamentalist imagery of war, as recurrently ordained by God. The holders of such images are joined by dogmatic believers in naive rationalism, who hold that the world needs federal world government, or free private enterprise, or some other institution which they consider reasonable, and who now may think of war as a last resort to impose it on the benighted and unwilling population of some foreign country. A variant of this image is the notion that foreign populations have no will and desires of their own, but will fall, like rows of dominoes, in the direction of the stronger and more determined push. A more inspiring-looking version is supplied by the members of various dogmas that exalt war now as a transitory historical necessity, and who summon their believers to a last battle in a war to end war, or to make the world safe for democracy, or for dogmatic Communism, depending on the details of each particular doctrine. These views then culminate in the quasi-Manichean images of Armageddon and the last battle between Good and Evil — images which may be held or temporarily adopted by many anxious individuals, not so much because they are looking forward to living to see the final victory of the Elect, or the side of Light, but because they derive from their imaginary or real participation in the struggle a sense of their own personal worth, affiliation and identity.

What of the possible coalitions among the holders of potentially peace-promoting images?

This coalition would be even more variegated. In the advanced countries of the West, it would notably include the Augustinian and Thomistic beliefs in the weakness and fallibility of men, who would distrust the claim that any human government was quite wise and righteous enough to take its people and the world on any road of escalation toward total war. To be an Augustinian or Thomistic Christian is to be an anti-escalationist. Believers in other great world religions, stressing both man's worth and his limitations, are likely to oppose escalation and total war for similar reasons.

In the same coalition are likely to be the modern humanists and agnostics, if they are realistic enough to believe that all-out war is obsolescent, and optimistic enough to think that man is not. Side by side with them we may find nondogmatic thinkers from both sides of the Cold War, including Marxists who are willing to believe that something decisive has changed with the coming of nuclear weapons and that all men, of whatever ideology or class, now have added to their old conflicting interests a new common interest in physical and cultural survival.

Finally, this coalition is likely to be joined by many social scientists. Whatever their preferred theoretical approach, and whether they are dealing with the psychology of individuals or groups or with the political behavior of governments or nations, most social scientists feel that man must increase greatly and rapidly his capabilities for understanding, communication, organization, control and self-control if his history is to continue. It is a major task of social scientists to do all they can to contribute to this growth in social, political and human capabilities. It is also their task, as it is the task of all men of good will to resist escalation toward all-out war and to make sure that mankind is given time enough to grow up to the point where he can control his conflicts and his fate.

REFERENCES

Angell, Sir Norman. *The Great Illusion, 1933*. New York: G. P. Putnam, 1933.

Arnold, Matthew. Dover Beach. In Lionel Trilling (Ed.), *The Portable Matthew Arnold*. New York: Viking Press, 1949, 165-7.

Augustine. *The City of God*. In Whitney J. Oates (Ed.), *Basic Writings of St. Augustine*, Vol. II. New York: Random House, 1948.

Barbusse, Henri. *Fire (Le Feu)*. Paris: E. Flammarion, 1917. [English translation: Fitzwater Wray (Tr.). *Under Fire: The Story of a Squad*. New York: E. P. Dutton, 1928.]

Batchelder, Robert. *The Irreversible Decision, 1939-1950*. Boston: Houghton Mifflin, 1962.

Chesterton, G. K. *Orthodoxy*. New York: Dodd Mead, 1924.

Cousins, Norman. *Modern Man Is Obsolete*. New York: Viking, 1946.

Deutsch, Karl W. *Political Community at the International Level*. New York: Doubleday-Random House, 1954.

————. *The Nerves of Government*. New York: Free Press, 1963. [See also David Easton. *A System Analysis of Political Life*. New York: Wiley, 1965; & John W. Burton. *International Relations: A General Theory*. Cambridge, England: Cambridge Univ. Press, 1965.]

Deutsch, Karl W., Burrell, S. A., et al. *Political Community and the North Atlantic Area*. Princeton: Princeton Univ. Press. 1957.

Hoffman, Stanley. *The State of War*. New York: Praeger, 1965.

Hughes, Henry Stuart. *Oswald Spengler: A Critical Estimate*. New York: Scribner, 1952.

Kant, Immanuel. *Perpetual Peace*. Indianapolis: Bobbs-Merrill, 1957.

Lasswell, Harold D. *Propaganda Technique in the World War*. New York: Knopf, 1927.

Spengler, Oswald. *The Decline of the West*. New York: Knopf, 1950.

Tennyson, Alfred Lord. Locksley Hall. *The Poems and Plays of Alfred Lord Tennyson*. New York: Modern Library, 1938.

Wright, Quincy. *A Study of War*, 2nd ed. Chicago: Univ. of Chicago Press, 1965.

Social Change and Social Pathology

Community Disintegration

The dependent variable in Goode's analysis — illegitimate birth — is not, by our definition, itself a pathology but rather a pathogenic condition for the individual affected by it. Illegitimacy contributes to violence, in part through the mother-based family structure which it tends to produce, and diminishes opportunities for acquiring "a sense of personal identity." In addition, it is an index of community disintegration, a condition that has frequently been regarded by sociologists as being responsible for destructive and self-destructive behavior but has rarely been measured in any way other than by citing statistics of destructive or self-destructive behavior presumably caused by it. If the illegitimacy rate is a valid index of community disintegration, it should be correlated with various pathologies. Community disintegration in general and illegitimacy in particular may indeed be among the main sources of the "culture of violence" in some of the regions discussed by Goode and may through this nexus contribute to their political pathologies.

Illegitimacy, Anomie, and Cultural Penetration

Since the family is a prime instrumental agency through which the needs of various institutional needs are met, and legitimacy is the keystone of the family system, an examination of family systems with high illegitimacy rates should yield useful data on the integration of societies. Analysis of high illegitimacy rates indeed suggests that some modifications may be profitably made in several segments of sociological theory: (1) the cultural and social conditions under which high illegitimacy rates occur; (2) the classical theory of the assimilation of both native rural and foreign-born immigrants in the United States; (3) effective procedures for destroying cultural and social systems; and (4) the relation between social and cultural integration.

Illegitimacy rates are, or have been, relatively high in three major areas: Northwestern Europe, industrializing sub-Saharan Africa, and the New World, from Tierra del Fuego to the non-white Southern population of the U.S. To consider these in turn, let us note that Iceland and particular regions in Sweden, Germany, and Austria have had rates of about twenty to thirty per cent in recent years.[1] In special studies of native urbanizing areas in sub-Saharan Africa, rates of forty per cent or more

Reprinted in abridged form by permission of the author and the American Sociological Association from "Illegitimacy, Anomie, and Cultural Penetration" by William J. Goode in the *American Sociological Review*, Vol. 26 (December 1961), pp. 910-925. A number of footnotes with bibliographical references have been omitted.

[1] Iceland's rate was 27.9% in 1950 (Meyer F. Nimkoff, "Illegitimacy," in *Encyclopedia Britannica*, 1954). The Swedish illegitimacy rate has been dropping over the past generation. The highest rates have been found in Stockholm (1841-1860, 43% illegitimate; 1901-1910, 34%; 1921-1925, 28%), but presumably these include many rural mothers. However, the regions of Gävleborgslän and Jamtlands län have continued to be relatively high (23% and 21% in 1921-1925; 17.6% and 18.5% in 1956). In Steiermark in Austria, the rate was 19% in 1956 (*Stat. J. Oesterreichs*, 1956). Oberbayern in Germany had a rate of 18.5% in 1954 (*Stat. J. Für Bayern*, 1955). I have recently found that certain regions of Portugal (Lisboa, Beja, Evora, and Setubal) have rates of 20%-30%, but I have found no special reports on them.

have been reported.[2] In the New World, particular provinces may have rates over eighty per cent, a handful of mainland countries have rates over seventy per cent, and a majority of all the political units have rates over thirty per cent. The non-white populations of the Southern states in the United States had rates of twenty to thirty per cent in 1957.[3]

Why did the New World rates become so high? They cannot be "survivals of native customs," since neither the native Indian groups nor the New World immigrants, whether white or African, had especially high rates of illegitimacy. Moreover, they had many *different* family patterns — patriliny and matriliny, low and high divorce rates, polygyny and monogamy — but the rates are *generally* high.

Another common explanation is that the consensual union, out of which such high rates grow, is part of the "development of a new subculture." That is, the union without benefit of wedlock is the "native," normatively supported equivalent of a legalized union. Consequently, Malinowski's Principle of Legitimacy, according to which every society has a rule condemning illegitimacy, is to be discarded. This explanation is not satisfactory, either. For at least the Caribbean, where this explanation has been widespread, it has been shown that both mother and child have a lower status outside the legal union, that women prefer to be married, and there is general agreement that the ideal family relationship

---

[2] The best surveys of recent changes may be found in *Social Implications of Industrialization and Urbanization South of the Sahara*, Paris, UNESCO, 1956, and *Survey of African Marriage and Family Life*, edited by Arthur Phillips, London: Oxford University, 1953. Twenty-three per cent of all unmarried women in certain Kxatla groups had borne children, 19% among the Ngwato and 17% among the Kwena (I. Schapera, *Migrant Labour and Tribal Life*, New York: Oxford, 1947, p. 173). An analysis of Bantu attitudes toward illegitimacy may be found in I. Schapera, "Pre-marital Pregnancy and Public Opinion," *Africa*, 6 (January, 1933), esp. pp. 83–89. Krige·reported an illegitimacy rate of 59% in three locations in Pretoria (Eileen J. Krige, "Changing Conditions in Marital Relations and· Parental Duties Among Urbanized Natives," *Africa*, 9 [No. 1, 1936], p. 4.) Janisch found that some half of the couples in a Johannesburg native township were "merely living together" (Miriam Janisch, "Some Administrative Aspects of Native Marriage Problems in an Urban Area," *Bantu Studies*, 15 [1941], p. 9.) In Capetown, illegitimacy rates of 26%-41% were reported in the period 1939-1944 (Ruth Levin, "Marriage in Langa Native Location," *Communications From the School of African Studies*, Capetown: University of Capetown, 1947, p. 41). The rate was 30% in Capetown in 1958. For Leopoldville, S. Comhaire-Sylvain reports almost half of the couples in certain native wards were living in concubinage, "Food and Leisure Among the African Youth in Leopoldville," *Communications From the School of African Studies*, N.S., No. 25, December 1950, p. 23. Similar processes of "living together" have been described in the urbanizing area of Kampala (A. W. Southall and P. C. W. Gutkind, *Townsmen in the Making*, East African Studies No. 9, Kampala: East African Institute of Social Research, 1956, pp. 72, 74, 79, 174-8.

[3] Data courtesy of U.S. National Office of Vital Statistics.

is that of marriage. Moreover, a majority eventually do marry in the Caribbean. The Principle of Legitimacy is, then, roughly correct. But we did correct Malinowski's Principle in certain respects and described the bargaining process of consensual courtship outside parental or peer group controls, by which the young girl, unprotected by a kin network, must risk an unstable union and childbirth in order to have a chance at eventually entering a legal union.

That analysis seems to be generally applicable, with only minor and obvious modifications, to the New World south of the Mason-Dixon Line: the consensual union is not the normative equivalent of marriage. Let us now consider the larger structural conditions under which such rates *develop*, to complement our previous analysis of the processes of individual social interaction which *maintain* these rates. From such a view, Northwestern Europe, urbanizing sub-Saharan Africa, and the New World exhibit very different patterns.

NORTHWESTERN EUROPE: A RURAL SUB-CULTURE

The relatively high rates in Northwestern Europe were the product of a courtship system which permitted considerable sex freedom to the young, under indirect but effective adult and peer group supervision. The choice of sex partners and of eventual spouse was restricted to a pool of eligibles, who were children of farmers. When premarital conception or even birth occurred, the young man was likely to be known as the girl's partner, and both were likely to be acceptable to both sets of parents. Illegitimacy was likely to occur mainly when there was some reason for delaying marriage (e.g., unavailability of farm or housing), rather than because either partner or set of parents had rejected the marriage.[4] Childbirth outside of marriage was not approved. Rather, the exact *timing* of the marriage, whether before or slightly after the birth of the first child, was not a focus of intense moral concern.

This pattern was a "native," rural custom, upheld within an integrated social and cultural system of norms which was *not* integrated with those of the dominant national society. Both the national state and Church opposed this pattern for centuries. It is not, then, a recent development, an index of "disorganization" in an urbanizing epoch. It is a subcultural difference, which has gradually been disappearing as isolated rural cultural

---

[4] And consequently, the rate of divorce for such marriages would be lower than for "forced" marriages in the United States. See Harold T. Christensen, "Cultural Relativism and Premarital Sex Norms," *American Sociological Review*, 25 (February, 1960), pp. 31-39. See also Sidney H. Croog, "Aspects of the Cultural Background of Premarital Pregnancy in Denmark, *Social Forces*, 39 (December, 1951), pp. 215-219.

and social systems have become more closely integrated with national cultural and social systems.

CLASSICAL ASSIMILATION THEORY

Studies of United States rural-urban migrants and of immigrant populations in the period 1910-1935 outlined a theory of assimilation and a theory of cultural destruction which fit both these cases of migration but which must be modified to fit the other two great cases of culture contact being analyzed in this paper, Africa and the New World south of the Mason-Dixon Line.

These migrants entered as *individuals* and families, so that their initial social systems were undermined. Thus, their cultural patterns could not be maintained by those social systems and were dissolved by an open-class, individualistic, secular culture which gave substantial rewards to those who assimilated. The in-migrating populations were culturally absorbed by the dominant, numerically larger group. In the transitional period, they also became somewhat anomic: they lost their allegiance to their native cultural patterns but for a while felt no great commitment to the norms of the dominant group. To some extent, in various cities they developed new social subsystems and kept some of their cultural integration by living in ghettos, from which individuals moved out as they became acculturated into the larger society. Younger and older generations were in conflict, since each was oriented to different cultures. Some people lived as "marginal men," being accepted by and accepting neither culture and neither social system fully.

These in-migrants typically entered society in the United States at the bottom of the class structure, where they were somewhat freed from both the older social controls and the controls of the new country. Some customs were difficult to obey under urban conditions and lost their force. Younger people could use either set of norms as a justification for any desired course of action. Generally, the native-born generation became acculturated, and the grandchild generation was *both* socially and culturally integrated in the larger society.

The cultural and social systems of the in-migrating peoples were undermined by these factors: (1) the dispersion of the immigrating social systems, (2) the political power and prestige standards of the receiving populations, which judged the migrants as belonging at the bottom of the class system, (3) the economic and social opportunities in the new system, which gave rewards to those who became acculturated and punished those who refused to do so, (4) the sheer numerical superiority of the receiving populations, and (5) the irrelevance of older customs to the new social situation.

Transitional populations exhibited, of course, relatively high rates of deviation in such areas as juvenile delinquency, adult criminality, desertion, illegitimacy, and so on. Unfortunately, the studies of that time did not make independent measures of "anomie," or "social disorganization," and correlate them with the usual rates of deviation in various areas of action. However, their findings do add corroboration to the modifications of Malinowski's Principle, offered in the paper on the Caribbean: (1) its foundation is not primarily the protection which the male gives the child, but the social importance which a kin or family line enjoys; i.e., it focuses on status placement, and (2) the strength of the norm commitment will vary with the importance of the kin line and thus will be higher toward the upper strata where the proportion of important kin lines is greater and where as a consequence illegitimacy rates will be lower.

AFRICAN ILLEGITIMACY: BREAKDOWN OF THE CULTURAL AND SOCIAL SYSTEMS

Classical assimilation theory was, then, an outline of the processes by which a given "native" system moves from (a) being internally integrated both socially and culturally to (b) being internally non-integrated or anomic *both* socially and culturally and then (c) eventually absorbed. *Individuals* moved from state (a), their original situation in their native region, to (b), losing their position in their native social system, but gaining one in the new United States social system and, for a considerable time, being part of the older cultural system but not part of the new one. Ultimately, of course, they became integrated in the new social and cultural system. That set of phases must be modified somewhat to fit urbanizing or industrializing sub-Saharan Africa and still more to fit the New World. On the other hand, both the suggested modification of Malinowski's Principle and the anonymous "bargaining" pattern of Caribbean courtship may be applied to the African situation.

The African anomie is like the older United States rural and foreign immigration in these respects (a) African individuals have been greatly dispersed in the urban locations, (b) native customs are often irrelevant and inconvenient in urbanizing areas, and (c) white standards and customs have higher prestige. It differs chiefly in these respects: (a) the original dominance of the white group was achieved by force, (b) those being assimilated outnumber the dominant group, (c) the African cultures were much more different from that of the dominant group than were the cultures of the United States in-migrants from that of the United States, and (d) because the Africans face caste barriers, they often cannot obtain substantial rewards for accepting European ways.

Important political consequences flow from these differences — for example, the inevitable creation of independent African nations throughout the continent — but here we shall confine ourselves to the matter of illegitimacy.

The natives in the African urban or industrialized locations have come from tribes in which elders were once powerful, marriages were arranged, and illegitimacy was rare. The skills and knowledge of the elders are not greatly respected in the urban areas, because they are no longer effective. Social control is therefore likely to be reduced to the formal controls of the outside, white society. Although there is some tendency for people from the same tribe to cluster together, as happened in urban ghettos in the United States, such groupings achieve less social control over the individual than do the economic and political imperatives of urban life, and at every turn the native is reminded that both his parental culture and community have no prestige and can be ignored. The kin lines that his family was once at pains to preserve need not be taken seriously. A young man need not worry that a girl's elders or male siblings will bring him to account for a pregnancy outside marriage. A girl need not wait until her sweetheart has saved enough for the bride price; nor is she, unprotected by a kin network, in any position to force him to wait. White governments in Africa, like those in the United States *ante-bellum* South, are little interested in maintaining legitimacy, since by caste definition African legitimacy has no relevance for white legitimacy. By contrast, U.S. white rural or foreign in-migrants could marry native whites so that public agencies were concerned about their legitimacy patterns.

The African couple need not bother with marriage. Indeed, marriage can no longer achieve its former manifest objectives: (1) it cannot maintain a respected lineage for yet another generation, since the kin line itself has lost its importance and because in an urban agglomeration the young man and woman may well be from different tribes, (2) it does not integrate a tribe by joining two lineages within it, since the tribe itself is disappearing and the tie may not be known to either lineage, and (3) it does not give a fully respected adult status to the young male, since under the Western caste pattern his rank will remain a lowly one, and whatever rank he does achieve will be based on his occupation and not his tribal position or the marriages he enters. Since, finally, both kin and elders have lost the authority on which social control once rested, both the young man and woman can and must make whatever individual role bargain with one another their circumstances permit.

In short, the political and economic dominance of the new urban world has begun to undermine that self-evident rightness of older family values which once guaranteed a legitimate position for the newborn child. The younger urban African generation has begun to feel a less intense commitment to those values, has acquired some opposing values, and in any event does not possess the means with which to achieve the older goals.

The anomie of native African urban life in some centers surpasses anything observed in United States immigrant life, because the original culture of the African was more different from the Western culture, to which he must adjust, and his present deprivation is greater than that of the United States immigrant. The latter was already part of Western Culture, so that the cultural destruction he experienced was minor by comparison. The native is at the bottom of a caste system and is no longer part of an integrated social group or cultural system which would permit him to assert his own worth or the worth of the family. Thus, the stigma of illegitimacy becomes minor.

In the urbanizing African areas, the native patterns are neither (1) socially or culturally integrated internally nor are they (2) integrated socially or culturally with the dominant societies. In this transitional period, when the social importance of kin lines has become minimal, illegitimacy is high because of casual liaisons, promiscuity, and delayed marriage. On the other hand, the consensual union has perhaps not become the *usual* pattern of marital unions. The numerical preponderance of the native population has prevented its being absorbed into white cultural patterns, but modern industrial and economic expansion has prevented the whites from "keeping them in their place," either in the tribes or in the stratification system. As a consequence, the phases of destruction have proceeded rapidly, and perhaps re-integration will occur more swiftly than in the New World.

THE NEW WORLD

The conquest of the New World seems at first to exhibit a very different pattern. First, no case of cultural penetration on so huge a scale can be found since Rome, unless the Islamic conquest be excepted. From Alaska to Tierra del Fuego, aside from a few tribal pockets, the hemisphere is Western in culture. The native cultural systems have been penetrated, undermined, and destroyed, though of course some elements of the older cultures do survive.

Next, two different forms of destruction may be distinguished. One of these, shared by the Southern United States and the Caribbean, was primarily a physical destruction and overwhelming of the native population, together with the substitution of alien slaves, who were so mixed geographically that their social systems were destroyed, and thus they could not maintain their African cultural heritage. These slaves, emancipated for the most part late in the nineteenth century, became Western in culture. Their descendants generally occupy the bottom social strata in the countries in which they were introduced, but in a few countries some occupy higher strata as well.

The second major pattern of destruction, socially more complex, was found on the Latin American mainland, from Mexico southwards. The main attacks were first concentrated on the three great population centers, the Aztec, Mayan, and Inca civilizations. Intent on political conquest and economic exploitation, the Iberians nearly undermined their own aims in the Conquest period by wiping out from one third to one half of their subjects, through disease, overwork, and underfeeding. At first, they ruled in part through native leaders, but by 1600 they had also removed this top stratum from power. Although the church often opposed those actions, its own efforts at destroying native religions were backed by political leaders, so that even when the Church attempted to save native bodies, it persisted successfully in its goal of undermining native cults and substituting some form of Catholicism. The Iberians, like the whites in Africa, were greatly outnumbered by native Indians until relatively late in the Colonial period, but within a hundred years after the first conquests most of the cultural destruction had already taken place.[5] The Iberians imposed their cultural patterns on the natives, unlike the Manchus in China, the Spanish in the Philippines, the Dutch in Indonesia, or the English in India.

Both the assimilation and destruction processes differed somewhat from those in Africa. The U.S. and the Caribbean masters dispersed the (forced, slave) immigrants, but the whites outnumbered them in the United States and did not in the Caribbean. On the mainland, the Indians outnumbered the Iberians, but their social systems were in part undermined by death and partly by forced dispersion and relocation in villages. There was no industrial expansion, and little economic expansion, so that there was little need (in contrast to modern Africa) to use the natives in higher level jobs. Native African customs are essentially irrelevant to the problems faced in urban and industrial situations, but since in the New World the natives or slaves were used primarily in an agricultural setting, their customs might have been maintained had the whites not opposed them. In all these cases, the rule of the whites was based to a considerable degree on face-to-face interaction rather than indirect rule.

The destruction pattern in these major cases is summarized [Table 1].

Before analyzing the consequences of these different patterns, let us comment further on the situation of the mainland natives. Although the Iberian rulers attempted to hold the Indians in economic and therefore political subjection and thus sought to keep a rigid caste line between the two groups, the emergence of two new classes in the stratification system

---

[5] See the estimates of the proportion of destruction by certain dates, in Sol Tax, *et al.*, *Heritage of Conquest*, Glencoe, Ill.: The Free Press, 1952, p. 264. Most of these groups are among the less acculturated peoples in the New World.

TABLE 1. COMPARISON OF CULTURAL AND SOCIAL DESTRUCTION AND ASSIMILATION PATTERNS: MODERN U.S. CITIES, MODERN INDUSTRIALIZING SUB-SAHARAN AFRICA, AND THE PAST NEW WORLD

Patterns	Immigration to U.S. Cities, Rural or Foreign	Africa, Modern	New World: Pre-1900		
			Ante-Bellum U.S. South	Caribbean	Mainland Iberian Countries
1. Physical Destruction of Acculturating Population	No	Some	Little or none	Some	Considerable at first
2. Dispersal of Social Groupings	Yes	Yes	Yes	Yes	Yes
3. Numerical Preponderance of Population Being Acculturated	No	Yes	No	Yes	Yes
4. Prestige Dominance of Absorbing Population	Yes	Yes	Yes	Yes	Yes
5. Caste System	No	Yes	Yes	Yes	Yes
6. Industrial Expansion	Yes	Yes	Yes	No	No
7. Economic Expansion	Yes	Yes	Yes	No	No
8. Relevance of Native Customs to New Situation	No	No	Yes	Yes	Yes
9. Situation of Culture Contact	Urban	Urban	Rural	Rural	Village and Urban

had considerable effect on the subsequent development of the family system. One new class, eventually to become the top stratum, was the Creoles, those born in the New World as legitimate offspring of Iberian families. As in the colonial United States, these rulers gradually loosened their ties with the Old World and led the revolutions which, in one country after another, freed all these possessions, except Puerto Rico and Cuba, from Mexico southwards, during the first quarter of the nineteenth century. The second class, which began at first from illegitimate unions between Iberians and Indians, were the mestizos, who gradually came to be a majority of the population in most Latin American countries. Likely to be intermediate in both appearance and culture between the rulers of pure descent and the Indians, this class reduced the strength of barriers against mobility.

More important for our understanding of cultural penetration, the mainland caste patterns permitted mainly only one form of mobility, what is called "passing" in United States white-Negro relations. This pattern is still found in the so-called caste relations between Ladinos and Indios in Guatemala and in the Andean Highlands of Bolivia, Ecuador, and Peru. That is, the individual could enter the Iberian world, for the most part in urban areas, only by becoming Iberian in all observable cultural characteristics, by ceasing to be Indian. He might starve as easily being all Iberian as being Indian, but without becoming Iberian the way upward was entirely closed. This structural pattern permitted some upward mobility without softening the low evaluation of Indian culture and without eroding the social barrier between Indian and Iberian.

In the New World, then, the native social and cultural systems were undermined by the steady economic and political pressures of a *closed*-class system, rather than by the open-class, expanding industrializing system of the modern world. The destruction was greatest among the slaves of the ante-bellum South, less in the Caribbean, and least on the Iberian mainland. Southern slaves were "seasoned" in the Caribbean first and were further dispersed on arrival in the U.S. Indians were able, especially in areas of less economic and political interest to the Iberians, to maintain some part of their social and cultural integration for many decades, and a few tribes still exist in remote regions, such as the upper Amazon. An index of the disorganization of Caribbean slaves is their failure to reproduce, so that slave-running continued to be profitable almost until the end of the slavery period. In general, the illegitimacy rates of former slave areas are still higher than the non-slave areas; and on the mainland countries rimming the Caribbean, the coastal provinces where Negro slaves were introduced have higher rates than the interior.

The caste barriers were most severe in the ante-bellum South, somewhat less severe in the Caribbean non-Iberian islands, and least severe on the Iberian mainland. As Tannenbaum has shown, the Iberian treatment of even Negroes was less rigid than the treatment by any of the other New World settlers.[6]

The Iberians also made the most conscious effort to indoctrinate their subject peoples, the Indians, in Western norms, especially those relating to religion. However, in all these cases the inculcation of the new, Western values proceeded slowly and inconsistently. It is difficult to socialize an individual unless he is assured of acceptance as a full member of the social system, but the Iberians refused to accept the Indian anywhere until recently. *Village* controls were weak, because norm commitment to either native or Iberian values was weak and because the local social system was truncated: the locus of economic and political power was in the Iberian world, and the religious system accepted the Indian as parishioner, not as priest. Rewards for becoming Iberian were low or non-existent. For example, the Indian might be exhorted to work hard, but he would be subjected to economic exploitation if he acquired any wealth. Learning to read would help little, since there were few positions open to him if he became literate. The Iberian pressures were directed toward keeping the Indians docile, not toward transforming them into Iberians.

In the slave areas, primarily the United States, Brazil, and the Circum-Caribbean, neither master nor slave had any concern about illegitimacy, since the slave kin line had no social importance: slavery undermines the status of the male as family head, more than that of the female, and it is precisely the male elders who would be (in an independent society) the guardians of the family honor. It was to the interest of the conquerors or masters to prevent the development of native systems of social control, whether family or community, for therein lay a potential threat to their dominance. Even in the twentieth-century United States South, whites have opposed the "pretensions" of Negroes in seeking certificates of marriage and divorce. Slavery was abolished only late in the nineteenth century, and we could expect that where the caste barriers against Negroes were stronger, especially outside the Iberian regions, concern about Negro legitimacy among both whites and Negroes would develop only slowly.

ILLEGITIMACY AND THE STRUCTURE OF COMMUNITY INTEGRATION

Our review to this point suggests that it is the *community*, not the individual or the family, that maintains conformity to or deviation from the norm of legitimacy. The community defines and confers legitimacy.

[6] Frank Tannenbaum, *Slave and Citizen*, New York: Knopf, 1947.

The individual decision, his or her role bargain, determines whether illegitimacy will be risked, and both family and individual may lose standing if illegitimacy results, but there is little stigma if the community itself gives almost as much respect for conformity as for non-conformity. Lacking integration, the community cannot easily punish the deviant. In any population, the maintenance of a high individual or family commitment to a given norm or conformity to the norm, is dependent on *both* the commitment of the community to the *cultural* norm and the strength of its *social* controls. In the New World during the Colonial Period and the nineteenth century, as in contemporary industrializing sub-Saharan Africa, both native community controls and the commitment to the norm of legitimacy were weak. Correlatively, neither conquerors nor masters were concerned, since such deviations had little effect on their primary interests, power and economic exploitation.

The failure of community social integration means, then, a high rate of illegitimacy, since (a) it is likely to occur along with a weakening of norm commitment and (b) even if norms are not greatly weakened, controls are weak. However, the nature of this community integration or non-integration must be *specified*. We cannot fall back on the frequent alternative term, "anomie." The classical definition of "anomie," *normlessness*, is not adequate because such a state is so extreme: almost no cases of it, perhaps none at all unless we accept the examples of Nazi concentration camps and of United States prisoners of the Chinese during the Korean War, have been described by modern investigators. Here we can more usefully think of anomie or non-integration as a matter of *degree*. However, sociological theory has not agreed on a clear meaning for "non-integration." Moreover, most analysts have viewed New World villages as "communities," i.e., as integrated. Thus, it is fruitful to specify the *several* structural points where "integration" may or may not exist.

We are asserting that for a period of about two centuries most of the slave and peasant populations of the New World lived in relatively stable, *non*-integrated settlements, kept from integration by United States, Iberian, and other European rulers. They were kept from either being integrated into the Western cultural and social systems *or* establishing independent, *internally* integrated cultural and social systems of their own. Here, of course, we necessarily go beyond the available data, but some of the specific descriptions can eventually be tested.

The points of non-integration can be outlined as follows:

> I. These villages were not internally *culturally* integrated. This statement also holds, of course, for the U.S. Southern Negro population, only a few of whom ever lived in separate communities.

Without even a geographical basis, cultural integration is most difficult to achieve. This general assertion means:

A. There was a commitment, though relatively weak, to a wide range of norms from *both* cultures: religious elements from both cultures, allegiance to both languages, songs and music, or local and "national" loyalties.

B. There was relatively low norm commitment to various *instrumental* norms, such as literacy, Western languages, skills in economic activities, etc., which might have been useful in fulfilling *other* Western norms to which there was some commitment.

C. Conditions for the achievement of norms in the villages were difficult (contradictions of norms and conditions).
   1. Costs of church marriage were high.
   2. Masters or conquerors were little interested in facilitating formal marriage.
   3. Costs of the *fiesta*, or reception, after marriage were high.
   4. There were few means for economic expansion, literacy, and even learning Church beliefs precisely.
   5. Conquerors and masters opposed native or slave efforts to pretend to the status honor enjoyed by rulers.
   6. European goods were urged on them, but prices were high.
   7. Responsibility for debts or labor was encouraged, but caste prohibitions against mobility were strong.

II. These villages were not internally *socially* integrated. Of course, where there is very low norm commitment, social integration may be low: there is little to be integrated *about*. Again, the Southern Negro population obviously fits this description, which means:

A. White rulers prevented the development of local leadership or self-rule, thus hindering community controls.

B. Natives were not generally permitted to participate in Church activities as priests or officials (the cofradías may be viewed as a partial exception, but they were organized to ensure proper contributions to the Church).

C. Any local community pressures, decisions, or rules were subject to being overridden by the whites.

III. The village *cultural* patterns were not integrated with "national," white patterns. This means:

A. The two patterns were differently oriented toward various important norms: the value of working and owning agricultural land, the value of living in the city, nationalism-patriotism, or belief in the details of Church doctrine.

B. Whites viewed the native or Negro patterns as alien, rather than as merely lower class or a variant of the dominant culture.

C. Whites viewed the native or Negro people as requiring acculturation or training (even when they wasted little energy on the task), not as having a different culture of equal validity.

IV. The villages were not *socially* integrated with the dominant social system of the whites or the larger social system of the nation.
   A. Natives did not generally feel part of the nation and had little interest in the changing political fortunes of the elite.
   B. Relatively few inter-community relations existed.
   C. The native was not viewed as a "citizen" everywhere in the nation, and many barriers to free movement existed.
   D. The economic system was locally oriented, for the most part.
   E. The wishes of the local villages were little taken into account in national planning or action.

All four structural connections have been specified, in order to avoid needless debate as to whether these populations were "anomic," or "non-integrated." The outline is thus partly a summary of the preceding analysis but emphasizes the special character of the non-integration of these populations, which also applies *mutatis mutandi* to the Negro population of the Old South in the United States. The caste pattern of India is different in that the local village is *internally* both socially and culturally integrated; and it is culturally integrated with the larger Indian cultural pattern, in that the local caste norms and patterns are viewed as a legitimate part of the national moral fabric. It seems doubtful, however, that until recently such local village castes were *socially* integrated with the national social system except through a lengthy series of intermediate steps. Under such circumstances, social control remains strong locally and so does the commitment to the norm of legitimacy.

Consequently, in the New World from the Old South in the United States to Cape Horn, the non-whites assimilated only slowly into the social and cultural patterns of the West. They accepted the superiority of these patterns or at least did not assert the contrary. However, the barriers to integration into the nationally dominant patterns and the forces arrayed against local social or cultural integration failed to yield the rewards which are necessary for effective acculturation, so that the process did not accelerate in most countries until the twentieth century. Consequently, both low norm commitment to legitimacy and weak community controls maintained relatively high illegitimacy rates.

PHASES OF ASSIMILATION: RURAL-URBAN ILLEGITIMACY DIFFERENTIALS

Although the foregoing outline of non-integration in the New World seems both theoretically and descriptively correct, it goes far beyond available data from individual community studies, which would test whether any large proportion of existing or historical villages were in fact non-integrated. However, some further conclusions can be derived and tested in this analysis, so that we are not left merely with speculations.

The first of these concerns the *phases* of non-integration. If the line of theory pursued so far is correct, then in the conquest period in the Iberian world the illegitimacy rates first began to increase in the urban centers where contact was first made and the primary undermining of the Indian patterns began. Thereafter, however, because urban centers were the source of Westernizing forces and the urban Indians were more likely to assimilate, the norm of formal marriage was more likely to be followed. In addition, of course, the cities contained Iberians who would usually follow this norm. Thus, while the rural areas were kept in a relatively non-integrated state or forced gradually into it as Iberian dominance spread, the urban regions moved toward Western norms.

We should, therefore, suppose that in most cases the urban illegitimacy rates would now be *lower* than the rural rates, even though the modern rapid urbanization of Latin America may be creating all those disruptions of social and cultural patterns which have elsewhere been recorded when rural peoples enter an urban milieu.[7] In the following table, the rural and urban rates are presented.

As can be seen, the conclusion is validated, except for Paraguay. If our theory of phases in disintegration and reintegration is correct, this means that Paraguay, the socio-economically least developed of independent Latin American countries, has not yet entered the phase in which urban rates have begun to drop below rural ones. It should do so in the future. Correspondingly, of the seven independent Iberian countries with very high rates (over 50%) all are little developed, and still show very low differentials between urban and rural rates. Finally, in the more ad-

[7] I am of course aware of the difficulties in interpreting illegitimacy rates in countries where recording procedures are undeveloped: (1) Official urban rates might be higher than rural rates, because recording procedures are more thorough. (2) In some rural areas, those classed as "Indios" may be generally ignored by officials. (3) Where social services are available in the city, as in San Juan, Puerto Rico, some illegitimacies may be recorded there, although the mothers come from rural villages. (4) The disorganization of urban slums may lead to much promiscuity and thus *override* any of the factors presented in my analysis (e.g., Caracas, Venezuela). (5) It is difficult to obtain true "rural-urban" breakdowns, because the political sub-units (provinces, departments, sections) of Latin American nations typically contain both an urban center and a surrounding rural countryside and the data are recorded for the sub-unit as a whole. Nevertheless, all of these except the last (whose effect is unknown) would bias the official rates *against* my hypothesis. Consequently it seems safe to use the data. Many analysts have claimed that consensual unions, and therefore illegitimacy, are more common in rural areas. As we shall see, however, that assertion is correct only for mainland, independent Latin America. (See, for example, Kingsley Davis and Ana Casís, *Urbanization in Latin America*, New York: Milbank Memorial Fund, 1946, pp. 39-40.)

Included under "illegitimate" are those born of a consensual union, whether or not the offspring are "recognized," as well as those born outside of any continuing marital relationship. These are official rates.

TABLE 2. DIFFERENCES IN ILLEGITIMACY RATES BETWEEN CAPITALS AND REMAINDER OF COUNTRY, MAINLAND INDEPENDENT COUNTRIES SOUTH OF THE RIO GRANDE

Political Unit	Year	Federal Capital Major Urban Province	Per Cent	Remainder of Country (23.8% for whole)	Highest Rate in Any Department or Province Per Cent
Argentina	(1957)	Federal Capital	10.4	27.0	60.3 (Formosa)
Brazil	(1952)	Capital Territory	12.4	15.0[a]	
Chile	(1958)	Valparaiso Province	16.3	25.2	30.2 (Coquimbo)
Uruguay	(1943)	Montevideo	18.4	27.5	66.7 (Florida)
Paraguay	(1946)	Capital	62.4	56.5	(No Figure Obtainable)
Colombia	(1956)	Cundinamarca Section	20.2	30.1	69.1 (Córdoba)
Ecuador	(1947)	Pichincha Province	22.3	34.7	84.9 (Los Ríos)
Peru	(1953)	Callao Department	30.9	43.9	59.6 (Loreto)
Venezuela	(1954)	Lima & Callao Departments	46.4	43.0	54.7 (Lambayeque)
Nicaragua	(1947)	Federal District	47.2	58.3	74.9 (Yaracuy)
Honduras	(1957)	Managua Department	57.5	62.3	70.4 (Chinandega)
Costa Rica	(1957)	Francisco Morazán	68.4	69.3	80.3 (Colón)
Mexico	(1956)	Province San José	14.2	28.1	49.1 (Limón)
El Salvador	(1955)	Distrito Federal	12.9	23.9	27.9 (Sinaloa)
		San Salvador Urban Area	30.8	59.3	67.6 (Santa Ana)
Guatemala	(1956-57)	Urban Areas	64.5	76.1[b]	
Panama	(1958)	Urban Areas	64.5	79.6[b]	

[a] Total for country as a whole.
[b] Rural areas.

vanced countries, such as Uruguay and Mexico, the differences should *diminish* in the future.

The mainland *dependent* countries do not fit this phase pattern (British and Dutch Guiana, British Honduras), nor do the Caribbean island countries. Of the three Caribbean countries that have been independent for more than half a century, Haiti, Cuba, and the Dominican Republic, we have been able to obtain rural-urban breakdowns for only one, the Dominican Republic, where the rural rate *is* slightly higher but has become so only recently (65.1%-63.9%, 1958).

In the Caribbean political units, the rural rates are almost the same as the urban and are very slightly *lower* in over half of them. This region differs from the mainland Iberian lands primarily in these characteristics: (1) almost all their population is descendant from slaves. Caste restrictions were more severe against Negroes than on the mainland against the Indios; (2) almost all of them have been dependencies until this century, so that there has been little basis for national integration; (3) most important, the phases which apply to the mainland Iberian countries do not apply here, since the initial disorganization *was as intense in rural as in urban regions*. The Indians were everywhere destroyed. The slaves who replaced them were no longer members of a community, and the bulk of them was used in agriculture. We should not expect the Caribbean, then, to follow all the phases of the mainland development, though we predict that the urban rates will become lower than the rural. Several of the differentials are given in the following table. The United States Southern Negro rates are also included, as following the Caribbean pattern.

TABLE 3. NEW WORLD RURAL-URBAN DIFFERENTIALS IN ILLEGITI-MACY RATES, SELECTED MAINLAND DEPENDENCIES AND CARIBBEAN COUNTRIES[8]

| | Illegitimacy Rates | |
	Urban	Rural
U.S. South, Non-White (1957)	18.6-32.7%	18.6-32.1%
Puerto Rico (1956)	34.6 (San Juan)	27.4 (Rest of Country)
British Guiana (1955)	43.8	33.6
Trinidad and Tobago (1956)	47.3	47.4
Dominican Republic (1958)	63.9	65.1
Surinam (Dutch Guiana) (1951)	43.0 (Paramaribo)	38.0 (Rest of Country)
Jamaica (1954)	73.1 (Capital)	71.5 (Rest of Country)
British Honduras (1956)	52.9 (Capital District)	49.8 (Rest of Country)
Barbados (1955)	65.2 (Capital Parish)	59.3 (Rest of Country)

[8] Rates calculated from figures furnished by Caribbean Commission, and from U.S. National Office of Vital Statistics.

ILLEGITIMACY AND DEGREE OF NATIONAL INTEGRATION

A second conclusion may be drawn from our earlier analysis. The New World countries have succeeded in varying degrees in integrating their formerly Indian or slave populations into the national cultural and social systems. Since their illegitimacy rates are in part a function of this variable, countries which have moved *further* toward such an integration should have *lower* rates. The degree of this type of integration is greatly dependent on the extent of industrialization and urbanization, since these variables require more interconnections between different parts of a nation and offer rewards to the individual for entering the cultural systems. Thus, it becomes both easier and more desirable to conform to the norm of legitimacy. However, the rank order of the illegitimacy rates has a Spearman-Brown coefficient of correlation of only .50 with the rank order of urbanization as measured by the percentage of the national population living in the major metropolitan areas.

In the following table, most of the New World political units are ranked by the degree to which their formerly slave or Indian populations have been brought into the dominant cultural and social systems. As can be seen, with few exceptions the conclusion holds: in general, where the formerly slave or Indian populations have been more fully integrated into the national cultural and social systems, the national illegitimacy rates are lower. [Table 4. Ed.]

ILLEGITIMACY AND THE INTERNAL INTEGRATION OF COMMUNITIES

A third deduction from our earlier analysis can be tested: because of the wide variety of geographical and sociological factors in New World history, some communities have either continued to be *internally* integrated both socially and culturally (but *not* integrated culturally or socially with the *national* systems) or else re-achieved such an integration after the initial dissolution. Such communities would then be the main source of individual or family honor and rank, and would be able and willing to ensure conformity to the norm of legitimacy. Thus, their illegitimacy rates would be low. Their *formal* official rates might be *high*, since the national registration system will recognize only the legal, civil ceremony; but their social rates would be low, since few people will enter a union without a public marriage ceremony of some kind in which both family lines participate. Such communities might be found, for example, in the Andean Highlands of Peru, Bolivia, and Ecuador, or the northwestern highland region of Guatemala and even here and there in the Caribbean. We should find low real rates of illegitimacy in such villages

Table 4. New World Political Units According to Their Degree of National Integration and Illegitimacy Rates[9]

Degree of National Integration	Illegitimacy Rates (Percentages)	Date
A. Higher Integration		
Brazil	15	1952
Chile	16	1958
Uruguay	20	1954
Mexico	22.5	1956
Costa Rica	25	1957
B. Medium Integration		
Argentina	28	1957
Colombia	28	1957
Cuba	30	1939
Puerto Rico	28.5	1955
U.S. Old South, Negro	19-32	1957
C. Lower Integration		
Ecuador	36	1956
Peru	43	1955
British Guiana	34	1957
Paraguay	48	1955
Surinam	34	1953
French Guiana	65	1956
Venezuela	57	1955
Guatamala	70	1957
Panama	71	1956
Jamaica	72	1954
Martinique	48	1956
British Honduras	48	1957
D. Not Classified		
Dominican Republic	55	1956
El Salvador	59	1953
Honduras	65	1957
Nicaragua	62	1945

and high rates in villages where such integration seems weak. In the following table, various places which have been the object of community studies are classified by illegitimacy rates and by the degree of integration, i.e., the extent to which the village forms a self-validating social and cultural system. [Table 5. Ed.]

[9] All rates were obtained from the *United Nations Demographic Year Book Questionnaire* for the respective dates, except the figure for Puerto Rico, which was obtained from the Caribbean Commission. It was not possible to obtain recent Cuban data and many smaller political units have been omitted.

Bolivia has been eliminated because any birth is recorded as legitimate if the couple has been living together for two years (personal communication from Dirección Nacional de Estadística). As noted later, in Guatemala many births are classified as illegitimate because no civil ceremony preceded them, though other types of marriage ceremonies may have occurred, so that its real rate is lower than its official rate.

With respect to the independent variable, there is reason to believe that this

TABLE 5. ILLEGITIMACY AND INTEGRATION IN SELECTED NEW WORLD
COMMUNITIES[10]

	High Rate of Illegitimacy	Low Rate of Illegitimacy[a]
High Integration:		Tzintzuntzán (Mexico)
		Cherán (Mexico)
		Cruz das Almas (Brazil)
		Tusik and Quintana Roo (Mayans of Mexico)
		Orange Grove (Jamaica)
		Nyame (British Guiana)
		Saucío (Colombia)
		Santa Eulalia (Guatemala)
		Peguche (Ecuador)
		Otóvalo (Ecuador)
Low Integration:	Rocky Roads (Jamaica)	Chichicastenango (Guatemala)
	Sugartown (Jamaica)	
	Moche (Peru)	
	Tobatí (Paraguay)	

[a] "Low" illegitimacy means, of course, relative to the level prevailing in the respective countries. Specific rates cannot be calculated from the descriptions.

classification would for the most part be conceded by New World specialists. Several such specialists have already accepted it.

The bases for the classification are these: (1) The maintenance of caste barriers, which remain strong in Guatemala and the Andean Highlands and are weak in Brazil and Mexico. (2) Extent of ethnic homogeneity. Uruguay and Costa Rica, for example, are very "Spanish" or "European," and in Mexico, Cuba, Chile, and Puerto Rico a thorough-going mixing has occurred, in contrast to Guatemala. (3) The status of political dependency. (4) The existence of national programs for education, literacy, economic development (Puerto Rico, United States, Argentina). (5) The existence of large pockets of geographically and socially isolated populations (Bolivia, Ecuador, Peru). (6) Comparison of comments by New World experts, with respect to how much the natives care about or take part in national political affairs or how long various forms of labor exploitation have continued (e.g., indentured labor was abolished in Jamaica in 1917). Too much weight may have been given to the relatively unintegrated Andean populations of Bolivia, Peru, and Ecuador. If so, they would move to "medium" integration, and their reported illegitimacy rates would "fit" better. . . .

Doubtless, many observers would classify *all* those in D. as "lower integration" units. I have no objection but simply have been unable to obtain sufficient data on them to be certain.

[10] . . . To classify a village as *non*integrated appears to be more difficult than to show its integration, possibly because there are many different ways in which a village may *not* be internally integrated. Indices such as these seem relevant: (1) how many of the young adults are attracted to city life and ways, (2) how well the elders still control the young, (3) how important is a "good name in the village," (4) how effectively non-legal, informal relationships may decide local issues, (5) how large a portion of the village participates in ceremonies and how much of village life centers around such ceremonies. . . .

As can be seen, we find relatively low rates of illegitimacy in specific communities which have achieved, or re-achieved, an internal social and cultural coherence, an acceptance of themselves as the source of prestige. Individuals in such communities are participants in their social systems and presumably also committed to their cultural norms. If prestige is earned within the system, then a family line or the community as a whole will insist on conformity with the norm of legitimacy. The communities which form a self-validating social system have low rates, and the communities which are less integrated have higher rates.

CONCLUSION

The present paper has attempted to relate cultural penetration, cultural and social anomie, and illegitimacy rates, by considering the main areas of high rates: Northwestern Europe, urbanizing Africa south of the Sahara, and the New World south of the Mason-Dixon Line. In the first case, the community retains control, and though some children are born outside of wedlock, they are likely to be only technically and temporarily illegitimate, not socially illegitimate. In urbanizing Africa, by contrast, Western culture has undermined the native cultural and social systems, and the Western community has not created conditions which permit the native to become a full member of the Western social and cultural system.

This situation is also observable in the history of the Western Hemisphere among both United States rural and foreign immigrants, where however the later phases in such a massive process of penetration have also taken place. The parallels among the United States and Latin American mainland, the Caribbean, and urbanizing Africa are striking, if we allow for the differences which the twentieth century political situation has imposed on Africa. At the same time, apparent differences suggest theoretical reformulations of the assimilation process. We see a conquering people who first rule indirectly through native leaders, and then directly, in Africa and the New World south of the Rio Grande; considerable destruction of native populations and forced migrations; destruction of the native cultures, but the erection of quasi-caste barriers to prevent the full achievement or even complete acceptance of Western norms by the native; the undermining of the *local* community as the source of prestige; bars to entrance into the conquering Western community; and the dissolution of native family systems, without granting the rewards for conformity to the new Western family norms. We have also outlined the differences among these cases.

Behind the New World, however, are four hundred years of assimilation, so that it has been possible to see what happens after the initial period of cultural penetration. It is in the cities that full assimilation of the peasant is possible, and under the later industrialization that assimilation is even useful to the upper strata. Thus, it is in the city that the Indian peasant may become not only culturally but also socially assimilated, while in the rural areas, the encomiendas, and villages he has taken over Western *culture* with less commitment, because he has been denied a part in the Western *social* community, with its concomitant rewards and punishments. Thus, it is in the urban areas that the rule of legitimacy begins to be imposed more stringently by the community, and the mestizo becomes willing to pay the price of marriage, such as the wedding feast which serves as both a community blessing and a ritual of passage.

In a parallel fashion, those countries in which strides have been taken toward integrating their populations into the national community will have lower illegitimacy rates.

And, finally, where the village becomes the cosmos, usually in isolated or mountainous areas, so that the individual in it is participating in both the cultural system and the social system of a genuine community, there again we find a stronger commitment to the norm of legitimacy, and greater community and family concern about marriage. The dominant value system does not set norms which the individuals cannot achieve; there is less contradiction between norms, so that there is a stronger commitment to them; and the coherence of the community permits more effective sanctions to enforce conformity to the norm of legitimacy.

Civil Strife

In the analytical framework employed by the Feierabends in the following article, social change (of a kind generally regarded as desirable, namely, "modernization") is treated as the cause of a pathogenic condition promoting internal political violence. In contrast to the preceding selection, however, the sources of pathological behavior are located not in the condition of society (lack of integration) but in the condition of the human mind (sense of frustration). These levels of analysis are somewhat interdependent but, of course, not identical. It is instructive to compare Beatrice Whiting's study with that of the Feierabends. Both seek to learn the causes of the behavioral tendency towards aggression; however, Whiting, who is concerned only with individual acts, looks to the "private" spheres of the social system, while the Feierabends, who are interested in both individual and governmental aggression, explore both the "private" and "public" spheres of the social system. They also differ in the kinds of psychodynamic mechanisms they employ to account for the causes of aggression. It would be desirable to combine their respective approaches in an overall, systematic analysis of the social sources of violence, measuring the relative weight of the several variables identified.

12   IVO K. FEIERABEND AND
        ROSALIND L. FEIERABEND

*Aggressive Behaviors within Polities, 1948-1962:
A Cross-National Study*

THEORETICAL FRAMEWORK

Although political instability is a concept that can be explicated in more than one way, the definition used in this analysis limits its meaning to aggressive, politically relevant behaviors. Specifically, it is defined as the degree or the amount of aggression directed by individuals or groups within the political system against other groups or against the complex of officeholders and individuals and groups associated with them. Or, conversely, it is the amount of aggression directed by these officeholders against other individuals, groups, or officeholders within the polity.

Once this meaning is ascribed, the theoretical insights and elaborations of frustration-aggression theory become available (Dollard *et al.*,

Reprinted in abridged form by permission of the authors and publisher from the *Journal of Conflict Resolution*, Vol. 10 (September 1966), pp. 249-271. This article forms a portion of the manuscript, "Systemic Conditions of Political Aggression: An Application of Frustration-Aggression Theory," awarded the 1966 Socio-Psychological Prize of the American Association for the Advancement of Science. The research was partially supported by a grant from the San Diego State College Foundation.

1939; Maier, 1949; McNeil, 1959; Buss, 1961; Berkowitz, 1962). Perhaps the most basic and generalized postulate of the theory maintains that "aggression is always the result of frustration" (Dollard *et al.*, 1939, p. 3), while frustration may lead to other modes of behavior, such as constructive solutions to problems. Furthermore, aggression is not likely to occur if aggressive behavior is inhibited through devices associated with the notion of punishment. Or it may be displaced onto objects other than those perceived as the frustrating agents.[1]

The utility of these few concepts is obvious. Political instability is identified as aggressive behavior. It should then result from situations of unrelieved, socially experienced frustration. Such situations may be typified as those in which levels of social expectations, aspirations, and needs are raised for many people for significant periods of time, and yet remain unmatched by equivalent levels of satisfactions. The notation:

$$\frac{\text{social want satisfaction}}{\text{social want formation}} = \text{systemic frustration}$$

indicates this relationship. Two types of situations which are apt to produce high levels of systemic frustration are investigated in this research, although certainly many other possibilities are open to study.

In applying the frustration-aggression framework to the political sphere, the concept of punishment may be identified with the notion of coerciveness of political regimes. And the constructive solution of problems is related to the political as well as the administrative, entrepreneurial, and other capabilities available in the environment of politics. The notion of displacement may furthermore be associated with the occurrence of scapegoating against minority groups or aggression in the international sphere or in individual behaviors.

The following general hypotheses are yielded by applying frustration-aggression theory to the problem of political stability:

1. Under a situation of relative lack of systemic frustration, political stability is to be expected.
2. If systemic frustration is present, political stability still may be predicted, given the following considerations:
   a. It is a nonparticipant society. Politically relevant strata capable of organized action are largely lacking.
   b. It is a participant society in which constructive solutions to frustrating situations are available or anticipated. (The effectiveness

---

[1] More recent analyses of aggression have placed increasing emphasis on the role of the stimulus in eliciting an aggressive response. (For a discussion of recent approaches, see Berkowitz, 1965.)

of government and also the legitimacy of regimes will be relevant factors.)

   c. If a sufficiently coercive government is capable of preventing overt acts of hostility against itself, then a relatively stable polity may be anticipated.

   d. If, as a result of the coerciveness of government, the aggressive impulse is vented or displaced in aggression against minority groups and/or

   e. against other nations, then stability can be predicted.

   f. If individual acts of aggression are sufficiently abundant to provide an outlet, stability may occur in the face of systemic frustration.

3. However, in the relative absence of these qualifying conditions, aggressive behavior in the form of political instability is predicted to be the consequence of systemic frustration.

A more refined set of hypotheses concerning socially aggressive behaviors and frustration can be achieved by interpreting the frustration-aggression hypothesis within the framework of theories of social and political action and political systems (Merton, 1949; Parsons and Shils, 1951; Lasswell, 1951; Almond, 1960; Parsons *et al.*, 1961; Deutsch, 1963; Easton, 1965a, 1965b; Gurr, 1965).

METHODOLOGY

The methodology of the studies is indicated by the scope of the problem. Concern is not with the dynamics underlying stability in any one particular country but with the determinants of stability within all national political systems. As many cases as possible, or at least an appropriate sample of cases, must be analyzed. Thus the present studies are cross-national endeavors in which data are collected and analyzed for as many as eighty-four polities. (The eighty-four nations are listed in Table 1.) The cross-national method is here conceived in similar terms as the cross-cultural studies of anthropology (Whiting and Child, 1953; Murdock, 1957; Feierabend, 1962).

A crucial aspect of the research is the collection of relevant cross-national data. Although data are available on ecological variables of political systems through the Yale Political Data Program, the Dimensionality of Nations Project, and the Cross-Polity Survey, data collections on the political stability dimension are scarcer.

In order to carry out the research, data on internal conflict behaviors were collected for eighty-four nations for a fifteen-year period, 1948-1962. The data derive from two sources: *Deadline Data on World Affairs* and the *Encyclopaedia Britannica Yearbooks*. They are organized into a particular format in which each instability event is characterized according to country in which it occurs, date, persons involved, presence or absence

of violence, and other pertinent characteristics (Feierabend and Feierabend, 1965). The data are on IBM cards, creating a storage bank of
some 5,000 events.[2]

STUDY 1. THE ANALYSIS OF THE DEPENDENT VARIABLE: POLITICAL STABILITY

WITH BETTY A. NESVOLD, FRANCIS W. HOOLE,
AND NORMAN G. LITELL

In order to evaluate the political stability–instability continuum, data
collected on internal conflict behavior were scaled. The ordering of
specific instability events into a scale was approached from the viewpoint
of both construct validity and consensual validation (Nesvold, 1964).

A seven-point instrument was devised, ranging from 0 (denoting extreme stability) through 6 (denoting extreme instability). Each point of
the scale was observationally defined in terms of specific events representing differing degrees of stability or instability. An illustration may be
given of one item typical of each position on the scale. Thus, for example, a general election is an item associated with a 0 position on
the rating instructions. Resignation of a cabinet official falls into the 1
position on the scale; peaceful demonstrations into the 2 position; assassi-
nation of a significant political figure into the 3 position; mass arrests
into the 4 position; *coups d'état* into the 5 position; and civil war into
the 6 position.

Consensual validation for this intensity scale was obtained by asking
judges to sort the same events along the same continuum. The level of
agreement among judges on the distribution of the items was fairly high
(Pearson $r = .87$). Other checks performed on the reliability of the
method were a comparison of the assignment of items to positions on the
scale by two independent raters. Their level of agreement for the task,
involving data from eighty-four countries for a seven-year time period,
was very high (Pearson $r = .935$).

Using this scaling instrument, stability profiles for the sample of
eighty-four nations were ascertained for the seven-year period, 1955-1961.
Countries were assigned to groups on the basis of the most unstable
event which they experienced during this seven-year period. Thus countries which experienced a civil war were placed in group 6; countries
which were prey to a *coup d'état* were placed in group 5; countries with
mass arrests were assigned to group 4, and so on. The purpose of this
assignment was to weight intensity (or quality) of instability events
equally with the frequency (or quantity) of events.

[2] The data bank of political instability events, including the *Code Index* to
the bank, instructions to raters, etc., is available through the Inter-University
Consortium for Political Research, Box 1248, Ann Arbor, Michigan.

Following the allotment to groups, a sum total of each country's stability ratings was calculated. Countries were then rank-ordered within groups on the basis of this frequency sum total. The results of the ratings are given in Table 1.[3]

In this table, it may be seen first of all that the distribution is skewed. Instability is more prevalent than stability within the sample of nations, and the largest proportion of countries are those experiencing an instability event with a scale weighting of 4. Furthermore, there is an interesting combination of countries at each scale position. The most stable scale positions, by and large, include modern nations but also a sprinkling of markedly underdeveloped polities and some nations from the Communist bloc. Again, the small group of extremely unstable countries at scale position 6 comprise nations from Latin America, Asia, and the Communist bloc. The United States, contrary perhaps to ethnocentric expectations, is not at scale position 1 although it is on the stable side of the scale.

Another approach to the ordering of internal conflict behavior was based upon frequency alone (Hoole, 1964).[4] The frequency of occurrence of thirty types of internal conflict behaviors was determined for the eighty-four countries for the time period, 1948-1962. Analysis in terms of frequency was used in three different ways:

(1) A global instability profile for all types of events, for all countries, was drawn to show changes in world level of instability during the time period under study. As may be seen in Figure 1, instability has been on the increase in recent years, reaching one peak in the late 1950s and an even higher level in the early 1960s.

(2) Frequencies of particular types of instability behaviors were compared for the entire sample of countries. The range of frequencies was from 18 (execution of significant persons) to 403 (acquisition of office). When the events were rank-ordered in terms of frequency of occurrence and the rank-ordering divided into quartiles, the first quartile, with the highest frequency of occurrence (1,555 occurrences) included events denoting routine governmental change (such as acquisition of office, vaca-

[3] These stability profiles correlate with the ordering of the same countries based on Eckstein's index, "Deaths from domestic group violence per 1,000,000 population, 1950-1962." The rank-order correlation between these two indices is Spearman $r = .69$. On the other hand, only a low correlation exists with Russett's index, "Executive stability: number of years independent/number of chief executives, 1945-1961." The rank-order correlation between these two indices is Spearman $r = .38$.

[4] The data used in Hoole's 1964 study were gathered from a single source, *Deadline Data on World Affairs*. The data bank as presently constituted comprises two sources, *Deadline Data on World Affairs* and *The Encyclopaedia Britannica Yearbooks*.

1955-1961 (STABILITY SCORE SHOWN FOR EACH COUNTRY)

STABILITY						INSTABILITY
N. Zea. 000	Norway 104	W. Germany 217	Tunisia 328	France 499	India 599	Indonesia 699
	Netherlands 104	Czech. 212	Gr. Britain 325	U. of S. Africa 495	Argentina 599	Cuba 699
	Cambodia 104	Finland 211	Portugal 323	Haiti 478	Korea 596	Colombia 681
	Sweden 103	Romania 206	Uruguay 318	Poland 465	Venezuela 584	Laos 652
	Saudi Ar. 103	Ireland 202	Israel 317	Spain 463	Turkey 583	Hungary 652
	Iceland 103	Costa Rica 202	Canada 317	Dom. Rep. 463	Lebanon 581	
	Philippines 101		U.S. 316	Iran 459	Iraq 579	
	Luxembourg 101		Taiwan 314	Ceylon 454	Bolivia 556	
			Libya 309	Japan 453	Syria 554	
			Austria 309	Thailand 451	Peru 552	
			E. Germany 307	Mexico 451	Guatemala 546	
			Ethiopia 307	Ghana 451	Brazil 541	
			Denmark 306	Jordan 448	Honduras 535	
			Australia 306	Sudan 445	Cyprus 526	
			Switzer. 303	Morocco 443		
				Egypt 438		
				Pakistan 437		
				Italy 433		
				Belgium 432		
				Paraguay 431		
				USSR 430		
				Nicaragua 430		
				Chile 427		
				Burma 427		
				Yugoslavia 422		
				Panama 422		
				Ecuador 422		
				China 422		
				El Salvador 421		
				Liberia 415		
				Malaya 413		
				Albania 412		
				Greece 409		
				Bulgaria 407		
				Afghanistan 404		
0	1	2	3	4	5	6

240   Ivo K. Feierabend and Rosalind L. Feierabend

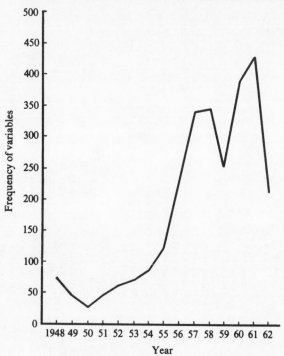

Fig. 1. Frequency of variables by year, 1948-1962.

tion of office, elections, and significant changes of laws). The second quartile (704 occurrences) appeared to be one of unrest, including such events as large-scale demonstrations, general strikes, arrests, and martial law. The third quartile (333 occurrences.) indicated serious societal disturbance, in the form of *coups d'état*, terrorism and sabotage, guerrilla warfare, and exile. And the fourth quartile (150 occurrences) consisted primarily of events connoting violence: executions, severe riots, civil war. Thus an inverse relationship was revealed between the frequency of occurrence of an event and the intensity of violence which it denotes.

(3) Finally, countries were compared for the relative frequency of occurrence of all thirty instability behaviors during this time period. The range was from 136 events (France) to one event (Switzerland). The median of this distribution was represented by Laos and Burma, with 28 and 26 events, respectively.

An additional refinement in the understanding of political instability is achieved by factor analysis, which reduces the large number of observed variables to a smaller number of underlying dimensions. Four previous factor analyses of internal conflict behaviors have been performed. Rummel (1963), factor-analyzing nine types of internal conflict behaviors for a three-year time period (1955-1957), emerged with three underlying dimensions: turmoil, revolution, and subversion. Tanter (1964, 1966), replicating the Rummel variables for the years 1958-1960, found a two-factor solution: turmoil and internal war. Recently, Rummel (1966) factor-analyzed thirteen variables obtained from Eckstein's collection of internal conflict behaviors (Eckstein, 1962) for the time period 1946-1950. This factor analysis again yielded three dimensions, which Rummel identifies with the three dimensions of the 1963 factor solution, namely, revolution, subversion, and turmoil. Hoole (1964) factor-analyzed thirty variables collected over a fifteen-year time span, 1948-1962, from a single source (see footnote 2), and emerged with five major and five minor factors. The five major factors were labelled: demonstrations, change of officeholder, riots, guerrilla warfare, and strikes.

Most recently, Feierabend, Feierabend, and Litell (1966), using Hoole's thirty variables for the fifteen-year period 1948-1962 and the complete data bank derived from two sources, performed a factor analysis with a principal components solution and an orthogonal Varimax rotation. (See Table 2 for the rotated factor matrix.) Nine factors emerged. The first three of these, ranked according to importance in terms of the amount of variance accounted for after rotation, were labelled, first, a turmoil dimension (characterized by violence and mass participation); second, a palace-revolution–revolt dimension (distinguished by a marked lack of mass support); and, third, a power-struggle–purge dimension (connoting violent upheavals and changes of office within regimes). It will be noted that there is definite correspondence between the first two factors revealed in this analysis and the factors discovered by both Rummel and Tanter.

Looking at the variables with the highest loadings on each factor, we see that the first factor comprises strikes of all types; demonstrations and riots, large and small, violent and severe; and also mass arrests and terrorism. One could say that it denotes serious, widespread disturbance, anomie, popular mass participation, and some governmental retaliation.

The second factor presents a sharp contrast to this mass turmoil dimension. It encompasses revolts, *coups d'état*, martial law, arrests of politically prominent leaders, and governmental action against specific groups. These events do not connote mass participation but rather extreme instability created by highly organized and conspiratorial elites and cliques. And the third factor presents yet another divergent pattern, including acquisition and loss of office, arrests and executions of politically significant figures, and some punitive action. Mass turmoil is not evident, as on the first factor; neither is the situation one of revolt and *coup d'état*. This is

TABLE 2. ROTATED FACTOR MATRIX OF DOMESTIC CONFLICT MEASURES

Variables	Factors[a]								
	Mass participation—turmoil	Palace revolution—revolt	Power struggle—purge	Riot	Election	Demonstration	Imprisonment	Civil war	Guerrilla warfare
1. Elections	29	-02	09	-18	70a	-10	-17	-05	-23
2. Vacation of office	38	08	74a	-14	20	-11	-15	-25	09
3. Significant change of laws	38	41	41	-01	31	15	-16	-23	-11
4. Acquisition of office	29	06	75a	-19	15	-04	-25	-19	22
5. Crisis within a nongovernmental organization	40	13	12	-21	04	-09	62a	07	-23
6. Organization of opposition party	08	10	-02	02	56a	36	19	-39	-10
7. Repressive action against specific groups	46	61a	27	01	-03	16	12	04	12
8. Micro strikes	67a	00	-15	-26	-16	05	03	03	23
9. General strikes	73a	13	04	-42	09	-06	-33	08	-18
10. Macro strikes	43	-22	-11	-35	15	-17	10	-12	-19
11. Micro demonstrations	61a	19	-02	02	20	59a	18	03	02
12. Macro demonstrations	73a	-01	00	26	06	19	-03	-21	03
13. Micro riots	46	11	-06	68a	27	-03	04	-15	11
14. Macro riots	69a	28	-04	33	20	02	-02	-08	-05
15. Severe macro riots	64a	-03	-04	53a	11	-19	23	-20	14
16. Arrests of significant persons	09	64a	64a	07	-14	-06	38	-10	-01
17. Imprisonment of significant persons	-14	12	49	17	-05	16	07	-33	-22
18. Arrests of few insignificant persons	42	09	05	-08	07	75a	-01	07	21
19. Mass arrests of insignificant persons	52a	33	14	54a	-12	-02	05	05	21
20. Imprisonment of insignificant persons	26	-08	09	08	-12	34	64a	-03	01
21. Assassination	17	40	23	06	24	23	-07	-10	56a
22. Martial law	11	71a	03	03	15	09	-27	-06	-08
23. Execution of significant persons	-08	01	54a	31	-26	14	-04	31	05
24. Execution of insignificant persons	01	-10	63a	32	-07	12	-02	47	-02
25. Terrorism and sabotage	62a	28	12	-21	13	-01	10	07	38
26. Guerrilla warfare	04	42	07	-19	19	-35	25	21	55a
27. Civil war	-14	25	31	14	45	08	-08	60a	02
28. Coup d'état	03	69a	07	01	-02	12	-40	07	-32
29. Revolts	06	75a	-01	11	07	-01	-10	32	16
30. Exile	-09	40	00	03	-36	32	-19	-13	04
Percentage of common variance	23.37	16.30	13.20	9.67	8.33	8.00	7.99	6.76	6.40 = 100.0
Percentage of total variance	23.33	11.11	7.52	6.77	5.89	5.32	4.18	3.82	3.62 = 71.46

an instability dimension of violent internal power struggles, purges, depositions, and changes within ruling parties and cliques, which nevertheless remain in power.

The nine factors in combination account for 71.5% of the total variance. After rotation the three first factors combined account for over half of the common variance (53%). The remaining six factors, accounting in combination for less than half of the common variance, seem to reveal the following patterns: a specific riot dimension; an election dimension; two factors connoting mild, limited unrest; and, finally, two separate dimensions of civil war and guerrilla warfare, respectively, the extreme forms of political instability.

STUDY 2. THE RELATION OF SOCIAL FRUSTRATION AND MODERNITY TO POLITICAL STABILITY

WITH BETTY A. NESVOLD

Once the data for the dependent variable, political stability, were collected, factor-analyzed, and scaled, the major step of seeking correlates of instability became feasible. In this attempt, two generalized and related hypotheses were investigated. (1) *The higher (lower) the social want formation in any given society and the lower (higher) the social want satisfaction, the greater (the less) the systemic frustration and the greater (the less) the impulse to political instability.* (2) *The highest and the lowest points of the modernity continuum in any given society will tend to produce maximum stability in the political order, while a medium position on the continuum will produce maximum instability* (Nesvold, 1964).

These hypotheses embody the basic propositions of the frustration-aggression theory, as well as insights gained from the literature on processes of modernization (Lerner, 1958; Deutsch, 1961; Cutright, 1963). In the first hypothesis, the discrepancy between social wants and social satisfactions is postulated to be the index of systemic frustration. The relationship is represented as follows:

$$\frac{\text{want satisfaction low}}{\text{want formation high}} = \text{high frustration}$$

$$\frac{\text{want satisfaction low}}{\text{want formation low}} = \text{low frustration}$$

$$\frac{\text{want satisfaction high}}{\text{want formation high}} = \text{low frustration}$$

A variety of social conditions may satisfy or leave unsatisfied the social wants of different strata of the population within social systems. In our present century the process of modernization is certain to create new wants and aspirations, as well as to lead in the long run to their satisfaction.

The notion of modernity denotes a very complex set of social phenomena. It includes the aspiration and capacity in a society to produce and consume a wide range and quantity of goods and services. It includes high development in science, technology, and education, and high attainment in scores of specialized skills. It includes, moreover, new structures of social organization and participation, new sets of aspirations, attitudes, and ideologies. Modern affluent nations, with their complex of economic, political, and social systems, serve best as models of modernity to nations emerging from traditional society. In these transitional nations, the growing, politically relevant strata of the population are all participants in modern life. Lerner (1957), for one, states categorically that once traditional societies are exposed to the modern way of life, without exception they desire benefits associated with modernity.

The acquisition of modern goals, although an integral aspect of modernity, is hardly synonymous with their attainment. The notion of "the revolution of rising expectations" (Lerner, 1958), also termed "the revolution of rising frustrations," points to the essentially frustrating nature of the modernization process. The arousal of an under-developed society to awareness of complex modern patterns of behavior and organization brings with it a desire to emulate and achieve the same high level of satisfaction. But there is an inevitable lag between aspiration and achievement which varies in length with the specific condition of the country. Furthermore, it may be postulated that the peak discrepancy between systemic goals and their satisfaction, and hence the maximum frustration, should come somewhere in the middle of the transitional phase between traditional society and the achievement of modernity. It is at this middle stage that awareness of modernity and exposure to modern patterns should be complete, that is, at a theoretical ceiling, whereas achievement levels would still be lagging far behind. Prior to this theoretical middle stage, exposure and achievement would both be lower. After the middle stage, exposure can no longer increase, since it already amounts to complete awareness, but achievement will continue to progress, thus carrying the nation eventually into the stage of modernity. Thus, in contrast to transitional societies, it may be postulated that traditional and modern societies will be less frustrated and therefore will tend to be more stable than transitional societies.

The most direct way to ascertain systemic frustration is through field work in the many countries, administering questionnaires (see Inkeles, 1960; Doob, 1960; Cantril, 1963, 1965; Almond and Verba, 1964). For the purpose of this study, an inexpensive and very indirect method was adopted.

The highly theoretical notions of want satisfaction and want formation were translated into observable definitions. For this purpose, available collections of cross-national statistical data were consulted and a few statistical items were chosen as appropriate indicators. The following selection of indicators was made. GNP and caloric intake per capita, physicians and telephones per unit of population were singled out as indices of satisfaction. Newspapers and radios per unit of population were also included. Many other indicators denoting material or other satisfactions could have served the purpose. The selection was guided by parsimony as well as availability of data.

The indicators, of course, have different significance in referring to the satisfaction of different wants. Furthermore, their significance may vary at different levels of relative abundance or scarcity. A great deal of theorizing is necessary to select and use the indicators wisely. For example, it is possible that a country with many physicians and telephones may still be starving. Or, beyond a certain point, caloric intake cannot measure the satisfaction of some other less basic needs than hunger, while GNP per capita may do so.

For want formation, literacy and urbanization were chosen as indicators. This selection was influenced by the notion of exposure to modernity (Lerner, 1958; Deutsch, 1961). Exposure to modernity was judged a good mechanism for the formation of new wants, and literacy and city life were taken as the two agents most likely to bring about such exposure.

These eight indices (GNP, caloric intake, telephones, physicians, newspapers, radios, literacy, and urbanization) were used to construct both a frustration index and a modernity index. The modernity index was formed by combining scores on all of the eight indicators. Raw scores were first transformed into standard scores and then a mean standard score was calculated for each of the eighty-four countries on the basis of the available data. The frustration index was a ratio. A country's combined coded score on the six satisfaction indices (GNP, caloric intake, telephones, physicians, newspapers, and radios) was divided by either the country's coded literacy or coded urbanization score, whichever was higher.[5]

The data on the independent variables were collected for the years 1948-1955 whereas the stability ratings were made for the years 1955-1961. It was assumed that some lag would occur before social frustrations would make themselves felt in political aggressions, that is, political instabilities.

[5] The difficulty of dividing these highly correlated indicators should be noted. Each contains some error component due to the unreliable reporting of cross-national data. For an estimate of error in cross-national data, see Russett (1964) and Rummel (1963).

RESULTS

The main finding of the study is that the higher the level of systemic frustration, as measured by the indices selected, the greater the political instability. The results are shown in Table 3. The stable countries are those which experience the least amount of measured systemic frustration. Conversely, the countries beset by political instability also suffer a high level of systemic frustration, although certain interesting exceptions occur.

Each indicator of want formation and satisfaction is also significantly related to political stability. The relationships between each indicator and stability are presented in Table 4 [omitted]. Another finding of interest in this table is that all eight indicators do not predict degree of stability with equal efficiency. Level of literacy is the best single predictor, as seen by the .90 degree of relationship (Yule's Q) between literacy and stability. Comparatively, GNP is one of the weaker predictors, along with percent of urbanization, population per physician, and caloric intake per capita per day.

These data on the predictors of political stability also determine empirical threshold values for each indicator. Above these values, countries are predominantly stable; below them, countries are predominantly unstable. The cutting point for each of the indicators was selected so as to reveal the maximum difference between stable and unstable countries.

From these empirical thresholds, a composite picture of the stable country emerges. It is a society which is 90 percent or more literate; with 65 or more radios and 120 or more newspapers per 1,000 population; with two percent or more of the population having telephones; with 2,525 or more calories per day per person; with not more than 1,900 persons per physician; with a GNP of 300 dollars or more per person per year; and with 45 percent or more of the population living in urban centers. If all of these threshold values are attained by a society, there is an extremely high probability that the country will achieve relative political stability. Conversely, if gratifications are less than these threshold values, the more they fail to meet these levels, the greater the likelihood of political instability.

In order to investigate the relationship between modernity and stability, countries were rank-ordered on the modernity index and the distribution was broken into three groups representing modern countries, transitional countries, and traditional countries. The cutting points for these three groups were to some extent arbitrary: the twenty-four countries which were highest on the modernity index were selected as the modern group. The traditional group was chosen to be equal in size to the modern group, while ranking at the opposite end of the modernity continuum. The remaining countries, falling between the modern and traditional groups, were designated transitional. The difficulty in determining the

TABLE 3. RELATIONSHIP BETWEEN LEVEL OF SYSTEMIC
FRUSTRATION AND DEGREE OF POLITICAL STABILITY[a]

DEGREE OF POLITICAL STABILITY	INDEX OF SYSTEMIC FRUSTRATION			
	Ratio of Want Formation to Want Satisfaction			
	High systemic frustration		Low systemic frustration	Total
Unstable	Bolivia Brazil Bulgaria Ceylon Chile Colombia Cuba Cyprus Dom. Republic Ecuador Egypt El Salvador Greece Guatemala Haiti India Indonesia	Iran Iraq Italy Japan Korea Mexico Nicaragua Pakistan Panama Paraguay Peru Spain Syria Thailand Turkey Venezuela Yugoslavia	Argentina Belgium France Lebanon Morocco Union of South Africa	40
	34		6	
	2		20	
Stable	Philippines Tunisia		Australia Austria Canada Costa Rica Czech. Denmark Finland West Germany Great Britain Iceland Ireland Israel Netherlands	New Zealand Norway Portugal Sweden Switzerland United States Uruguay	22
Total	36		26	62
Chi square[b] = 30.5, $p = <.001$			Yule's $Q = .9653$	

[a] The number of cases in this and the following tables varies with the data available in the UN statistical sources. This table includes only those countries with data on all eight indices.

[b] All chi squares in this and the following tables are corrected for continuity in view of the small frequencies in the nonconfirming cells.

true state of the countries lies not so much in finding the cutting point for the modern group as in selecting the traditional one. Truly traditional countries do not report data and hence have no way of being included in the study. The countries designated traditional are simply less modern than those classed as transitional, but they have nonetheless been exposed to modernity.[6]

A mean stability score was calculated for each group of countries. The differences between the mean stability scores for the three groups were then estimated. According to the hypothesis, the difference in mean stability score should be greatest between the transitional group and either of the other two groups. The difference in mean stability score between modern and traditional countries should not be significant. The results are given in Table 5.

TABLE 5. RELATIONSHIP BETWEEN MODERNITY AND STABILITY

Modernity level	N	Mean stability score	t	p^a	t	p^a
Modern countries	24	268	6.18	<.001		
Transitional countries	37	472			3.71	<.01
Traditional countries	23	420	1.53	>.05		

a Probability levels are two-tailed.

As may be seen in the table, the predicted difference between the stability level of modern and of transitional countries emerges as highly significant. The difference between modern and traditional countries is less but nonetheless also significant. And the difference between traditional and transitional countries does not reach significance. The difficulty in obtaining data on truly traditional countries undoubtedly contributes to the lack of significant difference between countries labelled in this sample as transitional and traditional.

In view of the lack of support in these eighty-four nations for the hypothesized curvilinear relationship between modernity and stability, the assumption may be made that all of the countries have been exposed to modernity. Hence want formation should be at a relatively high level throughout the sample. One might hypothesize that want formation reaches an early maximum with exposure to modernity, after which further awareness of the modern world can no longer increase desire for modernity. Under these conditions, the modernity index is also in fact a

---

[6] This modernity ranking, based on eight indices, is highly comparable to that of Russett et al. (1964) based on GNP alone. A Spearman r calculated between the two rank-orderings is .92.

frustration index, indicating the extent to which these measured economic satisfactions are present within a society which may be presumed to have already been exposed to modernity.

To compare the relative efficacy of these two frustration indices, product-moment correlations were calculated between each index and stability. The results show that while both indices are significantly correlated with stability, the correlation between the so-called modernity index and stability is the higher of the two. The product-moment correlation between modernity and stability is .625; the correlation between the so-called frustration index and stability is .499. An *eta* calculated between the modernity index and the stability index, to show curvilinearity of relationship, is $\eta = .667$, which is not significantly different from the Pearson *r* of .625. Thus again the hypothesis of curvilinearity between modernity and stability is not supported.

STUDY 3. THE PREDICTION OF CHANGES IN POLITICAL STABILITY OVER TIME

WITH WALLACE R. CONROE

In the previous study, stability, modernity, and the frustration index were all calculated as static measures. Each variable was represented by a single score, indicating an overall estimate of the level of the variable during the time period under study. The question raised in this study concerns the effect of relative rates of change over time in the ecological variables. It seeks to uncover dynamic relationships which would supplement the static ones.

The assumptions made in this study of dynamic trends are based on a view of change as essentially disruptive in character. The process of transition toward modernity, discussed in the previous study, is one during which, almost inevitably, goals and demands will exceed achievements. It is also a process during which former patterns of behavior, outdated technologies, established roles, statuses and norms, must all give way to new, unfamiliar patterns. The transitional personality is frustrated by this break-off from the past and the uncertainty of the present.

To this picture of a society in ferment is now added the notion of the relevance of time. Insofar as the transitional process is a gradual one, there is a possibility that new patterns may be adopted and adjusted to before old ones are completely abandoned. There is also the further possibility that achievements may begin to approximate the level at which aspirations are set, before aspirations move even further ahead. Where the transitional process is rapid, however, the effect will be to decrease the possibility of adaptation, thus increasing the probability of disruption, chaos, and feelings of personal discontent. Furthermore, the more rapid the process of change, the greater the likelihood of opening new perspectives of modernity, that is, of creating higher and higher levels of aspiration, thus inevitably increasing the gap between aspiration and achievement, at least in the early stages.

Thus the hypothesis promulgated in this study is that: *the faster (the slower) the rate of change in the modernization process within any given society, the higher (the lower) the level of political instability within that society* (Conroe, 1965).

As a first step in investigating this hypothesis, yearly changes in instability pattern for each of the eighty-four countries were calculated for the time period under study, 1948-1962. From the evidence accumulated on the global frequency of occurrence of instability events (Figure 1), it was clear that the world instability level increased sharply during the fifteen years, reaching its highest peak in the last six years. In order to compare countries as to their relative position on the instability continuum over time, the period was split in half and country instability scores were calculated for each seven-year period separately. The country scores for the second period tended to be higher than for the first one. A rank-order correlation between stability levels in the two seven-year periods for the eighty-four countries showed a moderate degree of relationship (Spearman $r = .43$). Not only was the instability level generally on the increase, but there was a tendency for countries to maintain their relatively stable or unstable positions over time.

As a further, more refined method of analyzing the stability–instability continuum over time, stability scores for the eighty-four nations were calculated on a year-by-year basis and plotted as a function of time. To characterize the time function, at least two measures were necessary: the slope of a best-fit line, indicating the average instability trend, over the fifteen-year period; and amplitude of change from year to year, as estimated by variance.

A calculation of the relationship between these two measures showed them to be independent and unrelated dimensions (Spearman $r = .06$). Of the two, only amplitude was related to static stability level as measured by the intensity scale (Spearman $r = .64$). This indicates that the meaning of instability as empirically ascertained in these studies is identified with the fluctuation of instability rather than with the average trend over time. Furthermore, it is the measure of amplitude and not the average trend over time which is directly related to rate of change in the independent variables. The average instability trend over time (increases or decreases) is related to the ecological variables only when combined with the data on yearly fluctuations in stability levels.

Turning to the predictors of instability, interest was in the effect of changes in levels of ecological variables upon changes in stability. The general hypothesis of this study was that rapid change will be experienced as an unsettling, frustrating societal condition and hence will be associated with a high level of internal conflict. To test the hypothesis, nine predictor indices were selected for study: caloric intake, literacy, primary and postprimary education, national income, cost of living, infant mortality, urbanization, and radios per thousand population. Data for these indices were collected for a 28-year period from 1935 through 1962. Plotting of the data revealed a consistent trend for substantially all countries in the sample to improve their position on all indices over time. Hence a yearly percent rate of change was calculated for each indicator.[7] These indicators are not identical to those of the previous study, although there is overlap. The new choice was determined by the availability of data for as many years as possible and for a maximum number of countries in the sample.

To summarize the results of the interrelationship between rates of change in the independent indices and rate of change in stability, it may be said that the higher the rate of change on the indices, the greater the increase in instability. A contingency table showing the relationship between mean rate of change on six or more of the nine indices and instability, as measured only by variation in pattern (amplitude), is given in Table 6.

As may be seen from the table, the countries experiencing a highly erratic instability pattern are those also undergoing a rapid rate of change in the ecological variables selected for study. On the other hand, countries experiencing political stability in the sense of a steady pattern are the static countries in which ecological change proceeds at a slower pace.

Furthermore, the rate at which modernization occurred from 1935 to 1962 is correlated with static stability level in the 1955-1961 time period (as measured in Study 1). A Pearson r of .647 was found between rate of change (calculated as a combined measure on six or more of the nine indices) and static stability score. Relationships were also calculated between rates of change on each of the nine independent indices taken separately and instability level, measured both as a static score and as a dynamic fluctuation (variance measure) for the 1948-1962 period (see Table 7).

The pattern is somewhat the same for both sets of calculations, indicating primary education to be the best single predictor of instability and literacy the worst.[8] The most interesting finding is the inverse relationship revealed between rate of change in national income and instability. In the

[7] The yearly percent rate of change on the ecological variables was calculated by subtracting the lowest value of the variable in the 28-year period from the highest value attained, dividing by the lowest value to convert to a percentage change, and then dividing by the number of years spanned to obtain the yearly percentage change.

[8] This finding is in contrast to the high level of relationship obtained between literacy and static stability level reported in Study 1. The explanation may lie in the observed inconsistency in the literacy data reported over the longer time period in various sources.

Table 6. Relationship Between Mean Rate of Change on Ecological Variables and Rate of Change in Stability

MEAN RATE OF CHANGE ON ECOLOGICAL VARIABLES (PERCENT)	CHANGE IN STABILITY			
	Amplitude of Fluctuations in Yearly Stability Scores			
	Low change (amplitude)		High change (amplitude)	Total
Low change	Argentina Australia Austria Bulgaria Canada Chile Denmark Ecuador Finland France Guatemala Iceland Ireland Israel Italy Luxembourg 31	Mexico Netherlands New Zealand Norway Pakistan Philippines Spain Sweden Switzerland Taiwan Un. of S. Africa United Kingdom United States Uruguay West Germany	Belgium Cuba Greece Hungary Paraguay 5	36
High change	Ceylon Ghana India Syria Turkey 5	Bolivia Brazil Burma Cambodia Colombia Costa Rica Dom. Republic Egypt El Salvador Haiti Honduras Indonesia Iraq	Japan Korea Malaya Morocco Panama Peru Poland Portugal Thailand Tunisia USSR Venezuela Yugoslavia 26	31
Total	36		31	67[a]

Chi square = 30.0; p = <.001.

[a] The N on this and some of the following tables is reduced to include only those countries with data on six or more indices, from which to calculate the mean rate of change score.

case of this indicator, the higher the rate of change, the greater the likelihood of stability. This finding may be understood when one contrasts the pattern of rate of change on national income to that for the nine indices taken together (see Tables 8 and 9).

TABLE 7. RANK-ORDER CORRELATIONS (RHO) BETWEEN RATE OF CHANGE ON ECOLOGICAL VARIABLES AND TWO MEASURES OF STABILITY, 1948-1962

	N	Static stability	Dynamic stability (amplitude)
Primary education	70	.61	.57
Calories per capita per day	39	.49	.35
Postprimary education	30	.36	.41
Cost of living	72	.36	.21
Radios	82	.34	.31
Infant mortality rate	60	.33	.36
Urbanization	69	.17	.14
Literacy	82	.03	.01
National income	70	−.34	−.45

From Table 8 it is clear that all countries except the modern show a high rate of change on ecological variables. (This again confirms the point made earlier that no truly traditional countries are included in the sample. By definition, a traditional country should be characterized by lack of change.) The modern countries are those undergoing the least amount of change. They are also those experiencing the least amount of instability.

In Table 9, however, we find the situation reversed for growth in national income. On this indicator, it is the modern countries which show the highest rate of change over time. National income may be viewed as a variable with no intrinsic ceiling and one on which marked improvement will not occur until a country is well advanced toward modernity and has achieved a relatively high standard on other ecological variables, such as literacy, education, caloric intake, and infant mortality. Thus again it is the modern countries which are the most stable and which show the greatest growth rate in national income.

.   .   .

In conclusion, one might speak of a syndrome which is exemplified by the modern group of nations. With interesting exceptions, they are relatively satisfied economically and relatively stable politically, no longer changing rapidly on many economic dimensions, although making sizeable gains in national income. In contrast are the transitional nations, some moving more rapidly toward modernity than others but, by and large, all characterized by relative economic deprivation, a high rate of change on many economic dimensions but a low rate of growth on national income, and a strong tendency to political instability, finding overt expression in many diverse events such as strikes, demonstrations, riots, *coups d'état*, and even civil war.

Table 8. Relationship Between Modernity Level and Mean Rate of Change on Ecological Variables

MEAN RATE OF CHANGE (PERCENT)	MODERNITY LEVEL			Total
	Traditional countries	Transitional countries	Modern countries	
Low change	Pakistan Philippines Taiwan	Bulgaria Chile Cuba Guatemala Hungary Italy Mexico Paraguay Spain Union of South Africa	Argentina Australia Austria Belgium Canada Denmark Finland France Iceland Ireland Israel Luxembourg Netherlands New Zealand Norway Sweden Switzerland United Kingdom United States Uruguay W. Germany	34
	3	10	21	
High change	Bolivia Burma Cambodia Ghana Haiti India Indonesia Iraq Malaya Morocco	Brazil Ceylon Colombia Costa Rica Dom. Rep. Ecuador Egypt El Salvador Greece Honduras Japan Korea Panama Peru Poland Portugal Syria Thailand Tunisia Turkey Venezuela Yugoslavia	USSR	33
	10	22	1	
Total	13	32	22	67

Chi square = 31.0; p = <.001.

TABLE 9. RELATIONSHIP BETWEEN MODERNITY LEVEL AND RATE OF CHANGE IN NATIONAL INCOME

RATE OF CHANGE IN NATIONAL INCOME (PERCENT)	MODERNITY LEVEL			
	Traditional countries	*Transitional countries*	*Modern countries*	*Total*
Low change	Burma, Cambodia, China, Ghana, Haiti, India, Iraq, Jordan, Indonesia, Malaya, Morocco, Pakistan, Philippines, Sudan — 14	Bulgaria, Colombia, Costa Rica, Dom. Rep., Ecuador, Egypt, El Salvador, Guatemala, Honduras, Lebanon, Panama, Poland, Portugal, Syria, Tunisia, Venezuela — 16	E. Germany, Ireland, Switzerland, USSR, United Kingdom — 5	35
High change	Taiwan — 1	Brazil, Chile, Ceylon, Cuba, Greece, Hungary, Italy, Japan, Korea, Mexico, Paraguay, Peru, Spain, Thailand, Turkey, Un. of So. Africa, Yugoslavia — 17	Argentina, Australia, Austria, Belgium, Canada, Denmark, Finland, France, Iceland, Israel, Luxembourg, Netherlands, New Zealand, Norway, Sweden, United States, W. Germany — 17	35
Total	15	33	22	70

Chi square = 17.8; $p = <.001$.

The results of these studies are an encouraging indication that cross-national, correlational, and scaling methods can profitably be applied to complex areas such as the analysis of internal conflict behaviors. The scaling, as well as the identification of the dimensions of internal conflict behavior, show that these events can be classified and disentangled.

Furthermore, the results of the studies provide empirical corroboration for many current notions regarding the determinants of political instability. The fact that change may lead to unrest has been suggested. By applying postulates drawn from the frustration-aggression model to this area of internal conflict behavior, and by subjecting the area to empirical analysis, new insights are also obtained. On the basis of these findings, it may be suggested that one compelling reason for the greater stability of modern countries lies in their greater ability to satisfy the wants of their citizens. The less advanced countries are characterized by greater instability because of the aggressive responses to systemic frustration evoked in the populace. It could be argued simply that the increase in instability resulting from a change in ecological conditions is due to the disruptive effect of change. But it is also possible that the satisfaction of wants has a feedback effect, adding to the strength of the drive for more satisfactions. As wants start to be satisfied, the few satisfactions which are achieved increase the drive for more satisfactions, thus in effect adding to the sense of systemic frustration. It is only when a high enough level of satisfaction has been reached that a country will tend toward stability rather than instability.

Although exploratory in nature, the findings are sufficiently striking and persuasive to argue for continuing with additional designs. A large-scale series of studies utilizing a wider scope of ecological, psychological, and political variables, an inventory of other, complementary aggressive behaviors, and a longer time period should lead to more refined results.

References

Almond, Gabriel A., and James S. Coleman (eds.). *The Politics of the Developing Areas*. Princeton: Princeton University Press, 1960.

———, and Sidney Verba. *The Civic Culture*. Princeton, N.J.: Princeton University Press, 1963.

Berkowitz, Leonard. *Aggression: A Social Psychological Analysis*. New York: McGraw-Hill, 1962.

———. "The Concept of Aggressive Drive: Some Additional Considerations." In L. Berkowitz (ed.), *Advances in Experimental Social Psychology*, Vol. 2. New York: Academic Press, 1965.

Buss, Arnold H. *The Psychology of Aggression*. New York: Wiley, 1961.

Cantril, Hadley. "A Study of Aspirations," *Scientific American*, February 1963, pp. 41-45.

————. *The Pattern of Human Concerns.* New Brunswick, N.J.: Rutgers University Press, 1965.

Conroe, Wallace W. *A Cross-National Analysis of the Impact of Modernization Upon Political Stability.* Master's thesis, San Diego State College, 1965.

Cutwright, Philips. "National Political Development: Measurement and Analysis," *American Sociological Review*, 28 (April 1963), 253-64.

Deutsch, Karl W. *The Nerves of Government.* New York: Free Press, 1963.

————. "Social Mobilization and Political Development," *American Political Science Review*, 55 (Sept. 1961), 493-514.

Dollard, John, *et al. Frustration and Aggression.* New Haven: Yale University Press, 1939.

Doob, Leonard W. *Becoming More Civilized: A Psychological Exploration.* New Haven: Yale University Press, 1960.

Easton, David. *A Framework for Political Analysis.* Englewood Cliffs, N.J.: Prentice-Hall, 1965a.

————. *A Systems Analysis of Political Life.* New York: Wiley, 1965b.

Eckstein, H. *Internal War: The Problem of Anticipation.* A Report submitted to the Research Group in Psychology and the Social Sciences, Smithsonian Institution, Washington, D.C., January 15, 1962.

Feierabend, Ivo K. "Exploring Political Stability: A Note on the Comparative Method," *Western Political Quarterly (Supplement)*, 15, 3 (Sept. 1962), 18-19.

————, and Rosalind L. Feierabend. *Cross-National Data Bank of Political Instability Events (Code Index).* Public Affairs Research Institute, San Diego State College, January 1965.

————, ————, and Norman G. Litell. "Dimensions of Political Unrest: A Factor Analysis of Cross-National Data." Paper delivered at the annual meeting of the Western Political Science Association, Reno, Nevada, March 1966.

Gurr, Ted. *The Genesis of Violence: A Multivariate Theory of the Preconditions of Civil Strife.* Ph.D. dissertation, New York University, 1965.

Hoole, Francis W. *Political Stability and Instability Within Nations: A Cross-National Study.* Master's thesis, San Diego State College, August 1964.

Inkeles, Alex. "Industrial Man: The Relation of Status to Experience, Perception and Value," *American Journal of Sociology* (July 1960), 1-31.

Lasswell, Harold D. *The Political Writings of Harold D. Lasswell.* Glencoe, Ill.: Free Press, 1951.

Lerner, Daniel. "Communication Systems and Social Systems: A Statistical Exploration in History and Policy," *Behavioral Science*, 2, 4 (Oct. 1957), 266-75.

————. *The Passing of Traditional Society.* Glencoe, Ill.: Free Press, 1958.

Maier, Norman R. F. *Frustration: The Study of Behavior Without a Goal.* New York: McGraw-Hill, 1949.

McNeil, Elton B. "Psychology and Aggression," *Journal of Conflict Resolution*, 3, 3 (Sept. 1959), 195-293.

Merton, R. K. *Social Theory and Social Structure.* New York: Free Press, 1949.

Murdock, George P. "Anthropology as a Comparative Science," *Behavioral Science*, 2, 4 (Oct. 1957), 249-54.

Nesvold, Betty A. *Modernity, Social Frustration, and the Stability of Political*

Systems: A Cross-National Study. Master's thesis, San Diego State College, June 1964.

Parsons, Talcott, and Edward A. Shils. *Toward a General Theory of Action.* Cambridge, Mass.: Harvard University Press, 1951.

————, ————, K. Naegele, and J. Pitts. *Theories of Society.* New York: Free Press, 1961.

Rummel, Rudolph J. "Dimensions of Conflict Behavior Within Nations, 1946-59," *Journal of Conflict Resolution*, 10, 1 (March 1966), 65-74.

————. "Dimensions of Conflict Behavior Within and Between Nations," *General Systems Yearbook*, 8 (1963), 1-50.

Russett, Bruce M. "Inequality and Instability: The Relation of Land Tenure and Politics," *World Politics*, 16, 3 (April 1964), 442-54.

————, et al. *World Handbook of Social and Economic Indicators.* New Haven: Yale University Press, 1964.

Tanter, Raymond. *Dimensions of Conflict Behavior Within and Between Nations, 1958-1960.* Monograph prepared in connection with research supported by National Science Foundation Contract NSF-GS224, 1964.

————. "Dimensions of Conflict Behavior Within and Between Nations, 1958-60," *Journal of Conflict Resolution*, 10, 1 (March 1966), 41-65.

Whiting, John W., and Irvin L. Child. *Child Training and Personality: A Cross-Cultural Study.* New Haven: Yale University Press, 1953.

Over-Population

All studies of social pathology have implications for its control, but Notestein's article focuses primarily on the control of a highly pathogenic condition characteristically found in economically underdeveloped countries. This condition — the over-production of people in relation to the resources necessary to sustain them — has been caused by a one-sided application of purposive rationality (medical and nutrition technology) to mortality control. The only effective method of reducing the excessively rapid growth of population and the social pathologies resulting therefrom is to apply purposive rationality to fertility control. The effectiveness of purposive rationality in the control of social pathology depends, however, on "irrational" factors: prevalent cultural attitudes and the adequacy of national political and ideological leaders. Not all pathogenic conditions can be alleviated by the application of rationality as, in principle, a distorted birth-death ratio can. But if this problem is successfully resolved, the solution may provide a model for coping with other pathogenic conditions on both the local and international scale.

The Population Crisis: Reasons for Hope

A discussion of the crisis of population growth must be organized around two sharply contrasting themes: one, of almost unrivaled dangers; the other, of new hope that it may be resolved during the remainder of this century. It is difficult to overstate the importance of either theme. The dangers threaten the entire process of modernization among the two-thirds of the world's people in the technologically backward nations, and thereby the maintenance of their political coherence; they threaten, indeed, a catastrophic loss of life. The hope lies in the fact that there is now new reason to think that, if the world is willing to bend its energies toward solving the problems, it can go far toward doing so during the coming decades. The time has passed when the problem must be viewed as insuperable.

In what follows, I shall be concerned with the technologically backward nations. The question here is not what population they might ultimately be capable of supporting if they achieve a high state of development. At present they are desperately poor, grossly uneducated and badly organized to make use of what knowledge they have. They have to start from where they are, and not from where they should like to be. The problem in the real world is that the rate of population growth is proving to be a major obstacle to economic development. Mounting rates of population growth are proving to be almost insuperable obstacles to the technological development on which our future hopes must depend. The heart of the demographic problem is that of slowing the rate of population growth sufficiently to permit the development of the lagging economies and of doing this in the next two or three decades.

The case is now too well known to require detailed documentation. Most of the newly developing nations have populations that are growing by at least 2.5 percent per year. Moreover, those with slower rates of growth have negligible health protection and will quickly come to that rate whenever rudimentary health services are developed. The rates of growth go up to 3.5 percent and occasionally higher. Growth continuing

Reprinted by special permission of the author and publisher from *Foreign Affairs*, Vol. 46 (October 1967), pp. 167-180. Copyright by the Council on Foreign Relations, Inc., New York.

at 2.5 percent doubles the size of the population in 28 years and growth at 3.5 percent doubles it in 20 years. In short, unless growth slows down, most of the technologically backward countries face the problem of dealing with double their present population well before the end of the century: that is, well before the children born this year have completed their own childbearing.

The sources of this rapid growth are easily identified. Birth rates are very much higher and death rates are very much lower than they were, for example, in the nineteenth-century period of modernization in Europe. There, populations seldom grew by as much as 1 percent per year. Whereas in Europe there tended to be about 35 births a year per 1,000 population, in today's newly developing countries birth rates generally range from 40 to 55. The source of this difference lies mainly in the universality of marriage in the developing nations and in the young ages at which it occurs.

Death rates differ even more spectacularly. In nineteenth-century Europe, death rates of 25 per 1,000 population were common and a rate as high as 30 was not unusual. In today's newly developing countries a rate of 25 is very high, 20 is common and the rates go as low as 6 per 1,000 population. A primary cause of these low figures is, of course, the new efficiency with which disease is controlled by sulpha drugs, antibiotics and insecticides. The expectation of life at birth has risen remarkably in most of the newly developing countries. Indeed, in a few areas it now exceeds 60 years — not so very much less than the U.S. figure of 70 years.

The low death rates also come from another and less commonly recognized source. The death rate is simply the annual number of deaths per 1,000 population and therefore is affected by the age composition of the population. Under anything like reasonable health conditions a young population tends to have a low death rate and an old population a high death rate. One of the important reasons that the newly developing countries have low death rates is that their very high birth rates have generated very young populations. It is this that accounts for the fact that the lowest death rates in the world today are found in newly developing countries that have relatively good health services. Taiwan, for example, has a lower death rate than the United States, and Ceylon has a lower death rate than France or England. Moreover, although death rates in the newly developing world are low by historical standards, many remain very high in the light of modern abilities to control disease. Hence we can expect that death rates will continue to be reduced.

It would be unwise, then, to expect even a very rapid decline of birth rates to reduce population growth below 1 percent by the end of the century. This figure is about the rate of natural increase in the United States at the present time. Barring catastrophe, and under the best possible cir-

cumstances, the newly developing world will have to achieve its modernization in spite of rates of population growth running from the present
figure of 2.5 to 3.5 percent down to 1.0 or 1.5 percent by the end of the
century. Any such trend will clearly require a very rapid reduction of
birth rates.

The cost of this growth must be met before new investment can be
made in educational and productive facilities. The dilemma is now widely
understood: if a nation is increasing its product by 5 percent a year — a
level that rather few of the developing nations have thus far been able to
sustain — and if its population is growing at 3 percent per year, then per
capita income rises at a rate of 2 percent. This means that incomes will
not have doubled until after the turn of the century. Per capita incomes
would rise from, say, $100 per year to only $200 per year over the next
35 years. But, meanwhile, the population would have increased by a factor of 2.7. In short, an excellent economic performance would result in
2.7 times as many people continuing to live in almost abject poverty, with
resources for the improvement of education and productive equipment
having increased only minimally.

In the densely settled regions of the world the problem is much more
difficult than these simple numbers suggest. Consider the situation of
India. A perpetuation of its present rate of growth of 2.4 percent would
mean that its present population of about half a billion would rise to one
billion before the end of the century. India already faces acute shortages
of food. Its agriculture is poorly developed. If it is to support such
growth, it must make strenuous efforts to enhance the production of the
land. A rapid but theoretically possible development of agricultural technology should enable India to meet at least its minimum needs. But to
increase production in this fashion requires very little more labor. It requires instead the rationalization of agriculture through development of
better crop practices, transportation, credit facilities, pest control and
fertilization. It does not require more people. And yet if its present population growth continues, India faces the problem of finding — within
about 29 years — the means to support another half-billion people outside
of agriculture. In an era of rising expectations how long can political coherence be maintained in the presence of unemployment on a possibly
unprecedented scale?

If political coherence cannot be maintained, the risks change — from
those of growth to those of a catastrophic loss of life. The margins of
safety are pathetically thin. It would not take much disorganization to
block transportation and public health activities so that famine and epi-
demic disease would stalk the land. To anyone inclined to point out that
this would at least be one solution to the problems of population pressure, the reply must be that massive upheavals also jeopardize every

aspect of the development process and every hope of representative government in unregimented societies. The risks of events of this kind are real in such densely settled areas as India, Pakistan, Indonesia and Egypt. Mainland China, about which we know very little, may already be experiencing these catastrophes.

II

In view of the foregoing it may seem reckless to turn to the optimistic side of the picture, but there is such a side which I think is persuasive. Optimism does not carry us to the point of forecasting that the problems will be solved without intervening tragedies. But we do have reason to believe that the problems can be solved by a world fully alert to the dangers and willing to devote serious resources and energy to attacking them. We now have a basis for expecting that a rapid decline in birth rates can be achieved in the next decades. The problems and the crisis need not be prolonged indefinitely. Much will depend on the scale of efforts both in developing the economies and in reducing birth rates in the next 20 or 30 years. We cannot argue that the solution is in sight, but we can argue that the prerequisites for a solution are at hand.

In this hopeful judgment four elements are important: (1) the development of national policies favoring family planning; (2) the demonstrated public interest in limiting childbearing; (3) the improvement of contraceptive technology; and (4) the fact that for the first time in history several Oriental populations have begun to cut their birth rates as a result of governmental programs to spread the practice of birth control. I shall consider each of these topics briefly.

A decade ago, India was the only country that had adopted a national policy to promote the practice of family planning, although for several years the plan had more words than substance. Today, more than half the people of the newly developing world live under governments that have decided to reduce their birth rates by family planning. These include Mainland China, Nepal, Pakistan, India, Ceylon, Malaysia, Indonesia (if still a bit ambiguously), Singapore, Hong Kong, Taiwan (in deed, if not in word), South Korea, Iran, Turkey, Egypt, Tunisia, Morocco, Kenya, Barbados, Jamaica and Honduras. Many other countries, such as Colombia and Chile, are setting up active governmental and quasi-governmental programs. In still other countries substantial efforts are going on in universities, public hospitals and in local health departments. These include, for example, Thailand, the Philippines and Venezuela.

It must immediately be said that a governmental policy does not guarantee an effective program; there has often been a lag of several years between the adoption of a policy and the beginning of effective work.

The point, however, is one of future relevance. The fact is that the newly developing nations have themselves been coming to an awareness of the seriousness of their population problems and of the extent to which their work in economic development is being frustrated by too rapid increases in the numbers of their people. Their awakening to the urgency of the problem has come with remarkable and accelerating speed. It foreshadows energetic work.

The second reason for optimism concerning the possibilities of reducing rates of population growth is that the public has been shown to be interested in limiting family size. The finding is surprising, for students of traditional agrarian societies have long reported that motivation for restricting fertility generally is not high. Many of the attitudes, customs, beliefs and familial arrangements remain those of centuries past in which survival, not overrapid growth, posed the problem. These factors continue today to weaken interest in family planning.

Nevertheless, sample surveys conducted in some 20 developing countries show that, without exception, substantial majorities of married couples want to restrict their childbearing. Moreover, these attitudes are found in the villages as well as in the cities — among illiterates as well as among the educated. The women want to limit their childbearing, not necessarily to only two or three children, for they may often want four or five and at least one son. But they want to curtail their childbearing, and this attitude is widespread even in communities in which there is little evidence of modernization.

Actually, these communities often have a great deal more modernization than first strikes the eye of the prosperous Western visitor. His overwhelming impression is that of poverty. But the villager has movies (either regularly or through traveling theaters), transistor radios and a desire to educate his children. He is aware that his children no longer die in infancy as they used to do, that sweeping epidemics no longer appear. He is also aware that more surviving children mean more difficulty in providing enough food, and he sees that today a medium-sized family will provide enough surviving adults to protect him in his old age. All these factors have increased the proportion of couples who say that they would like to practice contraception.

The demonstration of interest is based on much more than responses to surveys. In many societies a large number of crude and illegal abortions gives eloquent testimony to the motivations for restriction. Moreover, whenever there have been well-organized contraceptive services through which information and supplies are readily available, the response has been large. Where there is indifference, it usually has been to poorly organized services poorly supported by educational effort. Any lack of interest on the part of the public is less serious than the apathy of the middle classes and the lesser officials who cannot bring themselves to believe that their illiterate peasants are sufficiently intelligent to understand their own problems. Both surveys and the public response to services clearly demonstrate that ordinary people have a much better understanding of their own problems than their lesser officials appreciate.

The third encouraging fact is the improvement of contraceptive technology. During the past decade we have gained two methods which are safe, cheap and highly effective and that for the first time make no demands on the couple at the time of coition. One is the new plastic intrauterine device (I.U.D.) that, once inserted, remains indefinitely in place for those who tolerate it. Experience with it varies, depending on the quality of service and the extent to which the patient is warned to expect some initial discomfort. The weight of evidence is that with reasonable care (including re-insertion in some patients who expel it) some 55 or 60 percent of women continue to be completely protected after two years. The other 40 to 45 percent include women whose husbands have died, those who have decided to have a child and those who prefer other methods; only 20 to 30 percent cannot tolerate or retain it. The rate of pregnancy among users, including women who have unknowingly expelled the device, is 2 to 3 a year per hundred women. This is less than half the rate with conventional contraceptives under the best conditions.

The oral steroids offer the other most promising method. Until recently, they were too expensive to meet the needs of the majority in the developing countries. Recently, however, prices for bulk orders have dropped to about 15 cents per cycle, which permits their use in governmental programs, at least for those patients who cannot use the I.U.D. When the pill is systematically taken it is absolutely effective. We do not yet know how effective it is in actual use or what proportion of women will continue to use it. Preliminary indications in Taiwan and Korea are that the rates of discontinuation are, if anything, somewhat higher than those with the I.U.D.

The new methods go far toward meeting the needs of couples so weakly motivated that they will not take troublesome precautions. The limitations loom large only when they are compared with an abstract ideal rather than with earlier experience. Moreover, knowledgeable scientists from several laboratories are saying that we may come much closer to the abstract ideal within the next four years. Several possibilities are now being studied in animals. One of the more promising is an injection, or implant, that will prevent pregnancy for a year or more. It is hoped to release a progestin in such very small amounts that its effect is achieved exclusively at the uterine level without involving either the ovary or pituitary. If this proves to be possible, the reduction of dose and the elimination of estrogen should greatly reduce the undesirable side effects of the present combined pill and bring the cost to well under 50 cents a year. One cannot count on the success of anything in the early research stage, but there are now so many good leads that the prospects for major improvements in contraceptive technology in the near future are excellent.

The fourth reason for optimism about the possibility of reducing birth rates is that some countries have already done so. This is the case in South Korea, Taiwan, Hong Kong and Singapore, and perhaps in other countries where the evidence is more difficult to marshal.

South Korea offers no accurate birth rates, but consider the indirect evidence that they are falling.[1] Last year over 390,000 women had I.U.D.s inserted, bringing the total in the two-and-a-half-year program through 1966 to 737,000. Since 1962 there have been at least 80,000 male sterilizations. At the end of 1966 about 170,000 couples were receiving conventional contraceptive supplies from government stations. Altogether, with allowance for duplications, something like 900,000 couples have been served by the government effort. Since the program began (mostly since 1963), more than 20 percent of the women of childbearing age have taken part, and surveys indicate that about 20 percent of all couples are currently practicing contraception. Moreover, growing acceptance continues in 1967 with no indication that a saturation point has been reached.

According to year-end population registrations, of admittedly defective quality, the ratio of children under age five to women of childbearing age shows a sharp decline between 1962 and 1965, both nationally and in every province of the country. The Planning Board believes that the rate of natural increase has dropped from an estimated 3 percent in 1962 to about 2.5 percent in 1966; it has set a target of 2 percent by 1971. Clearly the birth rate has begun to fall rapidly in response to a strong governmental program.

In Taiwan the birth rate has been dropping for the last ten years, from 45 per 1000 in 1955 to 34.5 in 1964, 32.7 in 1965 and to a record low of 32.4 in 1966. (The actual and comparable figure would have been below 31 if a census in December 1966 had not brought in early birth registrations and omissions from the previous year.) The goal is to reach a birth rate of 20 by 1973. The program has depended heavily on the I.U.D. The target has been 600,000 Lippes loops inserted in five years, and at the half-

---

[1] The following discussion draws heavily on: Mauldin *et al.*, "Retention of IUDs: An International Comparison," and Chow and Freedman, "Taiwan: Births averted by the IUD program," from The Population Council's *Studies in Family Planning*, issues No. 18, April 1967, and No. 20, June 1967, respectively.

way point the actual number falls only 39,000 short of 300,000. The fertility rates of women 25 to 29 are beginning to drop and the proportion of I.U.D. acceptors with only three children is rising. The fact that 37 percent of the I.U.D. patients have discontinued after 18 months has led to efforts to improve the service and to make pills available. It appears, however, that even those who discontinue the I.U.D. control their fertility rather effectively. Chow and Freedman find that if they include all the experience of those who have had I.U.D.s inserted, regardless of subsequent use, the fertility rate of the group has been reduced by something between one-half and two-thirds. There can be no doubt that the family-planning program has been highly successful in speeding the reduction of Taiwan's birth rate. Similarly, in Hong Kong and Singapore, family-planning programs have been major factors in producing sharp declines in birth rates.

The glow of optimism that can come from considering these successful programs fades when we consider India and Pakistan. Those nations have had appropriate policies, but they cannot yet point to reduced birth rates with any certainty. It has been only in the last two or three years that the programs have had much substance. Now they are getting under way, and by the end of this year India will apparently have inserted more than two million I.U.D.s and Pakistan nearly one million. In both countries sterilization is beginning to take a significant place, and work with pills is beginning. If the programs continue to go forward at the new pace the efforts can become highly significant in a few years.

Equally encouraging is the breadth of interest around the world. The Population Council alone has filled requests for some 2.6 million Lippes loops from the governments or medical institutions of 39 developing countries, and has helped governments in South Korea, Taiwan, Hong Kong, India, Pakistan, Egypt and Turkey to establish local manufacturing. It has sponsored a coöperative birth-control program in the postpartum services of 26 large delivery hospitals of 20 cities in 15 countries, including the United States. Although this program is only about a year and a half old, some 25 percent of the obstetrical patients have used the contraceptive service, and they have been markedly younger and have had fewer children than the patients attending the usual service. They have flocked to the clinics whether in Alexandria, Ankara, Santiago, Caracas, Mexico City, New York, Manila, Singapore or Bangkok. From this and many other projects it becomes evident that the difficulties do not lie in lack of interest by the public. The main obstacles to the development of highly successful birth-control programs everywhere lie in the organizational and administrative field.

Newly developed nations offer examples of rapidly falling birth rates. Japan's birth rate, for example, had dropped by last year from a postwar high of 34 per thousand to 14; Japan now shares with Hungary the lowest birth rate in the world.[2] The decline was not the result of a governmental birth-control program; it was mainly due to abortion rather than contraception, and came almost in spite of the government. The public took such enthusiastic advantage of abortion permitted by the "Eugenic Protection Law" that it was politically impossible to interpret the law narrowly. At present there is a marked trend away from abortion and toward contraception, but Japan has shown that population growth can be drastically reduced by a prosperous people having few inhibitions against abortion and served by a competent medical establishment. The Japanese medical community's enthusiasm for abortion has seeped into Taiwan, South Korea, Hong Kong and Singapore, though it remains illegal.

Abortion is legal in the U.S.S.R. and all of Eastern Europe except East Germany and Albania.[3] As in Japan, it has been a major factor in reducing birth rates which were high before the war but now are for the most part lower than in the United States. Abortion is apparently legal under many circumstances in Mainland China, and there is a good deal of talk about making it legal in India and in Pakistan. In view of the dearth of medical personnel and facilities and the improved efficiency of modern contraceptives, it is doubtful that abortion will play the major role in reducing population growth in India and the Moslem world that it did in Japan, the Soviet Union and Eastern Europe.

Abortion is, nevertheless, important today. In Turkey, where until two years ago contraception was illegal, the Ministry of Health estimates that more than one in four pregnancies is terminated by illegal abortion. In Latin America, where church opposition has held back the development of governmental contraceptive services, abortion is rife. No one knows the number even approximately, but the obstetrical services of many hospitals devote from one-quarter to one-half of their beds to patients with incomplete or septic abortions. Professor Freedman suggests that in the world as a whole abortion is today the most common female method of preventing birth. Where abortion is common it is difficult to suggest the absence of motivation for family planning.

III

This, then, is the optimistic case for saying that the newly developing countries can, if they will, bring their rates of population growth to reasonably low levels in the next two or three decades provided that they

---

[2] The rate dropped from 19 to 14 last year, reflecting the fact that girls born in the year of the "fiery horse" have the worst horoscopes as brides of any for the last 60 years. The rate will probably rise this year, but the sharp response to astrological portents shows that fertility is under voluntary control.

[3] Since October, 1966, Rumania as well. [Ed.]

have the needed assistance from international, governmental and private agencies in the developed world. In absolute terms the assistance needed from the developed world is large, but it is small compared to that needed for economic development. Aid should include help with training at the professional and sub-professional levels in a wide range of biological, medical and social science specialties; assistance in building and enriching the medical infrastructure on which contraceptive services depend; assistance with organization, logistics, supplies and materials for informational and educational programs. Basic and applied research that seeks to attain new efficiency in the regulation of fertility needs to be increased throughout the world.

There are two kinds of major disagreement with the foregoing summary. One questions the objective of reducing the rates of population growth; the other accepts the goal but doubts that the appropriate means are being used for its attainment.

In both Sub-Saharan Africa and Latin America there is substantial opposition to family planning in official quarters. In most cases it is merely the continuation of the usual pre-modern view. When disease was uncontrolled, healthy and prosperous years produced rapid population growth. Bigger was, indeed, better. Things are still thought of in that light by many leaders who are impressed that they have large territories of undeveloped land. They are inclined to think in terms of traditional agriculture, and have little realization that a slower rate of population growth could mean a faster pace of educational and economic development, greater national prosperity and greater national power. This kind of opposition has been rapidly disappearing as governments gain new experience with the frustrations of development in the face of very rapid population growth.

There is also opposition from the more doctrinaire Catholics and communists, whose preoccupation with the defense of orthodoxy makes them slow to recognize the problem, and when recognizing it, inclined to prefer private and euphemistic to public and explicit solutions. When these groups are very strong, the governments tend to avoid policies and official programs, and the actual work goes on in the medical institutions and local health departments. Even then the assistance given is known not as contraception but as child-spacing, family health, pre-pregnancy health and anti-abortion service. Such opposition will undoubtedly delay somewhat the reduction of the rate of population growth, but everything on the horizon suggests it is rapidly disappearing.

Finally, there are dissident views among persons fully alert to the need for reducing birth rates. Objections have been voiced that too much of the effort is concentrated specifically on family planning, and that this overemphasis is particularly evident in the technical assistance from the developed world. This conclusion is based on a different reading of the record than that presented here. Overstated somewhat, this argument runs as follows: A number of countries such as India, Pakistan and Egypt have had national family-planning policies for a long time with inconsequential results; claims about public interest in family planning drawn from field surveys are worth little because they are too superficial to eliminate the favorable responses given mainly to please the perceived interests of the investigator; the majority of patients attracted to governmental programs are older women who will not have many more children in any event; the new contraceptive methods are proving unsuitable for a substantial proportion of people; and the only programmatic successes are in small Oriental nations.

The replies have been suggested. Nations with positive policies did not develop significant programs until the advent of the I.U.D. convinced their leaders that appropriate methods existed. Actual work is scarcely three years old. Responses to surveys are not to be taken at full face value, but the differences by education and income are in the expected direction, as are the changes of responses over time as programs develop. The real danger is that we do not take the surveys seriously enough, because, whenever put to the test, the public has backed its opinion with requests for service. Naturally older women with many children are the first to come for help. To them the problem is desperate. But one must start somewhere, and it can be argued that bringing the older and respected couples to the practice of family planning may well serve to legitimize the practice and to encourage imitation by younger couples for purposes of child spacing. Methods of contraception are less than perfect, but the important fact is that we now have methods with which more than 50 percent of women are happy and successful. For the 30 percent with real difficulties, there are the conventional methods, not to mention the new methods on the horizon. Finally, it is true that the beginnings of success have come only in small Oriental countries. The question, however, is not whether birth rates have been reduced in all the world, but whether they can be reduced by family-planning programs. The successful countries have shown what can be done. To me it seems that the skeptics are concentrating on the problems that remain to be solved rather than reading the lessons for the future in the recent and quite remarkable past.

Perhaps the basic reason for skepticism about the future significance of recent efforts lies in the conviction that institutional structures are too hostile to the very idea of family planning to permit any substantial success. One objection is that efforts to spread the practice of birth control ought to be reduced so that the resources could be devoted to economic development. Might not the construction of a school or a factory do more to spread birth control than the same funds devoted to family-planning services? The alternative is not a real one because of differences in the magnitude of the requirements. Efforts to promote economic development are grossly insufficient to avoid the danger of major catastrophe, and the modernized world, if it values its own interests, will awaken to that fact. The most powerful effort imaginable to spread birth control could not cost anything like 1 percent as much as the cost of economic development. Indeed, the cost of preventing one birth, probably about $20, falls far short of the cost of one year's schooling. Much more costly efforts to reduce birth rates than any that have been attempted can be shown to be worthwhile in speeding the process of development by cutting the burden of population growth.

Another suggestion is to go directly to the problem of institutional change. Some of the resources now devoted to birth control should, the argument runs, be devoted instead to changing the institutional setting in ways that would favor family planning. We should study the possibilities of changing marriage age, of finding ways in which the state can reward the parents of small families, and, perhaps, of penalizing the parents of large families (a policy now being debated in India). Undoubtedly, some support for such studies should be available, but before their results can have any influence on reproduction they will have to be carried through the entire political process. It is my impression that obtaining living examples of family planning will be much more important, even in changing social institutions, than efforts to change the governmental rules. Changes in the institutional setting are needed, but at this stage it seems more important to help those people who are willing to become the innovators.

Whatever happens, it is probable that, short of a major rise in the death rate, population growth will not be stopped for some decades. Given the necessary effort, however, it does seem likely that growth will be reduced to levels that can be coped with in a world of rapidly developing science and technology. In the long run, of course, growth must stop. Quite possibly it will not do so even if every couple is able to limit its childbearing to the precise number of children it wants. But a world in which all couples are able to choose the size of their family will be a world in which an alteration of institutional constraints would prove rather quickly effective. If the developing nations can move from their present growth rates of 2.5 and 3.5 percent to 1 and 1.5 percent while health improves, the problems will not all be solved, but the crisis will be passed.

It would be a great mistake to suppose that we will move into the future with a linear extension of past performance. No one ten years ago would have forecast the rapid changes of the past decade in policies, in contraceptive technology, in public interest and in programmatic successes. We must assume that the future will bring an accelerated pace of change. We have already moved from a position of public apathy to one of deep concern by many people. Today, governments, international agencies and private organizations are talking a great deal about major efforts and new groups are entering the discourse every day. Everything on the horizon suggests a further deepening of interest, both public and private. Our estimate of the future possibilities should be based on the premise that we are at the beginning of an accelerating trend. Almost all of the actual work, national and international, remains to be done. If our efforts are commensurate with our opportunities, however, we have reason to believe that by the end of the century the spectre of poverty perpetuated by population growth can be lifted from the earth.